T0330090

Leadership in Spaces and Places

Leadership in Spaces and Places

Edited by

Arja Ropo

Professor, University of Tampere, Finland

Perttu Salovaara

Adjunct Assistant Professor, New York University, USA and Research Fellow, University of Tampere, Finland

Erika Sauer

Adjunct Professor, University of Tampere, Finland

Donatella De Paoli

Associate Professor, Norwegian Business School BI, Norway

Edward Elgar
PUBLISHING

Cheltenham, UK • Northampton, MA, USA

Published by
Edward Elgar Publishing Limited
The Lypiatts
15 Lansdown Road
Cheltenham
Glos GL50 2JA
UK

Edward Elgar Publishing, Inc.
William Pratt House
9 Dewey Court
Northampton
Massachusetts 01060
USA

A catalogue record for this book
is available from the British Library

Library of Congress Control Number: 2015930138

This book is available electronically in the **Elgar**online
Business subject collection
DOI 10.4337/9781783477920

ISBN 978 1 78347 791 3 (cased)
ISBN 978 1 78347 792 0 (eBook)

Typeset by Servis Filmsetting Ltd, Stockport, Cheshire
Printed and bound in Great Britain by CPI Group (UK Ltd)

Contents

List of contributors   vii
Acknowledgements   xi

Why does space need to be taken seriously in leadership and
organization studies and practice?   1
Arja Ropo, Donatella De Paoli, Perttu Salovaara and Erika Sauer

PART I   WORKSPACES IN CHANGE

1   What can the coworking movement tell us about the future of
    workplaces?   27
    Perttu Salovaara

2   Work isn't where it used to be   49
    Siri Hunnes Blakstad

PART II   OPEN OFFICE SPACES

3   A spatial perspective to leadership in knowledge-intensive
    projects   71
    Anne Live Vaagaasar

4   Leading employee wellbeing by workspace experiences   87
    Niina Uolamo and Arja Ropo

PART III   VIRTUAL WORKSPACES

5   Virtual organizations: a call for new leadership   109
    Donatella De Paoli

6   Virtual spaces as workplaces: working and leading in virtual
    worlds   128
    Matti Vartiainen

PART IV   SERVICE SPACES

7   The symbolic dimension of space and artefacts in a bookstore:
leadership without a leader?   147
Kaisa Greenlees

8   Front stage with no front-stage employees: customer
perceptions of self-service hotels   163
Ritva Höykinpuro

PART V   CULTURAL SPACES

9   Cities lead   183
Erika Sauer

10 Culture matters: space and leadership in a cross-cultural
perspective   199
Tor Grenness

PART VI   INSTITUTIONAL SPACES

11 Leadership and space in 3D: distance, dissent and
disembodiment in the case of a new academic building   217
Karen Dale and Gibson Burrell

12 The hospital as a space of power: ownership of space and
symbols of power in the hospital setting   242
Erika Sauer

Index   265

Contributors

Siri Hunnes Blakstad is Vice President (Engineering and Architecture) at Reinertsen and tegn_3 and Adjunct Professor at NTNU, Norwegian University of Science and Technology, Norway. She combines work in practice with research and education. She has experience both as a workplace consultant and in corporate real estate and workplace strategy with Telenor, the multinational telecommunications company. She has been a Full Professor at NTNU and Research Director with SINTEF Building and Infrastructure, where she was involved in education and conducted research in workplace and facilities-management-related R&D projects. Her current research and practice aims at developing methods for strategic briefing and workplace design as well as evaluation of use of space and effects on the user organization.

Gibson Burrell is Emeritus Professor of Organization Theory in the School of Management at the University of Leicester, UK. His latest book is entitled *Styles of Organizing: The Will to Form*, published by Oxford University Press in 2013. For 2014–16 he has received a Leverhulme Emeritus Fellowship, awarded by the UK-based Leverhulme Trust, to undertake research in India and the USA.

Karen Dale is Senior Lecturer in the Department of Organization, Work and Technology at Lancaster University, UK. She has written about embodiment and organizations, most extensively in *Anatomising Embodiment and Organisation Theory* (Palgrave, 2001) and about architecture, space and social materiality as related to organization studies, including *The Spaces of Organisation and the Organisation of Space: Power, Identity and Materiality at Work* with Gibson Burrell (Palgrave, 2007).

Donatella De Paoli is Associate Professor at the Department of Leadership and Organization at Norwegian Business School BI, Oslo, Norway. Her research interests are the aesthetics of organizations and the organizing of the arts. She has written books and published scientifically on these issues. Currently, her main research interests are about leadership in virtual space, physicality of leadership, leadership images in architecture and the construction of leadership through spaces and places. She is teaching several Executive Master's programmes in leadership, has developed the field of Arts Management at BI, and is a regular speaker.

Kaisa Greenlees has a Master's degree both in Economics and Social Sciences and is a PhD student in the field of management and leadership at Jyväskylä University School of Business and Economics, Finland. As a graduate of social sciences she developed an interest in meanings attached to space and how they affect our behaviour and social relations. Currently, she is working on her PhD thesis on the experiences of space and leadership in a Finnish bookstore.

Tor Grenness is Emeritus Professor in International Management at Norwegian Business School BI, Oslo, Norway. He holds a Master's degree in Political Science from the University of Oslo and Doctor of Business Administration from Brunel University, UK. His research profile focuses on cross-cultural management and organization behaviour, Scandinavian culture and management and income inequality and trust within and between countries. He is currently engaged in a project focusing on the consequences of income inequality on levels of trust and economic performance across countries.

Ritva Höykinpuro is University Lecturer at the University of Tampere, School of Management, Finland. She has defended her PhD in the field of service management. Her research interests are service space, service design, service organizations and qualitative research methods, especially narratives. She is an experienced lecturer and she has been guest lecturing on service management and research methods in different universities, both in Finland and abroad.

Arja Ropo is Professor of Management and Organization at the School of Management, University of Tampere, Finland. Her continuing interest is leadership and embodiment. Recently she has studied the material aspects of leadership. Organizational aesthetics, art and cultural organizations and leading change are also her research themes. She has published in the *Leadership Quarterly*, *Leadership*, *Scandinavian Journal of Management*, *International Journal of Arts Management*, and *Journal of Management & Organization*. Her work has also appeared in a number of books in Europe and North America. She serves currently as an Editorial Board member for the *Scandinavian Journal of Management* and *Organizational Aesthetics*.

Perttu Salovaara is an Adjunct Assistant Professor at Stern School of Business, New York University, USA and a Research Fellow at the School of Management, University of Tampere, Finland. Having a background in philosophy his research interests focus on epistemological and ontological questions of leadership. He has recently published on embodiment in leadership, has produced two documentary films on leadership and is currently studying coworking spaces as locations of leadership. Prior to academic interests he worked as a management consultant and leadership trainer for 15 years.

Erika Sauer is Adjunct Professor and Senior Researcher at the University of Tampere, Finland. Her research interests are in the field of leadership: relational, embodied, emotional and aesthetic leadership, and also the construction of leadership through spaces and places. She has published in Scandinavian, European and North American journals, as well as written book chapters and co-written books on various aspects of leadership. She has produced a documentary film on leadership in Indonesia and in the USA. Erika is also an active consultant working with management teams and leadership capacity development in different organizations. She has recently been appointed Managing Director at the non-profit business association AmCham Finland in New York. She is a columnist for a Finnish business magazine.

Niina Uolamo is a recent MSc (Bus. Admin.) graduate from the School of Management, University of Tampere, Finland. Management and organization, and psychology, are her main academic interests. When beginning her Master's degree course three years ago, the literature on socially constructed and aesthetic leadership caught her interest. That literature and discussions with Professor Arja Ropo inspired her to write her Master's thesis on workspaces and employee wellbeing. The process challenged her to critically evaluate the research on employee wellbeing conducted in the fields of work psychology and environmental psychology.

Anne Live Vaagaasar is Associate Professor at the Norwegian Business School BI, Department of Leadership and Organization. She holds a PhD in Project Management. She teaches and conducts research on a broad range of themes related to project management including: learning and competence development in projects, organizing and coordinating large, complex projects and time and space issues in projects.

Matti Vartiainen is Professor of Learning Organization at the Work Psychology and Leadership Unit, Department of Industrial Engineering and Management, Aalto University, Finland. He is also the International Design Business Management Program Director at the Aalto School of Science. His research focuses on organizational innovations, new ways of working including mobile and multilocational work, distributed teams and organizations, collaborative working environments, knowledge and competence building and e-learning systems and reward systems. He is also the mentoring professor in the Virtual and Mobile Work and Work Psychology and Leadership research units at BIT Research Centre.

Acknowledgements

We wish to acknowledge a number of institutions and people who have supported our work in this book project. First of all, this book is an outcome of a four-year research project 'Leadership in "Place and Space"' (2011–14) funded by the Academy of Finland, which we are deeply grateful for. We would also like to extend our thanks to The Finnish Work Environment Fund, The Foundation for Economic Education and the Kiinko Real Estate Education. Furthermore, University of Tampere, Finland, Norwegian Business School BI, New York University, Stern School of Business, The Finnish Embassies in Jakarta and New York, and various coworking spaces in New York and Bellissimi, Italy have provided inspiring work environments for us. At Edward Elgar Publishing, a number of people have helped us finalize the book. Our thanks go to Fran O'Sullivan, Aisha Bushby, Megan Ballantyne, Karen Jones, Suzanne Giles and Dee Compson for their invaluable help to finish this project.

Arja Ropo
Tampere, Finland

Perttu Salovaara
New York, USA

Erika Sauer
Jakarta, Indonesia and New York, USA

Donatella De Paoli
Oslo, Norway and Bellissimi, Italy

Why does space need to be taken seriously in leadership and organization studies and practice?

Arja Ropo, Donatella De Paoli, Perttu Salovaara and Erika Sauer

CHANGES IN TODAY'S WAYS OF WORKING CALL FOR RETHINKING LEADERSHIP

Work is currently undergoing a major transformation in terms of where and how it is carried out. Traditional cell offices and fixed workspaces are not the only possibility. People work increasingly from their homes, trains, planes, airports, cafeterias and coworking spaces. In addition, virtual working is becoming the norm rather than the exception. At the same time, companies make efforts to plan and design workspaces to foster communication, collaboration and creativity. How do these different workspaces shape leadership and organizing, which traditionally call for individual leader presence and material boundaries? How do the practices of leading and organizing change in different spatial arrangements? As work transcends the office and is increasingly digitalized, globalized, dynamic and flexible, we must question where and how leadership happens and what leadership looks like when we think in terms of a spatially informed phenomenon. We have invited management and organization scholars to address some of these challenges. The following chapters try to answer the questions: What are the new changing workspaces? How is the virtual workspace used and what challenges for leadership does it pose? How do coworking and collaborative communities change the understanding of leadership, work and space? How do the different workspaces shape leadership roles and processes? What kind of symbolic roles do the workspace solutions imply? How does office space design convey corporate and leadership values in a cross-cultural setting? How do places and spaces influence employee wellbeing? What are the consequences of the spatial changes for leadership and organization?

We believe that a new way of understanding and practising leadership is needed when thinking of the above developments in the leadership landscape. Our view is that leadership is being shaped, modified and constructed by material workspace arrangements. The practical interest in the issue can be seen in organizations that have started redesigning their office spaces to be more dynamic, flexible, creative and collaborative. This change reflects the trend towards the '"high-involvement workplace" meaning operations with self-managed teams and other devices for empowering employees', as *Fortune Magazine* put it (Stewart and Jacob, 1992). Experimentation with alternative office spaces, home offices, software, new telecommunication devices and new perspectives on work practices during the past ten to 20 years argues for the need to understand leadership, work and organizing differently. In 2007, Gary Hamel claimed in his book *The Future of Management* that companies adhere to outdated models that do not tackle the current challenges and calls for management and leadership innovations. Following Donna Ladkin (2010) in *Rethinking Leadership: A New Look at Old Leadership Questions*, we conceive leadership as a relational construction between people, issues and the environment rather than as an individual quality. Traditional leader-centric practices do not fit with the changing work environment, and plural forms of leadership are increasingly being developed both conceptually and practically (for example, Denis et al., 2012). Following this line of thinking, we argue that future leadership is not only about leaders and followers, but about opening up to see how other 'things' in our environment lead us, such as architectural, design and layout solutions, physical objects, artefacts and even city-spaces.

Understanding leadership in this book builds on our earlier work on leadership, space and embodiment (for example, Ropo et al., 2013; Salovaara and Ropo, 2013). First, we make the distinction between leader and leadership (Parry and Hansen, 2007; Crevani et al., 2010; Salovaara, 2011) but note that there are still some undercurrents of individually centred leadership thinking in the chapters. Second, we join the social constructionist ways of conceiving leadership advocated first by Meindl (1995) and later developed by many others (for example, Grint, 2005; Collinson, 2006; Fairhurst and Grant, 2010). Interpretation and meaningmaking are central in this view (Smircich and Morgan, 1982). Third, to us, leadership is an aesthetic, embodied phenomenon, a subjective 'felt experience' rather than one person influencing another (Ropo et al., 2002; Sinclair, 2005; Hansen et al., 2007; Ladkin, 2008; Ropo and Sauer, 2008; Ladkin and Taylor, 2010; Koivunen and Wennes, 2011). Fourth, we view the relationship between leadership and space as a mutual construction, shaping and informing each other in an ongoing process (Wood, 2005; Taylor and Karanian, 2008; Van Marrewijk and Yanow, 2010).

By the term 'space', we mean physical or virtual environments people encounter in their work. We introduce two perspectives to space, distinguishing between the objective physically observed space (architecture, interior design, project software, technology and other material aspects) and the subjectively perceived space, that is, how each person perceives the environment with their senses, emotions and cognition (Ropo et al., 2013). These two perspectives represent different epistemological traditions, theoretical research disciplines and ways of thinking about space. The first, physically oriented objective space, is rooted in the architectural and organization behavioural field of study in the intersection of architecture and psychology (Steele, 1973; Becker and Steele, 1995). The subjective space is rooted in a social constructionist and phenomenological research tradition (Clegg and Kornberger, 2006; Dale and Burrell, 2008).

This book offers contributions to leadership and space from sociology, organizational aesthetics, cross-cultural management, project management, service management, architecture and facility management. The aim of the book is to point out the significance of the physical working environment and its subjective meaning for organizational life. The book broadens the scope of leadership and points out the vital relationship between leadership and material spaces. The book illuminates multiple ways of leading differently from a spatial perspective. The book is written for a variety of audiences interested in leadership, space and organization, including scholars and students of leadership and organization, educated practitioners, architects, facility managers and human resources (HR) professionals, who are willing to learn about the cutting-edge thinking in this field.

This book is rooted in the theoretical foundation of a four-year research project 'Leadership in Place and Space' (2011–14) funded by the Academy of Finland. The project aimed to develop a new understanding of leadership, emphasizing space, embodiment and aesthetics (www.leadspace.fi). The book develops the notion of 'spatial leadership', and the chapters illustrate various perspectives on how leadership and material spaces are related to and shape each other.

Even if leadership research has been conducted in many empirical settings and contexts, material places as such have not been conceptually treated at great length; neither has the relationship between physical and social space and organizational leadership been studied explicitly. By taking embodiment, emotions, power issues and politics into account, we wish to promote a new approach to leadership and space.

We will first outline some features of how spaces have been treated in the history of management thought and point out its limitations. Then we discuss the 'spatial turn' that is said to be taking place in organization studies and move on to discuss how it is emerging in the leadership field. We conclude and suggest that leadership could be understood as a socio-material phenomenon – a mutually constitutive relationship between the human and the non-human. Finally, we introduce the chapters of the book.

SPACES AND ORGANIZING IN THE HISTORY OF MANAGEMENT THOUGHT

With the development of the first organizations in the eighteenth century, the architecturally impressive and newly developed office and factory buildings were important manifestations, some might say power manifes-tations (Dale and Burrell, 2008), of the organizations themselves. It was with the new ideas of architecture and organizing that new forms of office buildings took shape, such as the tall office buildings with several floors housing the public bureaucracies or the modern corporations with the cell-shaped offices representing status, hierarchy and functionality. Engineers became involved in the design of organizations as new and more efficient modes of production, such as the assembly line and advanced specializa-tions. Architecture is one of the places where space and organization meet (ibid.). King (2004) states that 'it is within the space and form of the build-ing in which the social is most frequently constituted, in which its visual image announces its presence – in the city, in the nation, and in various distinct worlds' (p. 5).

More than just external appearance, the functional side of architectural buildings has been considered an important factor for organizing people, resources and activities. The development of production plants was linked with the idea of organizing, making the issue of space important for lead-ership processes. In the beginning of the industrial and managerial revolu-tion, the engineering and architect professions were important in setting the issue of place and space on the agenda for both public and private organizations. Forming an alliance, they made the factory and office buildings important symbols of the new industrial era.

The rise of management as a new profession started with people like Frederick W. Taylor (1911) launching 'scientific management' contain-ing new premises and models for production. The principles of organ-izing found their way to factory floor plans, which ultimately led to the mechanization, mass production and efficiency gains of the Industrial Revolution. The planning of the workspace was initially closely con-nected to production activities and processes, which gave the engineers a vital role in planning production spaces. This early development within management can be called a rational planning motive to study spaces and organizing.

According to Davis et al. (2011), the widespread introduction of open-plan and *bürolandschaft* (landscaped) offices in North America in the 1960s and 1970s animated organizational scholars to study the relationship between workers and their physical workspace (for an excellent review of the early development of office environments see Duffy, 1997). The effect that changes in established office design might have on the office occupants became a common concern, and journalists and scholars took up the issue. The open-plan concept soon became a vehicle for organizations to reduce their fixed costs (for example, Duffy, 1997; Vischer, 2005) and to increase the density of employees housed in previously enclosed spaces. Gradually, design features, such as the inclusion of plants and angled desk placements, were marginalized. At the same time, distances between neighbouring desks were reduced and circulation space was sacrificed for 'efficiency'. Flexible, open workspace solutions came to the attention of designers and managers in the 1990s (Cohen, 2007). Mobile phones, PCs and wireless networks made flexible work possible, and the rapid emergence of project work in knowledge-based organizations made possible new and more dynamic ways of working. Lefebvre (1991) uses the term 'conceived' space and Taylor and Spicer (2007) use the term 'planned' space to refer to architectural and managerial motives to point out the instrumental and objective thinking of organizational spaces.

The open-plan offices introduced a strategic perspective on workspace in seeing the physical contingencies of organizations as a means to achieve higher productivity, flexibility, business value and other performance measures. This perspective is particularly prevalent within corporate real estate and facility management, applied fields between engineering, architecture and management. Three strategic foci have been adopted: efficiency and competitive advantage, organizational change, and organizational branding. Within facility management, the cost-efficiency perspective has been a prevalent argument for introducing open and flexible workspace solutions, but the recent focus in facility management has been on the added value beyond efficiency and cost savings (for example, Lindholm and Leväinen, 2006). By paying attention to space in facility management, more focus is now on the effectiveness of facilities. For example, the work of Kampschroer and Heerwagen (2005) highlights the importance of aligning organizational objectives and desired changes with workplace strategies and design outcomes. The question remains, how open and flexible workspace solutions enhance value creation in organizations?

Arge and De Paoli (2000) found that organizational change and development was a top management motive for introducing new workplace strategies for three out of six large Norwegian organizations. Becker et al. (1994) studied the organizational implications of different implementation strategies related to new workspace designs. Their conclusions are that business-driven and process-oriented strategies by far outperform cost-driven and solution-oriented approaches in terms of user satisfaction, work effectiveness, lifetime of the workplace change and acceptance throughout the organization. Testing Becker's theory, Arge and De Paoli (2000) found that Norwegian senior managers in knowledge-based organizations had strategic, that is, business-driven, motives for introducing workplace changes and wanted to use workplace changes as a strategic tool to support organizational change and development.

Levin (2005) searched for a workplace design that connects with the strategy of the organization and is intended to support it. He refers to the congruence hypothesis defined by Nadler and Tushman (1997), that is, the degree to which the strategy, work, people, structure and culture of the organization are aligned will determine the organization's ability to compete and succeed. According to Levin, the role of the workplace as a facilitator and component of organizational congruence suggests a different paradigm for developing workplace design approaches or strategies. Blair and Wallman (2000) point out that assets are shifting away from physical ones, such as office buildings, towards intangibles as drivers of economic growth. The ramifications of this is that the workplace needs to be viewed in the context of a facilitator of the work processes that support knowledge work (Gjersvik and Blakstad, 2004) rather than as a physical asset itself that will create wealth for the organization. The literature shows that over time, the understanding of buildings and workspace design as facilitators and supporters of organizational value-added has increased, as has the understanding of how to design workspaces that support organizational performance and efficiency.

Branding corporate image and identity through buildings and workspace design became popular in the 1990s and 2000 (Appel-Meulenbroek et al., 2010). The importance given to corporate branding through architecture and aesthetics has been called 'corporate identity design' (Napoles, 1988) or 'corporate style in action' (Dickinson and Svensen, 2000). This is about the use of architecture and workspace design to promote and communicate the identity of organizations both inside and outside the company. Dickinson and Svensen (2000) argue that architecture serves as a 'visual symbol for the expression of a corporation's culture and personality' (p. 259). Architecture, art and design have been used to signal modernity and to attract the young and promising workforce to the organization.

In their article on 'funky offices', Deal and Kennedy (2000, cited in Van Meel and Vos, 2001, p. 2) write that 'a company's investment in bricks and mortar inevitably says something about its culture'. Becker (2001) points out that to prosper, organizations must reduce capital and operating costs and increase flexibility and adaptability, while creating a workplace that helps attract and retain the highest-quality staff and enables them to work to their fullest potential. Morgan and Anthony (2008) confirm that the corporate brand is now intrinsically linked to workplace strategy. Property change projects give an organization the possibility to reposition itself in the eyes of the market and to use workplace design to enforce its image and identity. Recent focus and research in workplace management and office design have highlighted the role of corporate aesthetics as a part of corporate branding. The discourse on office design has slowly entered the field of corporate strategy.

Another perspective on leadership, spaces and organizing has roots in the early Hawthorne studies in which the role of the physical work conditions for female assembly workers were studied. It was found that social and psychological factors were more important than the physical ones. This research programme paved the way for a rich and long history of human relations studies in organizations. However, paradoxically, it excluded physical work conditions, such as the workspace, for more than 50 years. According to a review by Davis et al. (2011), the physical environment of the office was a major topic for early industrial organizational psychologists (circa 1910 onwards), with attention predominantly on the effects of ambient conditions (for example, lighting, temperature, ventilation) on workers' productivity. This approach is still reflected in the more recent ergonomic and environmental psychology literature on workspace. The above contributions represent an organizational behaviour motive to study spaces and organizing.

SPATIAL TURN IN ORGANIZATION AND MANAGEMENT RESEARCH

Although spaces and places have been of interest to management and organization scholars, as discussed above, organization studies have emphasized the linguistic and social (constructionist) aspects of understanding organizations (for example, Fairhurst and Putnam, 2004). Recently, material aspects of organizational life – space included – have regained interest (for example, Barad, 2003; Dale, 2005; Orlikowski, 2007; Leonardi et al., 2012; Carlile et al., 2013; De Vaujany and Mitev, 2013). Van Marrewijk and Yanow (2010) and Beyes and Steyaert (2012), among others, argue that a 'spatial turn' is taking place in organization studies. In addition to studying the physical spatial designs of companies' headquarters and offices, this turn underlines values and symbolic meanings attached to spatial solutions and their effect on social relations and organizing at work.

There are several recent reviews of organizational space studies (Clegg and Kornberger, 2006; Elsbach and Pratt, 2007; Taylor and Spicer, 2007; Dale and Burrell, 2008; Van Marrewijk and Yanow, 2010; Stang Våland (2010). Based on these, Ropo et al. (2013) identified three major approaches in the literature: an objective approach that studies the physical environment from an architectural and managerial perspective (for example, Bitner, 1992; Elsbach and Pratt, 2007), a subjectively or phenomenologically oriented approach to space and how it is experienced (for example, Tuan, 1977; Berg and Kreiner, 1990; Gagliardi, 1990; Lefebvre, 1991; Bachelard, 1994; Guillén, 1997; Hatch and Cunliffe [1997] 2013; Yanow, 1998; Martin, 2002; Strati, 2007; Van Marrewijk, 2010) and a critical, post-structuralist approach emphasizing power, politics and control that spaces shape and maintain (for example, Foucault, 1977; Dale, 2005; Clegg and Kornberger, 2006; Dale and Burrell, 2008; Tyler and Cohen, 2010; Panayiotou and Kafiris, 2011).

The study of organizational space is also developing within an alternative and creative approach called 'the aesthetic perspective to leadership and organizing'. Discussion on organizational aesthetics started in the mid-1980s at the Standing Conference on Organizational Symbolism (SCOS) as a counter-movement to the positivist, objective understanding of organizational life. Antonio Strati (1992, 1999), Pascale Gagliardi (1990), Rafael Ramírez (1996) and Mauro Guillén (1997) were among the first contributors to this paradigmatically new approach to organizations and organizing. Hassard et al.'s edited volume *Body and Organization* (2000) paved the way to aesthetically address sensuously inspired and corporeal aspects of organizational life.

Certain topics related to space have been of particular interest in the organizational aesthetics literature (Strati, 2000, p. 28). The physical space of the organization is seen to emphasize corporate image and architecture as exercises of control. Furthermore, physical artefacts that constitute the organization's landscape are considered crucial for meaningmaking. As of now, there is a canonized body of knowledge on aesthetics and embodiment in organizations, which is also related to experiencing materiality and spaces (for example, Linstead and Höpfl, 2000; Strati, 2000; Martin, 2002; Strati and Guillet de Monthoux, 2002; Carr and Hancock, 2003; Taylor and Hansen, 2005). Despite this growth, we join Yanow (2010, p. 139) in remarking that space and embodiment (in Yanow's terms 'spatial sensibility') have not gained the same kind of terminological status within the last 20 years in the organization research.

LEADERSHIP AND SPACE

Material, embodied and aesthetic aspects have been recently addressed in the leadership field (Ropo and Parviainen, 2001; Sinclair, 2005; Ladkin, 2006, 2008; Hansen et al., 2007; Ropo and Sauer, 2008; Küpers, 2010; Ladkin and Taylor, 2010; Melina et al., 2013; Ropo et al., 2013; Special Issue on 'Materiality of Leadership' in *Leadership*, 2013). Broadly speaking, these studies consider leadership as a felt experience in the 'space between' rather than the effort of one person to influence another. Beyond emphasizing the emotional dimension of leadership over the mainstream rational and cognitive one, this view broadens leadership from happening between humans to include human and non-human encounters as well.

It is worth noting that leadership as a term is scarcely, if at all, mentioned in the space-related organization studies discussed earlier. This is a noteworthy omission, yet we believe – as this book will show – that studying organizational spaces from the perspective of leadership is a source of inspiration for understanding organizational life. Taylor and Karanian (2008), who study space as constructing relational leadership, are an exception. They conceptualize this as a 'working connection'. By this, they refer to the physical conditions where people can connect, collaborate and feel comfortable. In contrast to considering space and place as physical materiality, their critical approach discussed leadership as a structural, meta-level issue. The notions of power, politics, control, hierarchy, managerial practice and organizing principles are the terms used to elaborate on the relationship between leadership and space (for example, Hassard et al., 2000; Clegg and Kornberger, 2006; Dale and Burrell, 2008). For example, Hofbauer (2000) shows with empirical illustrations and architectural layouts how different office designs, such as office corridors or open offices, shape communication, collaboration and interaction. She also emphasizes the experience of space as a bodily experience (p. 166). Yet, as Elsbach and Pratt (2007) show in their literature review, no elements of the physical environment are consistently associated with certain particular outcomes in these work settings. This can be understood by Lefebvre's approach, according to which space is not an objective element that can be taken for granted, but rather the output of a social process. Lefebvre draws a distinction between three kinds of spaces: conceived (as discussed earlier as the rational and strategic motive to approach spaces and organizing), perceived and lived space. Taylor and Spicer (2007) identify the same type of distinctions and use the terms planned, practised and imagined space.

There are current discussions on leadership and place beyond the organization and management field. Researchers in the field of policy and regional studies (for example, Sotarauta, 2005, 2009; Gibney et al., 2009; Stimson et al., 2009; Liddle, 2010; Special Issue on 'Leadership and Place' in *Policy Studies*, 2010; Collinge and Gibney, 2011; Horlings, 2012), human geography (for example, Tuan, 1977), environmental psychology (for example, Gifford, 2007) and architecture have addressed this relationship. The question within regional studies is, how urban, rural or regional places are being shaped by leadership actions and processes. The term 'leadership of place' is widely used in this discussion (Collinge et al., 2010). As in the general leadership field, they also have varying perspectives on leadership, and both individually centred and relationally oriented shared views of leadership can be found (for example, Sotarauta, 2005; Mabey and Freeman, 2010). As the editors of the book *Leadership and Change in Sustainable Regional Development* (Sotarauta et al., 2012) state, leadership is important; however, it is still a sparsely researched area in terms of the reinvention of regions and their development. Deviating from the mainstream lines of thinking that consider leadership as an individualistic, top-down influence, they state that leadership needs to be seen as a multi-agency and multilevel culturally bound activity. They find themselves inspired by Scharmer (2008) who calls for passion, values, meaning, motivation and inspiration.

The field of human geography studies the world, its people, communities and cultures, with an emphasis on relationships across space and place. Human geography pays particular attention to human activities in spaces and places (Tuan, 1977) and uses mainly qualitative research methodologies to study the experience of space. Tuan, one of the founding fathers of human geography, argues that spaces, places and architecture 'instruct' us. For instance, in the Middle Ages, a great cathedral was usually centrally located and the mass of the construction alone immediately evokes bodily sensations. A cathedral was built to symbolically remind us of our smallness and of the greatness of God (especially in a time when there were no other competing high-rises around). In modern cities like New York, the skyscrapers may evoke similar feelings, or feelings of aggressiveness and arrogance or perhaps excitement, braveness and pulsating dynamism.

Twenty-first-century office architecture is going in new directions. The main features of the twentieth-century office – standardized, inflexible design, lack of human interaction and place dependency – are being replaced by different characteristics in the new millennium; offices are planned to be narrative, neighbourly and nomadic. In terms of leadership, it seems that architecture today regards itself as having a major influence on the inner workings of companies and practices. Productivity has become more important, and understanding human communication in other than mechanistic, machine-like terms produces a change to architecture and design.

Most of the architectural connotations to leadership are inherent and implicit to architectural process. Le Corbusier defined and influenced the architectural thinking of modern cities in his influential writings (for example, Le Corbusier, 1923). His approach is primarily based on certain normative ideals derived from mathematics and geometry and aesthetics (understood as the study of beauty). Architecture has multiple intentions, and within these intentions leadership is but one way to intentionally and actively lead people's behaviour.

Leadership theory and environmental psychology are indirectly related through their shared views on organization psychology, social psychology and sociology. Environmental psychology is interested in people's use and experience of place (Gifford, 2007). There are both written and unwritten rules and social codes, signs and symbols that guide us on how to be in a space and how to use it. How do we perceive the places? Are they attractive and pleasant? What kind of emotions and sensations do they evoke? Are we more creative or effective in certain spaces than others? These are some of the central questions in environmental psychology. Organizational leadership research that emphasizes places and spaces has a shared interest in these questions. Different schools and traditions within environmental psychology have slightly varied interests. Gestalt psychology is interested in how a person encounters the physical environment and acts on it. The ecology and social psychology researchers ask how the context organizes the action, whereas phenomenologically and analytically oriented environmental psychologists are keen on studying the experiences and meanings people have and attach to different places.

LEADERSHIP AS A HUMAN/NON-HUMAN RELATIONSHIP: SOCIOMATERIALITY OF LEADERSHIP

In the wake of a material turn in organization studies (Barad, 2003; Dale, 2005; Orlikowski, 2007), the notion of materiality has recently been discussed in the context of embodied, relational and plural leadership approaches (for example, Melina et al., 2013; Pullen and Vacchani, 2013; Ropo et al., 2013; Special Issue on 'The Materiality of Leadership' in *Leadership*, 2013). In that vein, sociomaterial concepts of leading and organizing are increasingly in the making (Orlikowski, 2007; Orlikowski and Scott, 2008; Von Marrewijk and Yanow, 2010; De Vaujany and Mitey, 2013; De Vaujany and Vaast, 2013; Oborn et al., 2013).

We see the sociomaterial nature of leadership as something that happens as we experience material places through our senses. While doing so, we attribute symbols, memories, feelings and physical qualities to places. The embodied experiences of the material spaces shape our way of relating to people and issues and the ways in which we act upon them. This is an emerging understanding of what we call 'spatial leadership' or 'spatiality of leadership'.

The way spaces and places lead us can be taken very literally. As we follow corridors, stairs and open doors but cannot walk through walls, the very materiality of the physical place leads or directs our action. Another more symbolic expression of spatial leadership can be experienced in self-service restaurants or in airports – even if there is no person telling us what to do, we find our way. This relationship between space and reading signs is based on cultural reading of symbols. The question is how to conceptualize this relationship so that it makes sense for organization and leadership research and practice.

In the long tradition of leadership research, leadership has been under-stood as a quality of an individual or a relationship between one or more subjects (leader–follower or within a team). In the notion of spatial leader-ship, leadership is not necessarily limited to human–human relations, as it can also be observed as taking place between humans and the physical materiality. A relationship between a person and his or her environment exists. This relationship has been conceptualized in organization research (even if not in leadership terms): the relationship between a person and a place manifests in an unfolding process and is formed as a mutual constitu-tion (Hernes et al., 2006; Van Marrewijk and Yanow, 2010; De Vajauny and Vaast, 2013) and through mutual enactment (Dale, 2005). These partly interchangeable terms do not refer directly to leadership, but the phenomenon they describe (the relationship between social and material) can be termed leadership. Following these authors, we are not giving space or place an independent agency but see it produced and being rematerial-ized over time (Lefebvre, 1991) and through the experiences of the spaces. The way spaces and their use change over time is well documented (for example, Peltonen, 2010; Van Marrewijk, 2010; De Vajauny and Vaast, 2013). Office environment and different workplace designs lead us through our constant interaction with environment, but they are neither neutral (Dale and Burrell, 2008; Carlile et al., 2013) nor constants (Lefebvre, 1991). The spaces lead through our subjective and embodied experiences (Hansen et al. 2007). This book offers several illustrations of this.

INTRODUCTION TO THE CHAPTERS

There is a long tradition of studying work in offices, illustrated by the research perspectives discussed above. We are opening up the 'office box' concept by introducing chapters describing many other kinds of places and spaces where work and leadership unfold today. We want to go beyond the regular office, as much of work and leadership is taking place elsewhere. Each chapter reveals new spaces for work and leadership and different perspectives from which to study and understand them. This book is divided into six parts. Part I looks at the changes in work and workspaces currently taking place with regard to new kinds of offices and coworking spaces. Part II looks at alternative or open offices, Part III at virtual workspaces and Part IV covers service spaces. Furthermore, Part V examines cultural spaces, such as cities and multinational companies, and the final part of the book, Part VI takes a close look at institutional spaces, in particular, a hospital and a university. The authors represent different disciplinary backgrounds in the management and organizational fields. The book shows that there are several ways to approach the subject of leadership, spaces and organizing.

Part I: Workspaces in Change

Work and workspaces are changing, which is illustrated in the first two chapters, describing new work and office trends. In Chapter 1, Perttu Salovaara describes an emerging and growing phenomenon – coworking as an office space and as a movement. The chapter introduces coworking as both a physical office space and as a movement with its own guiding principles and ideology. The discussion is framed within the larger context of new work and new 'sharing economy'. Based on a phenomenological leadership tradition, he uses his own experience as an academic hiring space in a coworking community in Bushwick, New York. He also questions whether coworking, having a core set of principles, that is, 'collaboration, openness, community, accessibility and sustainability', is building a community and what kind of benefits do coworking spaces bring to people, society and the economy. Finally, he asks what kind of leadership coworking spaces produce.

Siri Hunnes Blakstad, Chapter 2, is an architect from the facility management research tradition. She describes the history of workplace design and management from the perspective of organization and leadership. In workplace management and design, the discussion has focused on how to optimize space in order to support the user's activities and the organization's efficiency and effectiveness. She describes new ways of working and a new kind of office. She argues that increased mobility has, paradoxically, increased the meaning of the physical place. In spite of the trend towards more mobility and flexible ways of working, there seems to be even more focus on the workplace as a place that builds identity, meaning and the quality of an organization. Workplace management is therefore shifting into what is needed to support work. This means that the process of defining needs and discussing different ways of working becomes more important. Managers need to be able to assist the organization in a strategic process that defines their main ambitions and strategy related to the workplace and ways of working.

Part II: Open Office Spaces

From an established project management perspective, Anne Live Vaagaasar in Chapter 3 adopts a spatial perspective to leadership in knowledge-intensive projects. She has studied project managers located in team-based, open-plan, flexible office spaces. She argues that space is overlooked as an important resource in project work and that it can enable the prioritizing of project tasks, increasing motivation for project tasks, creating interdependencies between tasks, making knowledge and people more evident, sharing emotions and knowledge and providing team identity, team commitment and peer control. Additionally, the symbolic act of giving the project its own territory may lead to increased legitimacy of the project aims and work in organizations. Vaagaasar describes how the co-location of project teams in open-plan office space leads to knowledge work in the context of projects and makes it one of the preferred office spaces for project work.

In Chapter 4, Niina Uolamo and Arja Ropo describe a study on workspaces and employee wellbeing. They point out how the subjective and sensuous experiences of the physical work environment and the spatial changes lead to practices and feelings of wellbeing. The study uses narrative interviews as well as pictures taken by the participants. The authors emphasize that visual and other materials complement the interviews and are needed because people often find it difficult to talk about their feelings and the sensations of spaces. The chapter elaborates on the idea that leadership not only happens between humans but is also spatially informed. The chapter gives an empirical illustration on how leadership plays out as a sociomaterial phenomenon, that is, as a relationship between organizational space and employee wellbeing.

Part III: Virtual Workspaces

In Chapter 5, Donatella De Paoli writes about a relatively new kind of workspace – the virtual space. Coming from an organizational aesthetics and leadership perspective, she gives an extensive review of research on virtual leadership, questioning whether current researchers and practitioners are too pessimistic about leadership in virtual space. Inspired by an interview with a young entrepreneur running a company with several employees long distance, De Paoli argues that there is a call for new leadership. She draws a map of a new leadership landscape and approach based on the nature of technological networks favouring a more distributed, transparent, flexible and democratic leadership approach. She describes leadership theories, such as relational leadership, plural leadership, aesthetic and embodied leadership, and claims that the traditional leader-centric and centralized approach is no longer relevant for leadership in virtual space. Finally, she argues that physical places and spaces are important for virtual leadership, but in ways that differ from traditional workspaces.

Matti Vartiainen, Chapter 6, comes from the field of work psychology that is based on the technological sciences. He gives an accurate and descriptive account of how the Internet and an organization-wide intranet provide virtual tools called collaborative working environments (CWEs). Reviewing the technological literature on virtual work and cooperation, avatars (digital self-presentations), frames of reference, co-presence through shared three-dimensional place, an experience of immersion, multimodality, rich visual information and supporting tools are seen to provide creative work and interactions. He then discusses how personalized avatars influence the quality and character of work processes, for example, when the behaviour of an individual operating under a digital persona adapts to conform to that persona. The term 'avatar' is a generic term used to qualify an infinite number of possible representations of a person.

Part IV: Service Spaces

In Chapter 7, Kaisa Greenlees uses a symbolic, social constructionist perspective of space by doing an ethnographic study of employees in a bookstore. She shows how artefacts and their meanings are created in everyday practice by the people working and leading there. She describes symbolically powerful artefacts that are present all the time, including colours, uniforms and spatial arrangements. They give non-verbal cues and influence the actions of sales personnel. Using an organizational aesthetics approach to leadership, she describes and analyses both spaces and artefacts in the bookstore and how they construct leadership. She highlights the manager's room as evoking different feelings amongst sales personnel. She also describes the meaning of the sales desk area, which was considered to be a 'safe' place because the rules of social behaviour were clear, such as the physical distance to the customers.

Ritva Höykinpuro has a service management background within marketing. In Chapter 8, she discusses an emerging phenomenon of service space – self-service hotels – with a theatre metaphor. She takes a customer's perspective and analyses how the spaces lead the customers to act in a meaningful way. The customers are expected to follow a script (a service concept), but there are no front-stage actors to guide, train or inform them. Höykinpuro describes how the customer's role shifts from being a spectator to an actor or sometimes even to a lead actor on the stage. The study uses five explorative, narrative interviews and illustrates the interdisciplinary nature of understanding service space, namely service marketing and management, human resources management, leadership and hospitality management.

Part V: Cultural Spaces

Erika Sauer comes from an organizational aesthetics and leadership perspective and introduces two big, international cities in Chapter 9. She describes how New York and Jakarta lead their inhabitants in many ways. Through several interviews with a group, she draws a map of how culture, work, leadership and life are perceived in these two cities. In Jakarta, the traffic density, food and shopping lead people; in New York, the heterogeneity of the population, fast pace and the dynamic feeling of the city are important leading forces. The abundance of stimuli, the freedom of choice and anonymity are also characteristics of how these cities can lead people.

Tor Grenness comes from the cross-cultural leadership field and discusses in Chapter 10 how culture, especially national culture, influences perceptions of leadership. He has a keen interest in the Scandinavian leadership culture, which he explores from the perspective of workspace design. His chapter is based on research from a major international telecom company based in Norway that exported the architecture of its headquarters and its office design to subsidiaries in Asia. Grenness describes how the open-plan, flexible, transparent and standardized office solution is a manifestation of Scandinavian values of equality and leadership, emphasizing how leaders should be visible, open, accessible and involved. He questions and analyses how this may work in Asian work

culture. He argues that research on international human resource management – primarily focusing at staffing, performance appraisal and compensation systems – should also take into account the physical design of
subsidiaries' offices and make it an integrated part of international human
resource management studies and cross-cultural leadership.

Part VI: Institutional Spaces

Karen Dale and Gibson Burrell come from the critical organizational
research tradition, and in Chapter 11 they examine the process of launching and working in a new academic building where one of the authors
works. This is an interesting case of a lived workspace, described from
an 'insider' perspective that introduces the personal, subjective, lived and
embodied experience through stories of working in this new office facility.
They describe how the architects' notion of work and place are based in
architectural design ideals more than in the needs and perceptions of the
people inhabiting the workspace. The authors show an organizational
experiment of how and what should be done within the ever-present
tension between centralization and local autonomy in university settings.
They argue that the experience of formal leadership within this case was
one of distance, dissent and disembodiment.

Erika Sauer, in Chapter 12, uses a phenomenological, social constructionist and aesthetic approach to analyse hospital space to explore what
kind of power structures the architecture, design and the use of space
signal, symbolize and construct. Based on an ethnographic study of several
groups of people working in a hospital and her own experience visiting a
hospital as a relative of a patient, she gives an interesting account of many
of the 'taken-for-granted' symbolic artefacts, material places and ways of
organizing. She questions who this hospital space is made for and what
kind of hidden power structures it reveals. It is apparent that in hospitals
patients lose signs of individuality, dignity, privacy and autonomy. Losing
the personal space makes a person vulnerable. By invading personal space,
hospitals minimize individuality and power, thus turning the 'imprisoned'
patients, into 'docile bodies'.

REFERENCES

Appel-Meulenbroek, R., D. Havermans, I. Janssen and A. van Kempen (2010),
'Corporate branding: An exploration of the influence of CRE', *Journal of
Corporate Real Estate*, **12** (1), 47–59.
Arge, K. and D. De Paoli (2000), 'Strategic workplace design', in B. Nutt and

P. McLennan (eds), *Facilities Management Risks and Opportunities*, Oxford: Blackwell Science, pp. 149–56.

Bachelard, G. (1994), *The Poetics of Space*, Boston, MA: Beacon Press.

Barad, K. (2003), 'Posthumanist performativity: How matter comes to matter', *Signs: Journal of Women in Culture and Society*, **28** (3), 801–31.

Becker, F. (2001), 'Organisational dilemmas and workplace solutions', *Journal of Corporate Real Estate*, **4** (2), 129–49.

Becker, F. and F. Steele (1995), *Workplace by Design*, San Francisco, CA: Jossey-Bass.

Becker, F., K.L. Quinn, K.J. Rappaport and W.R. Sims (1994), *Implementing Innovative Workplaces: Organizational Implications of Different Strategies*, Ithaca, NY: Cornell University International Workplace Studies Program.

Berg, P.-O. and K. Kreiner (1990), 'Corporate architecture', in P. Gagliardi (ed.), *Symbols and Artifacts: Views of Corporate Landscape*, Berlin: De Gruyter, pp. 124–45.

Beyes, T. and C. Steyaert (2012), 'Spacing organization: Non-representational theory and performing organizational space', *Organization*, **19** (1), 45–61.

Bitner, M.J. (1992), 'Servicescapes: The impact of physical surroundings on customers and employees', *Journal of Marketing*, **56** (2), 57–71.

Blair, M. and S. Wallman (2000), *Unseen Wealth: Report of the Brookings Task Force on Understanding Intangible Sources of Value*, Washington, DC: Brookings Institute.

Carlile, P.R., D. Nicolini, A. Langley and H. Tsoukas (eds) (2013), *How Matter Matters: Objects, Artifacts, and Materiality in Organization Studies*, Oxford: Oxford University Press.

Carr, A. and P. Hancock (eds) (2003), *Art and Aesthetics at Work*, Basingstoke, UK: Palgrave Macmillan.

Clegg, S.R. and M. Kornberger (eds) (2006), *Space, Organizations and Management Theory*, Oslo and Copenhagen: Liber and Copenhagen Business School Press.

Cohen, L. (2007), 'Bridging of two streams of office research: A comparison of design/behaviour and management journal articles from 1980–2001', *Journal of Architectural and Planning Research*, **24** (4), 289–307.

Collinge, C. and J. Gibney (2011), 'Connecting place, policy and leadership', in C. Collinge, J. Gibney and C. Mabey (eds), *Leadership and Place*, Abingdon, UK: Routledge, pp. 13–25.

Collinge, C., J. Gibney and C. Mabey (2010), 'Introduction: Leadership and place', *Policy Studies*, **31** (4), 367–78.

Collinson, D.L. (2006), 'Rethinking followership: a post-structuralist analysis of follower identities', *Leadership Quarterly*, **17** (2), 172–89.

Crevani, L., M. Lindgren and J. Packendorff (2010), 'Leadership, not leaders: on the study of leadership as practices and interactions', *Scandinavian Journal of Management*, **26** (1), 77–86.

Dale, K. (2005), 'Building a social materiality: Spatial and embodied politics in organizational control', *Organization*, **12** (5), 649–78.

Dale, K. and G. Burrell (2008), *Spaces of Organization and the Organization of Space*, Basingstoke, UK: Palgrave Macmillan.

Davis, M.C., D.J. Leach and C.W. Clegg (2011), 'The physical environment of the office: Contemporary and emerging issues', in G.P. Hodgkinson and J.K. Ford (eds), *International Review of Industrial and Organizational Psychology, Vol. 26*, Chichester, UK: Wiley, pp. 193–235.

Deal, T.E. and A.A. Kennedy (2000), *Corporate Cultures: The Rites and Rituals of Corporate Life*, New York: Perseus Books Group.

Denis, J.-L., A. Langley and V. Sergi (2012), 'Leadership in the plural', *The Academy of Management Annals*, **6** (1), 211–83.

De Vaujany, F.-X. and N. Mitey (eds) (2013), *Materiality and Space: Organizations, Artefacts and Practices*, Basingstoke, UK: Palgrave Macmillan.

De Vaujany, F.-X. and E. Vaast (2013), 'If these walls could talk: The mutual constitution of space and legitimacy', *Organization Science*, **25** (3), 713–31.

Dickinson, P. and N. Svensen (2000), *Beautiful Corporations: Corporate Style in Action*, London: Pearson Education Limited/Prentice Hall.

Duffy, F. (1997), *The New Office*, London: Conran Octopus.

Elsbach, K.D. and M.G. Pratt (2007), 'The physical environment in organizations', *The Academy of Management Annals*, **1** (1), 181–224.

Fairhurst, G.T. and D. Grant (2010), 'The social construction of leadership: A sailing guide', *Management Communication Quarterly*, **24** (2), 171–210.

Fairhurst, G.T. and L. Putnam (2004), 'Organizations as discursive constructions', *Communication Theory*, **14** (1), 5–26.

Foucault, M. (1977), *Discipline and Punish: The Birth of the Prison*, New York: Pantheon Books.

Gagliardi, P. (ed.) (1990), *Symbols and Artifacts: Views of the Corporate Landscape*, New York: Aldine de Gruyter.

Gibney, M., S. Lanham-New, A. Cassidy and H. Vorster (2009), *Introduction to Human Nutrition*, 2nd edition, San Francisco, CA: Wiley.

Gifford, R. (2007), 'Environmental psychology and sustainable development: Expansion, maturation, and challenges', *Journal of Social Issues*, **63** (1) 199–212.

Gjersvik, R. and S.H. Blakstad (2004), 'Designing knowledge workspace: Archetypes of professional service work as a tool for change', in A. Carlsen, R. Klev and G. von Krogh (eds), *Living Knowledge: The Dynamics of Professional Service Work*, Basingstoke, UK: Palgrave Macmillan, pp. 134–46.

Grint, K. (2005), 'Problems, problems, problems: The social construction of "leadership"', *Human Relations*, **58** (11), 1467–94.

Guillén, M. (1997), 'Scientific management's lost aesthetic: Architecture, organization, and the Taylorized beauty of the mechanical', *Administrative Science Quarterly*, **42** (4), 682–715.

Hamel, G. (2007), *The Future of Management*, Boston, MA: Harvard Business School Publishing.

Hansen, H., A. Ropo and E. Sauer (2007), 'Aesthetic leadership', *Leadership Quarterly*, **18** (6), 544–60.

Hassard, J., R. Holliday and H. Willmott (eds) (2000), *Body and Organization*, London: Sage.

Hatch, M.J. and A. Cunliffe ([1997] 2013), *Organization Theory: Modern, Symbolic, and Postmodern Perspectives*, 3rd edition, Oxford: Oxford University Press.

Hernes, T., T. Bakken and P.I. Olsen (2006), 'Spaces as process: Developing a recursive perspective on organizational space', in S.R. Clegg and M. Kornberger (eds), *Space, Organizations and Management Theory*, Copenhagen: Liber & Copenhagen Business School Press, pp. 44–63.

Hofbauer, J. (2000), 'Bodies in a landscape: On office design and organization', in J. Hassard, R. Holliday and H. Willmott (eds), *Body and Organization*, London: Sage.

Horlings, L. (2012), 'Value-oriented leadership in the Netherlands', in M. Sotarauta, L. Horlings and J. Liddle (eds), *Leadership and Change in Sustainable Regional Development*, London and New York: Routledge, pp. 252–70.

Kampschroer, K. and J. Heerwagen (2005), 'The strategic workplace: Development and evaluation', *Building Research & Information*, **33** (4), 326–37.

King, N. (2004), *Spaces of Global Cultures*, London: Routledge.

Koivunen, N. and G. Wennes (2011), 'Show us the sound', *Leadership*, **7** (1), 51–71.

Küpers, W. (2010), '"Inter-place": Phenomenology of embodied space and place as a basis for a relational understanding of leader-followership in organizations', *Environment, Space, Place*, **2** (1), 81–121.

Ladkin, D. (2006), 'The enchantment of the charismatic leader: Charisma reconsidered as aesthetic encounter', *Leadership*, **2** (2), 165–79.

Ladkin, D. (2008), 'Leading beautifully: How mastery congruence and purpose create the aesthetic of embodied leadership performance', *Leadership Quarterly*, **19** (1), 31–41.

Ladkin, D. (2010), *Rethinking Leadership: A New Look at Old Leadership Questions*, Cheltenham, UK and Northampton, MA, USA: Edward Elgar Publishing.

Ladkin, D. and S.S. Taylor (2010), 'Enacting the "true self": Towards a theory of embodied authentic leadership', *Leadership Quarterly*, **21** (1), 64–74.

Leadership (2013), Special Issue: 'The Materiality of Leadership: Corporeality and Subjectivity', **9** (3).

Le Corbusier (1923), *Toward an Architecture*, trans. J. Goodman, London: Frances Lincoln Ltd Publishers.

Lefebvre, H. (1991), *The Production of Space*, Oxford: Blackwell.

Leonardi, P.M., B.A. Nardi and J. Kallinikos (eds) (2012), *Materiality and Organizing: Social Interaction in a Technological World*, Oxford: Oxford University Press.

Levin, A.C. (2005), 'Changing the role of workplace design within the business organisation: A model for linking workplace design solutions to business strategies', *Journal of Facilities Management*, **3** (4), 299–311.

Liddle, J. (2010), '21st century public leadership: Some reflections', *Policy and Politics*, **38** (4), 657–64.

Lindholm, A.-L. and K.I. Leväinen (2006), 'A framework for identifying and measuring value-added by corporate real estate', *Journal of Corporate Real Estate*, **8** (1), 38–46.

Linstead, S.A. and H.J. Höpfl (eds) (2000), *The Aesthetics of Organization*, London: Sage.

Mabey, C. and T. Freeman (2010), 'Reflections on leadership and place', *Policy Studies*, **31** (4), 505–22.

Martin, Y. (2002), 'Sensations, bodies, and the spirit of a place: Aesthetics in residential organizations for the elderly', *Human Relations*, **55** (7), 861–85.

Meindl, J.R. (1995), 'The romance of leadership as a follower-centric theory: A social constructionist approach', *The Leadership Quarterly*, **6** (3), 329–41.

Melina, L.R., G.J. Burgess, L.L. Falkman and A. Marturano (eds) (2013), *The Embodiment of Leadership*, San Francisco, CA: Jossey-Bass.

Morgan, A. and S. Anthony (2008), 'Creating a high-performance workplace: A review of issues and opportunities', *Journal of Corporate Real Estate*, **10** (1), 27–39.

Nadler, D.A. and M.L. Tushman (1997), *Competing by Design: The Power of Organizational Architecture*, Oxford: Oxford University Press.

Napoles, V. (1988), *Corporate Identity Design*, Hoboken, NJ: John Wiley & Sons, Inc.

Oborn, E., M. Barrett and S. Dawson (2013), 'Distributed leadership in policy formulation: A sociomaterial perspective', *Organization Studies*, **34** (2), 253–76.

Orlikowski, W.J. (2007), 'Sociomaterial practices: Exploring technology at work', *Organization Studies*, **28** (9), 1435–48.

Orlikowski, W.J. and S.V. Scott (2008), 'Sociomateriality: Challenging the separation of technology, work and organization', *Annals of the Academy of Management*, **2** (1), 433–74.

Panayiotou, A. and K. Kafiris (2011), 'Viewing the language of space: Organizational spaces, power, and resistance in popular films', *Journal of Management Inquiry*, **20** (3), 264–84.

Parry, K.W. and H. Hansen (2007), 'The organizational story as leadership', *Leadership*, **3** (3), 281–300.

Peltonen, T. (2010), 'Multiple architectures and the production of organizational space in a Finnish University', *Journal of Organizational Change Management*, **24** (6), 806–21.

Policy Studies (2010), Special Issue: 'Leaderships and Space', **31** (4).

Pullen, A. and S. Vacchani (2013), 'The materiality of leadership', *Leadership*, **9** (3), 315–19.

Ramírez, R. (1996), 'Wrapping form and organisational beauty', *Organization*, **3** (2), 233–42.

Ropo, A. and J. Parviainen (2001), 'Leadership and bodily knowledge in expert organizations: Epistemological rethinking', *Scandinavian Journal of Management*, **17** (1), 1–18.

Ropo, A. and E. Sauer (2008), 'Corporeal leaders', in D. Barry and H. Hansen (eds), *The Sage Handbook on New Approaches in Management and Organization Studies*, London: Sage, pp. 469–78.

Ropo, A., J. Parviainen and N. Koivunen (2002), 'Aesthetics in leadership. From absent bodies to social bodily presence', in J. Meindl and K. Parry (eds), *Grounding Leadership Theory and Research: Issues and Perspectives*, Greenwich, CT: Information Age Publishing, pp. 21–38.

Ropo, A., E. Sauer and P. Salovaara (2013), 'Embodiment of leadership through material place', *Leadership*, **9** (3), 378–95.

Salovaara, P. (2011), *From Leader-Centricity Toward Leadership: A Hermeneutic Narrative Approach*, Tampere: Tampere University Press.

Salovaara, P. and A. Ropo (2013), 'Embodied learning experience in leadership development', in L.R. Melina, G.J. Burgess, L.L. Falkman and A. Marturano (eds), *The Embodiment of Leadership*, San Francisco: Jossey-Bass, pp. 193–215.

Scharmer, C.O. (2008), 'Uncovering the blind spot of leadership', *Leader to Leader*, **47**, 52–79.

Sinclair, A. (2005), 'Body possibilities in leadership', *Leadership*, **1** (4), 387–406.

Smircich, L. and G. Morgan (1982), 'Leadership: The management of meaning', *Journal of Applied Behavioral Science*, **18** (3), 257–73.

Sotarauta, M. (2005), 'Shared leadership and dynamic capabilities in regional development', in I. Sagan and H. Halkier, *Regionalism Contested: Institution, Society and Governance*, Aldershot, UK: Ashgate.

Sotarauta, M. (2009), 'Power and influence tactics in the promotion of regional

development: An empirical analysis of the work of Finnish regional development officers', *Geoform*, **40** (5), 895–905.
Steele, F.I. (1973), *Physical Settings and Organization Development*, Menlo Park,
CA: Addison-Wesley.
Stewart, T.A. and R. Jacob (1992), 'The search for the organization of tomorrow:
Are you flat, lean, and ready for a bold new look? Try high-performance teams,
redesigned work, and unbridled information', *Fortune Magazine*, 18 May,
accessed 20 January 2015 at http://archive.fortune.com/magazines/fortune/
fortune_archive/1992/05/18/76425/index.htm.
Stimson, R., R.R. Stough and P. Nijkamp (eds) (2009), *Endogenous Regional
Development: Perspectives, Measurement, and Empirical Investigation*,
Cheltenham, UK and Northampton, MA, USA: Edward Elgar Publishing.
Strati, A. (1992), 'Aesthetic understanding of organizational life', *Academy of
Management Review*, **17** (3), 568–81.
Strati, A. (1999), *Organization and Aesthetics*, London: Sage.
Strati, A. (2000), 'The aesthetic approach in organization studies', in S. Linstead
and H. Höpfl (eds), *The Aesthetics of Organization*, London: Sage, pp. 13–34.
Strati, A. (2007), 'Sensible knowledge and practice-based learning', *Management
Learning*, **38** (1), 61–77.
Strati. A. and P. Guillet de Monthoux (2002), 'Organizing aesthetics', *Human
Relations*, **57** (7), 755–66.
Taylor, F.W. (1911), *The Principles of Scientific Management*, New York: Harper.
Taylor, S. and A. Spicer (2007), 'Time for space: A narrative review of research
on organizational spaces', *International Journal of Management Reviews*, **9** (4),
325–46.
Taylor, S.S. and H. Hansen (2005), 'Finding form: Looking at the field of organi-
zational aesthetics', *Journal of Management Studies*, **42** (6), 1211–31.
Taylor, S.S. and B. Karanian (2008), 'Working connection: The relational art of
leadership', *Aesthesis. International Journal of Art and Aesthetics in Management
and Organizational Life*, **2** (2), 15–22.
Tuan, Y.-F. (1977), *Space and Place: The Perspective of Experience*, Minneapolis,
MN: University of Minnesota Press.
Tyler, M. and L. Cohen (2010), 'Gender in/visibility and organizational space', in
P. Lewis and R. Simpson (eds), *Revealing and Concealing Gender*, Basingstoke,
UK: Palgrave Macmillan, pp. 23–38.
Van Marrewijk, A. (2010), 'The beauty and the beast: The embodied experi-
ence of two corporate buildings', in A. van Marrewijk and D. Yanow (eds),
Organizational Spaces: Rematerializing the Workaday World, Cheltenham, UK
and Northampton, MA, USA: Edward Elgar Publishing, pp. 139–58.
Van Marrewijk, A. and D. Yanow (eds) (2010), *Organizational Spaces:
Rematerializing the Workaday World*, Cheltenham, UK and Northampton,
MA, USA: Edward Elgar Publishing.
Van Meel, J. and P. Vos (2001), 'Funky offices: Reflections on office design in the
"new economy"', *Journal of Corporate Real Estate*, **3** (4), 322–3.
Våland, M. (2010), *What We Talk About When We Talk About Space*, Copenhagen:
Copenhagen Business School Press.
Vischer, J.C. (2005), *Space Meets Status: Designing Workplace Performance*,
Oxford: Taylor and Francis/Routledge.
Wood, M. (2005), 'The fallacy of misplaced leadership', *Journal of Management
Studies*, **42** (6), 1101–21.

Yanow, D. (1998), 'Space stories; or, studying museum buildings as organizational spaces, while reflecting on interpretive methods and their narration', *Journal of Management Inquiry*, **7** (3), 215–39.

Yanow, D. (2010), 'Giving voice to space: Academic practices and the material world', in A. van Marrewijk and D. Yanow (eds), *Organizational Spaces: Rematerializing the Workaday World*, Cheltenham, UK and Northampton, MA, USA: Edward Elgar Publishing, pp. 139–58.

PART I

Workspaces in change

1. What can the coworking movement tell us about the future of workplaces?

Perttu Salovaara

> One of the unintended consequences of modern capitalism is that it has strengthened the value of place, aroused a longing for community.
> (Sennett, 1998, p. 138)

INTRODUCTION

Here is the picture [Photo 1.1] of what coworking means to me. I actually took this when I first started working there and was in awe of this new place. It's the door that you see right before you walk into New Work City. It has the logo and some fun quotes about coworking on it. It is so happy and colourful, funny against the industrial background of this metal door you find after going up some rickety stairs in a random building on Broadway. You see this, and then you open the door to this beautiful big space with so many busy and productive people. So coworking is like this surprise, exciting world you just walk into, with great colourful ideas and a sense of community. (Interviewee 1, 2014)

This chapter studies today's work-life by exploring the relatively new phenomenon of coworking. For this purpose the chapter links three streams of research. First, the concept of office space has undergone a major shift since the 1970s, and today open-plan and flexible office space designs have become a dominant trend (Davis et al., 2011; also see Blakstad, Chapter 2 in this book). Coworking spaces mainly rely on the open-plan concept, yet they serve different purposes than company offices. Second, as a result of the globalization of economy and the widespread use of technology and the Internet, new ways of working have emerged and challenged the traditional definitions of where, how and for whom we work and how we get paid (Sennett, 1998; Castells, 2000; Ehrenreich, 2001). Third, leadership has recently been conceptualized as plural – not only individual managers but also groups are creating leadership (Denis et al., 2012).

Source: Sabina de Matteo; with permission.

*Photo 1.1   Entrance to New Work City, a coworking space on Broadway,
           New York*

These three streams of research can be useful in studying coworking – sharing a workspace with other members. Here (Photo 1.2) is the
coworking space where I wrote this chapter (when I was not working from
home, in a café or the university). Being employed by a university and
having a remote work contract allows me to complete my research work
– mainly reading and writing – anywhere, and I have chosen the Bat Haus
in Bushwick, Brooklyn.

Apart from being associated with physical coworking spaces, coworking,
Spinuzzi (2012b) argues, can be understood 'as part of a larger movement

Source: Author's own photograph; with permission.

Photo 1.2   The Bat Haus follows the open-space office design

toward distributed work and perhaps a way to examine and predict further work trends'. An interviewee in Strauss's (2013) research claims that the coworking movement 'is teaching corporate America a lot about how people interact, what makes them effective at creation and is really defining the future of how companies interact with each other on a deeper level'. Yet as popular and widespread as it is in 2014, coworking spaces would have been difficult to find even five years ago.

The empirical materials for this study were collected through participant observation (150 days spent in the Bat Haus), research diary entries (30), interviews (10) and reviewing the literature on coworking spaces and the coworking movement. The key questions in the context of this book on leadership, spaces and organizing are: What kind of phenomenon is coworking? How does it inform leadership studies?

In this chapter I first introduce coworking as seen from the perspectives of spaces and people and as a movement. This is followed by a short review of plural leadership theories – an approach that fits with coworking, as is argued. Next the chapter presents three organizations whose workplace design and leadership practices show similarities with coworking principles. To conclude, this chapter critically discusses coworking in the context of new work and the new sharing economy in which the idea of sharing physical commodities and services has expanded into various kinds of peer-to-peer models. The chapter contributes to discussions on workplace design, plural leadership approaches and the concepts of new work.

COWORKING: SPACES AND PEOPLE

Were human beings meant to spend most of their time awake in cubicles called offices? More precisely, do modern white-collar workers need to sit in an office the whole day in order to get their intellectual capacity to work? Most researchers and writers exploring new office designs, work concepts and coworking disagree with the traditional definition of work as going to the office from 9 to 5. However, the office has been a central part of developed countries' post-industrial work imagery in the twenty-first century (Davis et al., 2011). It is no surprise then that the office and the associated behavioural and organizational patterns – the office culture – have even become a source of comedy, as shown in the UK television series *The Office* (featuring Ricky Gervais), the US film *Office Space* (1999) and Scott Adams's popular cartoon character Dilbert, who with his colleagues is trapped in a windowless office landscape filled with cubicles (and, by any standards, absurd leadership). Despite the normalization of the office and what it represents, Jones et al. (2009) in their book *I'm Outta Here!* claim that coworking is making the office obsolete. This is an interesting notion from the developers of the coworking movement because coworking spaces tend to be some kind of an office. On the other hand, the traditional concept of office work is undergoing change, as will be discussed. What then is coworking?

Coworking space refers to a workspace that has shared desks, a good Internet connection, usually at least one open-plan space, a common kitchen area and meeting facilities. One can join a space on a daily, weekly, monthly or yearly basis. Often there are no dedicated spaces, desks or chairs, and one can/must choose anew every morning: Where do I sit? With whom? For nomads who do not need a fixed office but seek a more professional work environment than the home or a café or want to avoid the risk of becoming isolated as solo workers, coworking offers a viable, affordable option.

Yet, working with others and sharing space and tools with them are nothing new under the sun: artisan and artist communities have existed in varied forms for hundreds, if not thousands of years, Jones et al. (2009) remind readers. The corporate world has also toyed with these concepts, as a 1971 report on IBM's experiment with the non-territorial office shows:

> Under this concept, not only are all office walls removed, but most desks and other permanent stations are eliminated as well. . . All work is performed at laboratory benches and large round tables, and an individual may choose to work anywhere in the area that suits him or [is] convenient. (Allen and Gerstberger, 1971, p. 2)

These principles well describe today's corporate practices and the coworking spaces, too. In contrast to the corporate world's planned change initiatives and corporate objectives, though, many coworking spaces originate from casual working events called 'Jellies'. These are informal meetings where (somewhat) same-minded people gather to work together in someone's home, a coffee shop or an existing office. Participants bring their tools (for example, laptop, pens, paper) and the space provides wireless Internet, chairs and the company of other people in a similar situation. What is their similar situation? The common user groups of coworking spaces are freelancers, entrepreneurs, start-ups and micro-enterprises. As one of the main motivations for coworking many users mention the professional setting (compared to a home or café) and the community.

According to a Deskmag (2013) study some 2500 coworking spaces exist in 81 countries, while the number of coworking spaces and coworkers more than doubled from 2012 to 2013. Considering that the term 'coworking' with its current meaning was coined in 1999, that the first official full-time coworking space was established in 2006 and that the first peak in Google searches for the term occurred in October 2007 (Spinuzzi, 2012a; Deskmag, 2013), the coworking movement and industry are in a notable growth stage.

Apart from users, interest in coworking spaces is shared by stakeholders, including 'coworking space operators, facility managers, real estate pundits as well as city councils representatives, public development agencies, universities or startup incubator managers', as the organizers of Coworking Conference Europe (2013) describe their approximately 350 participants.

A first-hand reason for the growth of coworking requires looking at its benefits: from the perspective of individuals it offers a more professional environment than the home, as well social connections and a community, and it allows start-ups to keep fixed costs down and to create networks (Strauss, 2013). Sometimes labelled the 'unoffice', the coworking model 'integrates flexible office space with possibility to interact with other workers and clients' (Spinuzzi, 2012a, p. 412). The unoffice combines unlimited use of office space with features (meeting rooms, networking, new people) that one does not usually have at home or in a café.

One can differentiate among various kinds of coworking concepts. First, Jellies represent a pre-form of coworking spaces as they are based on the pure interest in sharing a workspace. Second, there are traditional coworking spaces where one can pop in at any time and pay a daily, weekly, monthly or yearly fee. These tend to attract a pretty diverse customer base with broad demographics, ranging from artists, graphic designers, coders and researchers to private entrepreneurs and micro-businesses. Third, there are more specialized spaces that market themselves as hubs for specific groups of professionals, such as writers, artisans and information technology and tech start-ups. Fourth, there are invitation-only spaces that are aimed at stimulating high-growth start-ups; they allow new small companies to inspire and connect with one another and offer value chains. In the search to finance operations and benefit from innovations, universities have also increasingly employed this concept of connecting people, ideas and business proposals (compare Welch, 2012). Finally, there are coworking spaces that come close to being office hotels by offering a combination of private office spaces and free communal space (compare Bacigalupo, 2011).

Coworking spaces also have negative features. Blog articles and commentaries frequently mention problems such as a lack of privacy, noise, the inability to establish a common culture and many overcrowded and dirty spaces (for example, Leforestier, 2009; Murphy Paul, 2012; Duffy, 2014). These complaints match some disadvantages linked to open-plan offices: 'Open-plan offices in general have been associated with less persistence at challenging tasks, lower motivation, higher stress and blood pressure' (Kim and De Dear, 2013; see also Taylor and Spicer, 2007 for a review).

Academic research on coworking spaces and coworkers is still extremely limited. Spinuzzi (2012a) and Hurry (2012) relied on interviews (Spinuzzi: 17 interviews, Hurry: 5 interviews) and written sources but not primarily on observations. In addition to these methods this research involved participant observation. I also conducted 10 interviews at two coworking spaces.[1]

Coworking is based on a juxtaposition of 'working alone together' (Spinuzzi, 2012a). The end users are pretty divided: instead of working from home or cafés, about half only want a more productive setting while the other half also seek community. In my interviews many users attest that 'work opportunities do arise', and my observations confirm this. In opposition to constant or nomadic movement most users do not consider moving out in the near future (Deskmag, 2013).

COWORKING: MOVEMENT

To understand coworking better, it is essential to look at the larger picture of work-life and see how coworking is part of that shift and movement. Sociologists including Manuel Castells (2000) and Richard Sennett (1998) argue that work-life is changing from long-term employment to constant shorter-term projects. Coworking can be regarded as a consequence of the new capitalism in which the 'virtues' of flexibility, downsizing, low loyalty and part-time work offer benefits and disadvantages for individual workers (Sennett, 1998). Spinuzzi (2015) uses the term 'projectification' to describe the shift from stable departmental organizations to project-based organizations, and in this respect, for many coworkers their job is 'projectified'. In Sennett's (1998) explanation the meaning of work has changed: 'The word "job" in English of the fourteenth century meant a lump or piece of something which could be carted around. Flexibility today brings back this arcane sense of the job, as people do lumps of labor, pieces of work, over the course of lifetime' (p. 9). A growing class of people in short-term jobs find that their work identity is created in horizontal shifts between project work of various natures, rather than by following the vertical career ladders of their parents' generation (Standing, 2011). My interviewees confirmed that the majority of independent coworkers have several occupations and multiple sources of income. An illustrative example is an interviewee who holds part-time jobs as a production assistant in a film crew, as a laboratory assistant in a photo studio, as an independent freelance wedding photographer, as a webpage designer and as painter and sculptor.

According to a 2011 study (MBO Partners, 2011), the independent workforce in the United States numbers 17.7 million and is projected to reach as high as 24 million by 2018. By 2020, so the MBO (2011) survey projects, around half of the private workforce will have worked from the position of an independent worker. This trend will continue because these workers 'want control over their lives, including the ability to determine when, where and what type of work they do' (ibid.). That study argues that the steady growth of the independent workforce can be regarded as a structural change in employment. Working independently is based on freedom, and Edelberg (2010) argues that it is precisely freedom that leads people to coworking spaces:

> Freedom in the labor market carries a high price. Lack of competition and social interaction may lead to professional isolation and sustained loss of creative and innovative capacity. In order to forestall these threats a new work mode has emerged – coworking, whereby a group of

professionals hired individually by different employers share workspace and
benefit from a common logistics and technology platform. (Edelberg, 2010,
abstract)

Coworking apparently fits today's economic landscape in which more
and more independent workers need some sort of professional work
setting. Taking this development in the number of independent workers
into account offers an explanation of why coworking refers not only to
physical spaces but also to a movement, a global community of people,
and to a verb, to cowork (Jones et al., 2009). Summarizing various sources
on the nature of the coworking movement, Coworking Wiki asserts that
the community aspect is at the core:

> Coworking is not only about the physical space, but about establishing the
> coworking community first. Its benefits can already be experienced outside
> of its spaces, and it is recommended to start with building a coworking com-
> munity first before considering opening a coworking space. However, some
> coworking spaces don't build a community: they just get a part of an existing
> one by combining their opening with an event which attracts their target group.
> (Coworking Wiki, n.d.)

Coworking Wiki emphasizes that coworking spaces 'are about
community-building and sustainability'. Other sources reassure that 'the
goal[s] of the co-working spaces [are] to create a sense of community
among users' and to bring 'the social back into the workplace' (Leforestier,
2009, p. 5). While other, similar kinds of spaces (rental offices, start-up
incubators) are directed at businesspeople, coworking, Bacigalupo (2011)
argues, attracts 'people who do something they care about' and creates
communities of practice.

There seems to be an inherent need for community building in these
days of independent working and of flexible capitalism. Sennett (1998)
observes: 'One of the unintended consequences of modern capitalism is
that it has strengthened the value of place, aroused a longing for community' (p. 138). In a survey on coworking, participants regarded community
as the main benefit of a coworking space and the three most important
features as the atmosphere, community feeling and collaborative environment (Global Coworking Blog, 2007). All my interviewees also viewed the
social aspect of coworking as an asset. Interestingly, this trend supports
the argument for a movement from independence to interdependence.

A writer in the first issue of a newly established (2014) e-journal *New
Worker Magazine* asserts that the concept of coworking is not fully realized without the community aspect: 'Realize you are choosing this lifestyle
and workstyle. Make it worth it. If you're just using a coworking space

as a space to work, you're missing the point' (Segreti, 2014). Anticipating (and socially constructing) this ethos, one of the early coworking spaces, Citizen Space in San Francisco, came up with values that many sources identify as coworking principles: collaboration, openness, community, accessibility and sustainability (Coworking Wiki, n.d.; Jones et al., 2009; Leforestier, 2009; Pachego-Vega, 2013).

Elaborating upon these values reveals more about the nature of coworking. First, collaboration is the key value, indicating a diverse group of people with varied sets of backgrounds and knowledge. Openness refers to an open flow of ideas and an attitude of sharing, giving and reciprocity. Community emphasizes mixing together like-minded people with different backgrounds. Accessibility means having opportunities to interact both physically and mentally. Sustainability is important ecologically, eco-nomically and socially: it applies to keeping the structure financially and socially sustainable and making ecologically responsible choices.

Jellies, too, start from the platform of interactions: 'People come to Jelly for the purpose of working alongside others, sharing ideas, and meeting new people – it's much more interactive and concentrated in that respect because people come with the intent to interact' (Gupta, in Jones et al., 2009, p. 14). What makes Jelly a pre-form of coworking is that, if people see the need and desire to further organize these meetings, they can found a coworking community or space. As organic gatherings based on organic growth, Jellies represent the basic ideology of coworking in a nutshell. Jones et al. (2009, p. 3) contrast the ideals of coworking and the Industrial Age in Table 1.1.

There is some evidence that those who choose coworking subscribe to coworking values, rather than corporate values (Spinuzzi, 2012a; Bacigalupo, personal communication, 12 December 2013; Strauss, 2013). My interviews also confirm that in today's work-life there are many opportunities to live an independent existence outside big corporations. Advocates of the coworking movement do not hold employer–employee relations in high regard due to the idea of dependency:

> If you work for someone, you depend on that person, and that can lead to unhealthy relations. I think there are a lot of people who love to have the security and structure of a traditional job, but I think a lot of people don't feel like they were conscious agents in choosing their path. Eventually you need to make money to live, and a traditional 'job' was the only visible path. That leads to potential for all sorts of resentment and bad feelings. (Bacigalupo, personal communication, 12 December 2013)

Traditionally (as in Hegel's dialectics of master and slave relations) workers have been defined by their master (company owner, manager),

Table 1.1   Ideals of coworking and the Industrial Age

Corporate values	Coworking values
We are your employer	You are my client
You will come to my office	I will set my own hours
You will stay in your cube	I will work where it fits me best
Talking to other coworkers distracts you from your work	Talking to other people energizes my work, helps me collaborate and solve problems and is essential for my social well-being
You will work on whatever project we put in front of you	I will work on projects that are meaningful to me
You will put in face time so I know you are working and not messing around	I will work until the project is completed
Your work and your life outside work are separate	My work and my life are intertwined

Source: Jones et al. (2009).

thus their identities originate from that dependency relation. In an interview, however, Bacigalupo (ibid.) explains the core of this movement through the terms 'dependent', 'independent' and 'interdependent'. Not being dependent means being free of traditional work relations restrictions, but in addition to having freedom, independent workers also have responsibility. Joining a coworking space is a voluntary choice and, when associated with the social aspects of coworking, indicates that the value of interdependency is taken seriously. Interdependency means accepting dependency relations, this time formed by choice – out of mutual respect and acceptance, not obligation.

Turner (2006) traces some of the community-based coworking ideals to 1960s' communal idealism. While computers in the 1950s to 1960s were largely associated with the military, control and the Cold War, from the late 1960s to the early 1970s a counterculture that adopted personal computing as a tool for personal liberation arose in the San Francisco Bay area. This 'digital utopia' (exemplified in the *Whole Earth Catalog* counterculture magazine) foresaw that linking individuals together by personal computing would empower 'humans in their day-to-day lives and, in that way, would change humanity' (Cornelissen, 2013, p. 704). Blended with hippies' communal ideals of living and working together and flower power, this movement influenced many early tech enthusiasts, including Steve Jobs (Turner, 2006; Isaacson, 2011; Cornelissen, 2013).

Virtual communities such as MySpace and Facebook have challenged the definition of community, as belonging and not-belonging have become more difficult to define and a lack of physical or face-to-face meetings makes the degree of emotional ties unclear (Reich, 2010). One of my interviewees compared the coworking movement to the 'open source movement' in which 'people are doing things for free to contribute to something meaningful'.

On the other hand, not all coworking spaces create communities. In my materials three coworking proprietors I interviewed raised the concern that movement is driven by the coworking industry in which business-people do not necessarily emphasize movement and participants thus get only a little taste of movement. On a more positive note it was mentioned that the coworking industry brought coworking from a niche to the mainstream and created access to the movement for a larger population.

Despite consisting of a loose collection of members, the spaces tend to be central to the coworking movement and features such as localism – understood as working in a local community and contributing to the local economy (Pachego-Vega 2009) – make these more physical communities. The interviews conducted in this research support the view that the physical place, collaboration and sometimes location play crucial roles in determining the success of a coworking space.

COWORKING THROUGH THE LEADERSHIP LENS

Following the community-based ethos of coworking, I will not dwell on the numerous definitions of leadership but concentrate on plural leadership. In the twenty-first century a shift has occurred in leadership theories. Leadership has long been studied as a quality of an individual, but the post-heroic theories consider leadership as a plural phenomenon (Denis et al., 2012) based in the mundane activities and relations of members of an organization (Uhl-Bien, 2006; Hosking, 2007; Carroll et al., 2008; Fairhurst and Grant, 2010; Grint and Jackson, 2010) and encompassing any leaderful actions by organizational members (Raelin, 2011). Effective leadership, in this perspective, does not need to consist of heroic explicit actions but can be subtle and informal (Karp, 2013). These post-heroic leadership theories (Crevani et al., 2007, 2010; Avolio et al., 2009) define leadership as constructed in a process, as a continuation of social activities, rather than as a momentary action (for example, showing assertiveness, taking leadership), and they thus subscribe to process ontological approaches (Chia, 1997; Tsoukas and Chia, 2002; Wood, 2005).

Plural leadership examines leadership not as a property of individuals and their behaviours but as a collective phenomenon that is distributed or shared among different people, potentially fluid and constructed through interaction (Denis et al., 2012). Already in 1954 Gibbs argues for leadership that is 'probably best conceived as a group quality, as a set of functions which must be carried out by the group' (quoted in Denis et al., 2012, p. 212). This ethos is described well in Mabey and Freeman's (2010) words 'as a distributed and interdependent set of practices enacted by all rather than specific traits possessed by figureheads at the apex of a hierarchy' (p. 513). From the four research streams on plural leadership resulting from Denis et al. (2012), 'producing leadership through interactions' (p. 215) comes closest to the reality of coworking.

Applying plural leadership to coworking spaces means locating leadership in the members of the space. We first need to be clear about the context. Leadership in coworking spaces is a two-fold issue: practically all members are part of other groups outside the physical space, so plural leadership touches both external networks outside the coworking community and the internal ones within the physical space. The focus here is on aspects of internal leadership within the coworking space community and how independent workers relate to (plural) leadership. The first question this focus raises is, what kind of phenomenon is leadership in coworking spaces?

From the internal perspective, leadership traditionally would be attached to anyone who officially runs the place (for example, the proprietor, hired help). However, from the plural leadership perspective, many other informal leadership actions take place on the level of members' activities. The interviews indicate that, even if the proprietors organize events and play a crucial role in creating a specific atmosphere, members also organize events or meetings and the informal organization creates a sense of place, as the following interview excerpt shows:

> What happens when no one [of the owners or assistance] is there? Lots of people walk in and out. When the post guy comes, some people pick the post up, and some not. Some people ignore new people entering the space; some give guidance. It is tacit leadership: I step forward and take a little bit of responsibility. In my first coworking space part of responsibility of being [a] coworker was to open the door for the buzzer. You let that person in and talk about the space. If no official is there you took that responsibility. This little responsibility made a huge impact. The difference is that between service and community. As soon as people stop feeling [that] it is service and see it as community, they start to behave differently. (Interviewee 2, 2014)

This kind of thinking is very much in line with plural leadership: when there is not one person at the apex of things, some responsibilities are intentionally left for members to attend to. This requires that those who run the space truly subscribe to coworking values and approach these from the plural leadership perspective.

Another example of coworker ownership initiatives is cotivation, which started in the New York-based New Work City. Cotivation is a weekly meeting of members who want to accomplish something and to discuss with the group what is holding people back from achieving their tasks (Bacigalupo, 2013). In the Bat Haus where I cowork, the weekly social hour on Thursday evenings is an initiative of members too.

The main organizing principle behind these initiatives is a decentralized form of leadership: the participants/members share the responsibility for the social life in their space. The spaces that more resemble office hotels do not necessarily encourage these kinds of activities, let alone expect clients to ask for it: after all, they pay for these services. Whether one joins a space with the attitude of a client or a member seems to contribute to participation in plural leadership. It remains to be seen what directions leadership in coworking will take in the future. The four coworking principles described earlier match the post-heroic understanding of leadership as a collective task. Notably, the rise of post-heroic leadership research has coincided with the emergence of the coworking phenomenon.

CASES: COWORKING PRINCIPLES IN BUSINESS ORGANIZATIONS

As noted, organizations have experimented with flexible office solutions for a long time. Here I look at a few company practices and coworking principles that coincide in modern organizations. In the Netherlands and Finland, Microsoft has reorganized its open-plan offices according to the so-called 'new way of working'. The physical office space is divided into different kinds of places that one chooses according to personal needs and likings, and no one – not even the chief executive officer (CEO) – has a designated workspace (Meerbeek et al., 2009). In the interior of the offices Microsoft has created spaces with various looks and feels. For instance, Bistro is a café-like environment for relaxing and casual meetings, the Beach a working room with groovy background music and large windows overlooking the sea, the Library is dedicated to quiet work and has a ban on talking, and the Playroom a creative and colourful space with toys, Lego and gym balls (Photo 1.3). At the heart of this re-design is a concept called 'presence work'. In opposition to teleworking this concept emphasizes cooperation instead of distance. 'We wanted to focus on the idea of trust; that people are present even when they are not close by', the Microsoft marketing communications manager explains. The

Source: Author's own photograph; with permission.

Photo 1.3   Microsoft has created spaces with various looks and feels

concept aims at 'colliding' people: 'We want people to meet, new ideas to be born, and we want to get rid of various boundaries' (Salovaara, 2014). The process of designing the space at Microsoft was based on participative design principles (compare Meerbeek et al., 2009).

The way Frantic, a small Finnish tech company with approximately 50 employees, figured out its relocation to new office space reflects the same principles. Frantic formerly had a long space, physically divided into two ends connected by a kitchen area and meeting rooms in the middle. Keen on getting rid of the silos that this structure endorsed, the company moved to a (smaller) space consisting of one large room. In the middle there is a long table for coworking and the space allows small teams to gather on the sides and talk without disrupting others too much (Photo 1.4). The relocation was highly anticipated and the workers had both negative and positive experiences. The move to new, higher, lighter, more modern open space changed the working culture, people communicated more, and cooperation became smoother. The new space, even if smaller, is not much cheaper, but at the same time the company's financial results have improved, according to interviews, due mainly to improved cooperation among employees (Salovaara, 2014).

The sales manager at Technopolis, a company offering office-space-related services, confirms that there are two trends in workplace design: 'tribes' and 'one café'. The term 'tribes' refers to free-floating, self-managed,

Source: Author's own photograph; with permission.

Photo 1.4   At Frantic people do not have individual workspaces

usually project- or interest-based teams that can meet and work anywhere. The office space is planned to allow the tribes to meet – an arrangement well known to anyone familiar with current office design. The 'one café' trend stands in opposition to an earlier practice of designing several café corners (small café areas with a coffee machine) throughout the office. The new trend is to build only one, larger café that can also be used for corporate meetings and events. When the departments had their own cafés, sales, marketing and accounting departments tended to remain separated in their silos. The benefit of connecting these silos is that only one set of information spreads throughout the office, instead of several, sometimes conflicting ones (ibid.).

On the other hand many spaces do not support this kind of group work. In this research's interviews a university professor complained of how buildings' metal exteriors, long corridors and closed doors evoke a sense of researchers 'in their ivory towers, distanced from the real life' (ibid.). The layout of the offices within departments also supports the university hierarchy: professors have the most spacious offices, which are located first along the corridor. My university's School of Management has a full floor of space – but apart from one cramped space in the corridor *outside* the department doors there is no space designed for students.

Telecommunications company Telenor, a Norwegian formerly state-owned telephone company, boasts buildings with glass-and-metal architecture, open-space design and open-plan offices. Despite the positive image of open-plan offices, the research on them reveals mixed reactions:

> [The o]pen-plan office layout is commonly assumed to facilitate communication and interaction between co-workers, promote well-being at work and workplace satisfaction, and to enhance team-work effectiveness. On the other hand, open-plan layouts are widely acknowledged to be more disruptive due to uncontrollable noise and loss of privacy... Enclosed private offices clearly outperformed open-plan layouts in most aspects...particularly in acoustics, privacy and the proxemics issues. Benefits of enhanced 'ease of interaction' were smaller than the penalties of increased noise level and decreased privacy resulting from open-plan office configuration. (Kim and De Dear, 2013, p. 18)

As the design of modern office buildings is meant to serve various organizational and human resource purposes, architecture alone is less able to respond to these needs (Heerwagen et al., 2004). The drawbacks, to some degree, might stem from the architecture's focus on the physical structure, not productivity or organizational goals. This focus is often reflected, for instance, in architectural pictures of buildings; they usually do not include people but only physical constructions. I share an impression with Shortt (2013), who says that in her observations most workplace discussions are about functional and physical aspects of space while emotions and the people side of things remain marginal topics in workplace research. Applying Lefebvre (1991), Taylor and Spicer (2007) distinguish among planned, practised and imagined space and note the drawback that architecture and space design often identify themselves chiefly with the planned structures, not those practised or imagined.

In designing new, attractive workspaces companies seek a delicate balance between employee motivation and profits. Sometimes this leads to conflicting ideologies. For instance '[f]irms like Apple are new age in their imagery and old school in their business practices' (Heller, 2013, p. 70). As much as communication is the at the core of new company practices an anecdote about Amazon's then CEO Jeff Bezos tells how he seemingly became irritated and called 'for teams to communicate less with each other, not more' (ibid.). Even if Bezos's point was that small customer teams should respond directly to the client and that internal communication 'is a sign of dysfunction' (ibid.), the story shows more than anything how manager centred some high-tech companies still are.

How do coworking values match with organizational practices? At Microsoft, collaboration, openness and access to information are valued. In the refurbished office, employees can also feel a bit like a tribe that has managed to conquer the space and to turn it into their home turf. At Technopolis the manager clearly emphasized that, in the midst of changing workspaces and mobile work 'every man needs his own turf' (Salovaara, 2014). On the other hand the creative manager at Frantic asserts that despite the fears, the company has experienced an unexpected growth spurt since relocating to the new, open office space (with the purpose of breaking up silos and increasing communication) and has been forced to seek extra space in the same building. Open office space clearly has benefits and disadvantages.

Overall, this short overview challenges Jones et al.'s table above that places corporate and coworking values in opposition. The same new principles can be adapted to corporate practices too (and are sometimes piloted by companies, as in the IBM example from 1971).

SUMMARY AND DISCUSSION

As the amount of distance work and virtual teams increase, workers seem to long for physical relations and communities. Coworking spaces are a pioneering way for humans to interrelate to one another as the coworking movement emphasizes its community-building aspect. Coworking seems to address some basic human needs that people working independently desire.

A shared workspace that also fulfils social needs is not new, but the concept of plural leadership might offer a way to analyse the internal dynamics of coworking spaces and community building. Leadership produced through interactions paves the way for more participatory practices in coworking spaces. As pointed out, there are different kinds of coworking spaces supporting the coworking movement to varying degrees. The coworking movement, it seems, will accept plural leadership more readily than traditional forms of leadership, whereas in most business-like spaces plural leadership is neither an issue nor a desired feature.

The coworking movement shares features with the sharing economy (for example, sharing cars, bikes, apartments) (Sacks, 2011), open source movement (in software programming) (Lerner and Tirole, 2001), Occupy movement (Piven, 2012), crowdsourcing and crowd funding (Mollick,

2014) and the maker movement (Ohanian, 2013; Hatch, 2014). These movements favour the bottom-up approach over top-down leadership approaches. In general, these movements support a shift from the idea of individual ownership (independence) to a form where possible collective uses (interdependence) instead of possession is important and thus suggest a move from competition to cooperation (Malone, 2004).

At the same time, most if not all visionary sources anticipate that the uses of office space will change. Office design is no longer ruled by fixed relationships between groups of office workers located in specific buildings in predetermined places; instead there is talk about multi-use and networked offices (Duffy and Tanis, 1993; Duffy, 2013). While work-life is expected to become less centralized and more mobile and flexible, the future office will be more of a place for cooperation instead of working alone – a hub instead of an individual retreat. This pattern closely resembles the basic idea of coworking, where the reason for going to work is not to sit alone behind closed doors but to connect with others. Even in traditional environments such as universities, turning faculty groups into communities of caring scholars has been shown to have positive effects (Heinrich, 2010).

A desk to work at and a café with an Internet connection are easy to find, but a random discussion with a half-stranger does not fulfil the human emotional need to connect with others. There is something very intriguing at the heart of coworking: in a very old-fashioned way it brings people together, yet coworking spaces function only in today's world of endless virtual connections.

NOTE

1. At the time of writing this chapter the research project is ongoing and more interviews will be conducted.

REFERENCES

Allen, T.J. and P.G. Gerstberger (1971), 'Report of a field experiment to improve communications in a product-engineering department: The non-territorial office', Working Paper, Cambridge, MA: Massachusetts Institute of Technology.
Avolio, B.J., F.O. Wakumbwa and T.J. Weber (2009), 'Leadership: Current theories, research, and future directions', *Annual Review of Psychology*, **60** (1), 421–49.
Bacigalupo, T. (2011), 'What are the differences between office rental facilities,

startup incubators, and coworking spaces?' [blog], 7 November, accessed 20 May 2014 at http://happymonster.co/2011/11/07/what-are-the-differences-between-office-rental-facilities-startup-incubators-and-coworking-spaces/.

Bacigalupo, T. (2013), 'New memberships, now with more awesome' [blog], 19 April, accessed 20 May 2014 at http://happymonster.co/2013/04/19/new-memberships-now-with-more-awesome/.

Carroll, B., L. Levy and D. Richmond (2008), 'Leadership as practice: Challenging the competency paradigm', *Leadership*, **4** (4), 363–79.

Castells, M. (2010), *The Rise of The Network Society: The Information Age: Economy, Society and Culture*, Chichester, UK: Wiley-Blackwell.

Chia, R. (1997), 'Essai. Thirty years on: From organization structures to the organization of thought', *Organization Studies*, **18** (4), 685–707.

Cornelissen, J.P. (2013), 'Portrait of an entrepreneur: Steve Jobs, Vincent van Gogh, and the entrepreneurial imagination', *Academy of Management Review*, **38** (4), 700–709.

Coworking Conference Europe (2013), accessed 30 May 2014 at https://coworkingeurope.net/2013/05/16/coworking-europe-2013-conference-takes-place-in-barcelona-11-13-november-early-bird-registration-is-open-until-july-31st/.

Coworking Wiki (n.d.), accessed 30 May 2014 at http://en.wikipedia.org/wiki/Coworking.

Crevani, L., M. Lindgren and J. Packendorff (2007), 'Shared leadership: A post-heroic perspective on leadership as a collective construction', *International Journal of Leadership Studies*, **3** (1), 40–67.

Crevani, L., M. Lindgren and J. Packendorff (2010), 'Leadership, not leaders: On the study of leadership as practices and interactions', *Scandinavian Journal of Management*, **26** (1), 77–86.

Davis, M.C., D.J. Leach and C.W. Clegg (2011), 'The physical environment of the office: Contemporary and emerging issues', in G.P. Hodgkinson and J.K. Ford (eds), *International Review of Industrial and Organizational Psychology, Vol. 6*, pp. 193–235.

Denis, J.-L., A. Langley and V. Sergi (2012), 'Leadership in the plural', *The Academy of Management Annals*, **6** (1), 211–83.

Deskmag (2013), *3rd Global Coworking Survey*, accessed 6 February 2015 at http://www.deskmag.com/en/1st-results-of-the-3rd-global-coworking-survey-2012.

Duffy, F. (2013), 'Justifying place in a virtual world', accessed 20 May 2014 at http://www.aecom.com/deployedfiles/Internet/Capabilities/Design%20and%20Planning/Strategy%20Plus/FDuffy_Connected%20Real%20Estate.pdf.

Duffy, J. (2014), 'Get organized: 5 tips for working in a co-working space', *PCMag.com*, accessed 20 May 2014 at http://www.pcmag.com/article2/0,28 17,2457130,00.asp.

Duffy, F. and J. Tanis (1993), 'A vision of the new workplace', *Site Selection*, **38** (2), 427–32.

Edelberg, G.S. (2010), 'Coworking', *Debates IESA*, **15** (4) 6–7 [in Spanish], English abstract, accessed 30 May 2014 at http://connection.ebscohost.com/c/articles/59803501/coworking.

Ehrenreich, B. (2001), *Nickel and Dimed: On (Not) Getting By in America*, New York: Henry Holt & Company, LLC.

Fairhurst, G.T. and D. Grant (2010), 'The social construction of leadership: A sailing guide', *Management Communication Quarterly*, **24** (2), 171–210.

Global Coworking Blog (2007), 'The results of the coworking survey' [blog], 21 April, accessed 23 May 2014 at http://blog.coworking.com/the-results-of-the-coworking-survey/.

Grint, K. and B. Jackson (2010), 'Toward "socially constructed" social constructions of leadership', *Management Communication Quarterly*, **24** (2), 348–55.

Hatch, M.J. (2014), *Maker Movement Manifesto: Rules for Innovation in the New World of Crafters, Hackers and Tinkerers*, New York: McGraw-Hill.

Heerwagen, J.H., K. Kampschroer, K.M. Powell and V. Loftness (2004), 'Collaborative knowledge work environments', *Building Research and Information*, **32**(6), 510–28.

Heinrich, K.T. (2010), 'Passionate scholarship 2001–2010: A vision for making academe safer for joyous risk-takers', *Advances in Nursing Science*, **33** (1), 50–64.

Heller, K. (2013), 'Naked launch. What's really new about the big new tech companies?', *The New Yorker*, 25 November, 68–76.

Hosking, D.M. (2007), 'Not leaders, not followers: A post-modern discourse of leadership processes', in J.R. Meindl and B. Shamir (eds), *Follower-Centered Perspectives on Leadership: A Tribute to the Memory of James R. Meindl*, Greenwich, CT: IAP, pp. 243–64.

Hurry, C.J.P (2012), 'The Hub Halifax: A qualitative study on coworking' (a Major Research Project submitted to St. Mary's University, Halifax, Nova Scotia in partial fulfilment of the requirements for the Degree of Master of Business Administration), accessed 30 May 2014 at http://library2.smu.ca/handle/01/24826#.U6pArxaD7N5.

Isaacson, W. (2011), *Steve Jobs*, New York: Simon and Schuster.

Jones, D., T. Sundsted and T. Bacigalupo (2009), *I'm Outta Here! How Coworking is Making the Office Obsolete*, Austin, TX: Not an MBA Press.

Karp. T. (2013), 'Studying subtle acts of leadership', *Leadership*, **9** (1), 3–22.

Kim, D. and R. de Dear (2013), 'Workspace satisfaction: the privacy–communication trade-off in open-plan offices', *Journal of Environmental Psychology*, **36**, 18–26.

Lefebvre, H. (1991), *The Production of Space*, Oxford: Blackwell.

Leforestier, A. (2009), 'The co-working space concept', accessed 20 May 2014 at http://www.iimahd.ernet.in/users/anilg/files/Articles/Co-working%20space.pdf.

Lerner, J. and J. Tirole (2001), 'The open source movement: Key research questions', *European Economic Review*, **45** (4–6), 819–26.

Mabey, C. and T. Freeman (2010), 'Reflections on leadership and place', *Policy Studies*, **31** (4), 505–22.

Malone, T.W. (2004), *The Future of Work: How the New Order of Work Will Shape Your Organization, Your Management Style, and Your Life*, Boston, MA: Harvard Business School Press.

MBO Partners (2011), *The State of Independence in America – Independent Workplace Index*, accessed 30 May 2014 at http://www.mbopartners.com/state-of-independence/docs/MBO-Partners-Independent-Workforce-Index-2011.pdf.

Meerbeek, M., K. Randolph, D.W. Rasmus, J. van Wilgenburg, H. van der Meer, J. Witkamp and H. Kompier (2009), 'A new way of working: The 7 factors for success, based on Microsoft Netherlands experience', *Slideshare*, accessed 30 May 2014 at http://www.slideshare.net/markmeerbeek/whitepaper anewwayofworkingmicrosoftnetherlandsexternal1.

Mollick, E. (2014), 'The dynamics of crowdfunding: An exploratory study', *Journal of Business Venturing*, **29** (1), 1–16.

Murphy Paul, A. (2012), 'Workplace woes: the "open" office is a hotbed of stress', *Time*, 15 August, accessed 25 November 2013 at http://ideas.time.com/2012/08/15/why-the-open-office-is-a-hotbed-of-stress/#ixzz2lmfYOEOU.

Ohanian, A. (2013), *Without Their Permission: How the 21st Century Will Be Made, Not Managed*, New York: Hachette Book Group.

Pachego-Vega, R. (2009), 'Thinking about guiding principles for coworking spaces', *The Network Hub* [blog], accessed 26 November 2013 at http://thenetworkhub.ca/vancouver/2009/10/02/thinking-about-guiding-principles-for-coworking-spaces/.

Piven, F.F. (2012), 'Occupy's protest is not over. It has barely begun', *The Guardian*, 17 September, accessed 20 May 2013 at http://www.guardian.co.uk/commentisfree/2012/sep/17/occupy-protest-not-over.

Raelin, J. (2011), 'From leadership-as-practice to leaderful practice', *Leadership*, **7** (2), 195–211.

Reich, S.M. (2010), 'Adolescents' sense of community on MySpace and Facebook: A mixed-methods approach', *Journal of Community Psychology*, **38** (6), 688–705.

Sacks, D. (2011), 'The sharing economy', *Fast Company*, accessed 30 May 2014 at http://www.fastcompany.com/1747551/sharing-economy.

Salovaara, P. (2014), 'Video: Leadership in spaces and places', *Organizational Aesthetics*, **3** (2), 79. Available at http://digitalcommons.wpi.edu/oa/vol3/iss1/8.

Segreti, A. (2014), 'How coworking can help you live your passions', *New Worker Magazine*, accessed 30 May 2014 at http://newworker.co/mag/coworking-self-actualization.

Sennett, R. (1998), *The Corrosion of Character. The Personal Consequences of Work in the New Capitalism*, New York: W.W. Norton and Co.

Shortt, H. (2013), 'Workplace trends 2013 – what's new in work space?', accessed 20 May 2014 at http://harrietshortt.wordpress.com/2013/10/28/workplace-trends-2013-whats-new-in-work-space/.

Spinuzzi, C. (2012a), 'Working alone together: Coworking as an emergent collaborative activity', *Journal of Business and Technical Communication*, **26** (4), 399–441.

Spinuzzi, C. (2012b), 'Writing: Working alone, together' [blog], accessed 30 May 2014 at http://spinuzzi.blogspot.com/2012/05/writing-working-alone-together.html.

Spinuzzi, C. (2015), *All Edge: Inside the New Workplace Networks*, Chicago, IL: University of Chicago Press.

Standing, G. (2011), *The Precariat – The New Dangerous Class*, London: Bloomsbury Publishing.

Strauss, K. (2013), 'Why coworking spaces are here to stay', *Forbes.com*, 28 May, accessed 30 May 2014 at http://www.forbes.com/sites/karstenstrauss/2013/05/28/why-coworking-spaces-are-here-to-stay.

Taylor, S. and A. Spicer (2007), 'Time for space: A narrative review of research on organizational spaces', *International Journal of Management Review*, **9** (4), 325–46.

Tsoukas, H. and R. Chia (2002), 'On organizational becoming: Rethinking organizational change', *Organization Science*, **13** (5), 567–82.

Turner, F. (2006), *From Counterculture to Cyberculture: Stewart Brand, the Whole*

Earth Network, and the Rise of Digital Utopianism, Chicago, IL: University of Chicago Press.

Uhl-Bien, M. (2006), 'Relational leadership theory: Exploring the social process of leadership and organizing', *Leadership Quarterly*, **17** (6), 654–76.

Welch, J. (2012), 'The power of collaboration', *Economic Development Journal*, **11** (4), 36–41, accessed 25 January 2014 at http://www.jasperwelch.org/jasperwelch/assets/File/EDJ-Fall12-final-2-36-41.pdf.

Wood, M. (2005), 'The fallacy of misplaced leadership', *Journal of Management Studies*, **42** (6), 1101–21.

2. Work isn't where it used to be

Siri Hunnes Blakstad*

INTRODUCTION

I am a user of offices. In my 'workplace career' I have used almost all pos-sible office types. I have had cellular offices (from the smallest ones to the big boss's office with a personal meeting table and the best view towards the sea). I have sat in noisy open-plan offices with my own desk and docu-ments and stuff piling up around me. I have lived the life of a workplace nomad, occasionally checking in to my department's 'home base' in the open-plan activity-based office, with no work desk of my own and every-thing I needed accessible anytime and anywhere through my computer. I have shared a cellular office with a colleague. I have worked from a home office, and from numerous hotel rooms and lounges. My best reading is always on the plane. This means that I know, first-hand, the richness of the information you get from working in the same space, the distractions of people running through the office landscape while you are trying to work, the focus and the loneliness of a cellular office by an empty corridor. . .

I have also researched offices. My research has been in real estate and facility management, but my educational background is in architecture. I have always been interested in the effects of our buildings on people, organizations and use. This has coloured my view on workplace research. As part of my PhD, which was concerned with adaptability in office build-ings, I became aware of the new ways of working, and the new work tech-nology that emerged in the last decade before the new millennium. I still remember one of the first conferences, in Stockholm in 1995, dedicated to 'the alternative office'. Born-again managers described how work would never be the same, and how they had changed their organization radically by applying 'the alternative office'. I immediately knew that I needed to learn more about this, to look for knowledge behind the success stories. Since then, I have interviewed hundreds of office workers, seen thousands of desks in many countries and in different organizations, and analysed loads of data from user surveys.

My third perspective on offices is that of a consultant and as a workplace manager in corporate real estate. I have been involved in the development, design, implementation and management of workplaces for different organizations. I have met users and have heard about their needs and worries. I have met leaders with very different agendas – the offensive leader who is determined that 'change is good', and that a new workplace concept will improve his or her business; the hesitant leaders, who in silence choose not to implement the latest corporate workplace policy. The leaders who need both to save money and to change the organization in order to survive. I know the trade-offs that are needed in order to balance the creation of workplaces when it comes to needs and aspirations against the efficient use of money and the physical constraints of buildings.

Today, I am a manager of people working in offices. I have people in my team at seven different locations. We work together, but we are seldom in the same workplace or even in the same city. We use video, chat, phone and email. Sometimes we meet, and are able to get to know each other better. When we meet physically, we create common experiences. Experiences in which I know place matters. . .

From all these perspectives, I have spent most of my professional life occupied with how workplaces support the organization and the individual user. Ironically, new technology makes organizations and people less dependent on space. As more work becomes mobile and dispersed, the places for work have changed. In this chapter I will explore how this affects the workplace and how it is managed and designed, and last but not least, how distributed workplaces affect leadership.

PLACES FOR WORK?

The topic of leadership and the workplace has been rather overlooked in research. Still, the effects of place on organizations and on leadership, behaviours and relationships are potentially important issues for managers. Much recent work in workplace management and design highlights the effects of the workplace on organizational performance, and the strategic potential of using space as a tool for organizational development (O'Mara, 1999; Arge and De Paoli, 2000; Yttri and Bakke, 2003; Becker, 2004; Appel-Meulenbroek, 2010; Haynes and Nunnington, 2010; Blakstad and Andersen, 2013).

Through the history of workplace design and management, the main issue has been to create environments that support knowledge work. During the last 20 years, discussions have been related to how space supports interaction, and how to create possibilities for people to meet, learn and work together. The focus has always been on how physical workplace solutions affect work and knowledge workers, and rarely about leaders and leadership.

In the 1990s, we witnessed a change in office design, as the possibilities of new information and communication technology opened up to other ways to organize work and connect different spaces for working. The technology optimists predicted the demise of the office, and there was an assumption that, for some organizations, one could get rid of most of the real estate and replace it with telework. But even in the 'alternative offices' of the 1990s, such as Digital and Ericsson in Sweden and SOL in Finland, the technology was immature. Flexible working and mobile work supported by technology had its limitations. But the early developments of flexible working paved the way for new solutions and experimentation with different physical settings for different types of work and activities. Twenty years later, the technology has overtaken the rhetoric, and it is actually possible for everyone to work from almost anyplace. The connectivity and the user friendliness of the smartphone and tablets, wireless networks and 4G, truly enable mobile work. Most people can read and write their email or participate in video meetings from where they choose. Almost! Knowledge work is truly freed from place, and most workers take advantage of the possibilities. But knowledge workers still come to the office. Why? How does the office, a physical place to meet, still survive in the virtual world? And how do workplace managers and leaders find meaningful ways to support and lead mobile and dispersed work?

This chapter is about places for work in the 'modern, mobile' organization. I will start with a historical review of the office, work and leadership, and continue to look at the office today, as a network of places to work. The underlying question is: How does the design and management of workplaces affect leadership?

THE OFFICE – AS IT USED TO BE

Traditionally, the office has been either cellular or open plan. Early offices were related to finance and public administration. The office buildings were often monumental, and located in central sites in the cities. The majority of the workers were located in open-plan landscapes, while managers had their own cellular and comfortable offices, the kind of workspace design that supported the bureaucratic legitimacy and status of managers (Weber, 1947). Later came other types of administrative work, like post services, and later the telegraph, which were housed in similar buildings. In early commercial buildings, for trade, the administrative space was often located in residential-like environments, with a series of 'living rooms' in which the clerks would work, standing up. The first organizational theories were about the division of work, authority, order and discipline (Fayol [1919] 1949), with managers executing orders and subordinates paying obedience to those in power. This hierarchical and centralized form of organizing and leading with managers at the centre of control was supported by a physical structure highlighting and elevating those in power with separate, bigger and centrally placed status offices. The organizational space supported an elitist and leader-centric approach to leadership, with managers either hidden behind large mahogany desks in large offices, or, as in factories, in their own glass cubicles monitoring and controlling workers through glass windows. Managers had their own offices, spacious and furnished to show off status.

Nikolaus Pevsner points to the Country Fire Office from 1819 in London as the first modern mono-functional office building (Pevsner, 1970). With the rise of administrative work in the early 1900s, the number of staff working in offices increased (Flagstad and Laustsen, 1983; Albrecht and Broikos, 2001), and the office building as we know it today emerged. More work was routine, and the status of the office workers declined. Employees were located in huge, densely furnished halls, with rows and rows of work desks. In Sweden, this was referred to as 'the sea of slaves' (Bedoire, 1979). The leading management theory was scientific management (Taylor, 1947), which had a structured, formalized approach that divided work, including management work, and gave it a more visible and operational role. Taylorism has been important for more efficient mass production, including in offices, and paved the way for capitalism on a large scale. The focus on workspace design was not explicit, but rather implicit, and architects and engineers were important contributors in developing more functional and efficient factories and offices. The Larkin Administration Building (Buffalo, New York 1903–05), designed by Frank Lloyd Wright, illustrates the Taylorist approach very well with its line of office clerks in large, open environments, and at the front, managers in control. Employees were seated according to which part of the work process they worked on. The work process, in this case, mail-order sales, was broken down into individual operations, like an assembly line. Place, role and operation were all clearly defined to such an extent that every chair was bolted to the floor. The management supervised work. The building and the interiors were designed to support this way of working. This fits well with the architect Wright's own words only a few years earlier: 'The tall modern office building is the machine – pure and simple' (in Trachtenberg and Hyman, 1986). Form followed function, or rather, form followed management theory, the new and modern scientific management theories giving control over workers and production

(Taylor, 1947). This perspective is indirectly still influencing today's views on the office and organizational space as a tool to influence and control people, although recently, critical views on the use of organizational space have arisen within the organizational field from researchers like Dale and Burrell (2008), who are also contributing to this book (see Chapter 11).

In the late 1950s, the Quickborner Team in Germany (Duffy, 1992) developed a new ideology, highlighting the importance of working in teams. They also developed a workplace typology to support this way of working: the office landscape. The theory had its origins in the human relations school from the 1930s (Mayo, 1949), and highlighted the social psychological aspects of work motivation as well as informal aspects, such as group work and group morale. According to these newer perspectives on work and organizing, employees should be organized in social networks and teams, with a focus on enhancing communication. The office was organized according to these organizational perspectives and architectural ideals about 'open space', with open and flexible floor plans with clusters of desks. The office landscape developed into a type of office usually associated with large, deep floor plans with little daylight. The building technology was not able to efficiently service the air in such deep floors, and the indoor environment was bad in many cases. The employees used typewriters and desktop telephones, which meant that their work was rather fixed; they were limited to working only from their own desk in the landscape. There was a lack of space for conversation, focus and informal cooperation.

In the Anglo-Saxon world, as well as in Asia, the descendants of the office landscape, open-plan offices have been the norm since the office developed as a distinct building type. The ideals about the office landscape and open space were fertilized by the perspectives of Taylorism, and by a strong focus on efficiency and return on investment. The main objective was to optimize value for business. This is what we may label the 'shareholder value' tradition in modern office design. Workplaces support hierarchy. Managers are separated from their employees, and occupy large cellular offices with ample daylight, while their 'people' are sitting in dense landscapes, often in cubicles with no outside view or daylight. The office landscapes are highly efficient, and support a hierarchical corporate culture, flexibility, return on investment and business efficiency. Although the human relations school had advocated for better working conditions, the view on leadership found in these work spaces was still very much based on a hierarchical, authoritative and centralized model of management and leadership inspired by the first theories of organizing.

In workplace history, we observe a tradition that is parallel to 'shareholder value'. This is what we might label 'stakeholder value', which prevailed in Northern Europe and especially in Scandinavia (Duffy, 1997). Here, more focus was on the autonomy of the individual user, and on good physical and psychosocial work environments. Workplaces were arranged according to democratic ideas; work environment acts ensured user involvement in design and changes in the office. Regulations by law ensured daylight, good indoor air quality and reduced noise levels in work environments. In the 1980s, the North European office was mostly cellular or combi-office. Most offices were cellular and individual, and each user had control over their 'territory', as well as the freedom to use and adapt the office according to individual preferences. The users controlled, to a large extent, their environment. Most managers had larger offices, but there were modest differences between employees and leaders when it came to services and furniture. In this workplace tradition, the office was rather egalitarian.

A hybrid between the open-plan and cellular offices emerged in the 1970s. The combi-office is seen as a Scandinavian contribution to the history of offices. The concept was first published as sketches by Svante Sjöman in 1977, and later implemented for the first time in the Canon office in Stockholm (Doxtater, 1994). Sjöman's sketches show how individual cellular spaces could be combined with shared space and functions. The concept combined the best of two worlds: the individual space with a good indoor environment and personal control from the cellular tradition, and the communal space and places for communication from the office landscape. The SAS Frösundavik office building in Solna, by architect Niels Torp, became the best-known example of the combi-office (Duffy, 1997). Here, the ideals of a more transparent, communicative and open leadership approach came through with transparent, separating glass walls and more equal furnishings between managers and followers. The Scandinavian leadership approach (Grenness, 2003) also became more present through these more modern, open, transparent workspace designs. Later in this book, Tor Grenness will exemplify and explain how the Scandinavian leadership approach received support through the office architecture (see Chapter 10).

The space efficiency of the cellular and combi-offices was in many cases rather low, and the density in the combi-office was not high enough to justify the large amount of communal shared space. This meant that the space was often perceived to be 'empty', and rather expensive for the business.

In the 1990s, a wave of 'alternative office design' emerged, fuelled by new management ideas like 'liberation management' (Peters, 1994). Again, Scandinavian companies took the lead in developing new solutions and concepts, with offices for SOL, Ericsson and Digital as well-known

examples. Technology and new ways of working were supposed to trans-
form the workplace. Office workers were to be liberated from the tyranny
of the office and the empty corridors. Focus was on the knowledge work
economy, and sharing knowledge and interactions. Since technology
enabled work 'everywhere' there was no need for work desks anymore;
instead, alternative places for work emerged. You could work away from
the office and in alternative settings within the office. There was no need
for one desk each: sharing desks was more efficient and allowed for organizational dynamics, change and flexibility. Although the Scandinavian
influence on the 'alternative office' was strong in the beginning, other
countries, such as the Netherlands, soon took the lead and implemented
'new ways of working' on a larger scale. One of the most influential
examples has been the Interpolis in Tilburg. The Interpolis office defined
conceptual solutions, a clear set of functions as well as a style in interior
design, which has been copied in numerous projects and almost developed
as a 'new ways of working' style.

Juriaan van Meel traces the origins of 'new ways of working' back to the
1960s (Van Meel, 2011). Still, the terms 'the virtual office'/'the alternative
office'/'the new office' all communicate a strong belief in a 'new beginning' for workplace design in the 1990s. But in reality, information and
communication technology was not yet able to deliver the kind of freedom
it promised. It took another 15–20 years before technology truly enabled
mobile work for a large number of employees.

The alternative offices that developed around the turn of the millennium were flexible and open, and in some cases people shared desks,
like the flexible, open-plan offices exemplified in the telecommunication
company of Telenor, more widely described in the chapters of this book
by Grenness and Vaagaasar (Chapters 10 and 3 respectively). An emerging interest in workplace design and management, as well as a growing
demand for a more knowledge-based design of new solutions, has fuelled
an increasing amount of research into the effects of the new office solutions. There has been a strong focus on how open-plan offices affect users,
and some evaluations have shown increased levels of knowledge sharing,
benefits from learning and social cohesion, and more problems with noise
and concentration in the new, more open offices than in their cellular
counterparts (Arge and Landstad, 2004; Heerwagen et al., 2004; De Croon
et al., 2005; Kampschroer and Heerwagen, 2005; Danielsson and Bodin,
2008; Blakstad et al., 2009; Maarleveld et al., 2009; Danielsson, 2010).
Interestingly, among the many studies analysing office solutions, there
is hardly any emphasis on how leaders experience their office environment specifically, and how they lead in the more open-plan offices. The
only study, known to the author, of leadership in relation to different

workplace types focuses on the employees' perceptions of their leaders in different settings (Danielson et al., 2013).

THE WORKPLACE TODAY: A NETWORK OF PLACES FOR WORK

Today, information and communication technology is making true mobility at work possible. The new 'office' is 'Net Work', or distributed work (Harrison et al., 2004). You can work from multiple locations. This means that it is possible to have more geographically distributed organizations. This results in a 'network of places for work'. You can work from the office (first place), from home (second place) or from 'anywhere' (see Figure 2.1). When 'anywhere' is a social meeting place, such as an airport or a public café, it is referred to as the third place for work. Interestingly, the network model of an organization is increasingly put forward as a metaphor for the new organization, inspired and supported by the network structure of information technology (Hastings, 1996).

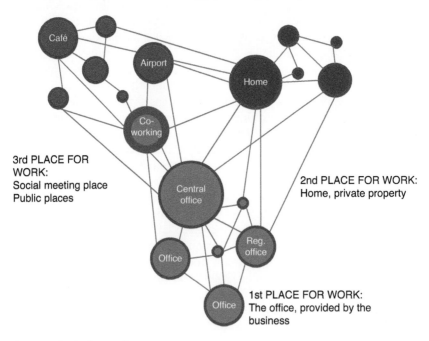

Source: Author's own diagram.

Figure 2.1   Net Work. A network of places for work

In *Work and the City*, Frank Duffy argues that industrialization forced co-location and synchrony on the workforce (Duffy, 2008). To produce goods in the mill, one needed workers to be at the same place and in regulated shifts. The same way of regulating work has been the case for office work, checking into your dedicated workplace at regular 'office hours'. With technology and the ways we work today, this is not necessarily the case anymore. In theory you can work wherever you want – and whenever you like.

These days, most people are used to being 'connected': they expect easy and fast connectivity, anytime, anywhere. 'Net Work' and mobility means that you can work from multiple locations, if your organization allows you. In practice, we see that most organizations prefer to make people commit to coming into the office (at least some of the time). In many ways, the new possibilities make the office more of a place to meet than a place to perform your individual tasks. The work you can do on your own can be performed everywhere. But when you need other people to help solve your tasks, to learn, to cooperate – you go into the office. This has made the design and provision of spaces for interaction more important than before.

In distributed organizations, people cooperate from separate locations. This means that you don't meet your colleagues physically every day. And as a leader, you don't see your employees every day. Technology allows you to cooperate; it supports interaction and collaboration (unified communication and collaboration). In truly distributed organizations, space, management and technology support the social network within the organization, and between people who cooperate regardless of location. Still, there may be a strong focus on 'interaction' and working together.

In the early days of the 'office revolution', computers were expected to change how and where we worked, and the office building was expected to become extinct. There was a strong belief in the notion that organizations would become less dependent on locations, and, indeed, on buildings. Even so, 20 years later, we still build offices. Organizations still lease space. But the focus in office design and management has developed from the supply of space for work desks, to the provisioning of spaces for interaction and for a variety of places to meet. The mobile office is characterized by diversity in spaces and locations. There are places for routine work, for informal and formal meetings, for workshops, and for project work. Space is designed for a variety of activities (Van Meel et al., 2010). Cases where organizations choose not to have designated work desks, but share workplaces in a non-territorial manner, are often labelled as 'activity-based offices'. The employees can choose where to perform their tasks. This requires more places specifically designed to support a variety of different activities. In evaluations, the flexible, activity-based office performs quite well when it comes to user satisfaction, probably because it provides more control and freedom for the individual (Danielsson, 2010) and is better equipped with supporting space and custom-made places for the different activities.

In many ways, increased mobility has, ironically, increased the meaning of place. In spite of the trends of more mobility and flexible ways of work, there seems to be even more focus on the workplace as 'place' that adds identity, meaning and quality to the occupying organization as well as to the individual. Office design is used as marketing, to brand organizations, to create identity and shape culture. When you can choose wherever you would like to work, you will probably choose to be close to people you work with and like, and in places that have some sort of meaning and quality for you. The workplace becomes a place to express the company's identity, for branding and a sense of belonging. The office is supposed to tell a story, both externally and internally. It seems like the new possibilities to work everywhere actually strengthen organizations' determination to express themselves and to provide 'organizational gravitation' – to draw people together and create a common 'corporate culture'. If we look at designing workplaces as a potential strategic activity, the main potential is to create places for mobile workers to meet, and to develop a work environment through technology, space and organization that supports work and leadership – wherever you are.

WORKPLACE MANAGEMENT

Joroff et al. (1993) describe real estate as the fifth resource for production, the others being capital, people, information and technology. The single most important argument for an increased focus on workplace design and management has been that the physical environments affect the organization, and thus can contribute to the strategic development of the user organization. In facilities management (FM), the main focus is on supporting the core business. Workplace management grew as a part of FM, and quickly became one of the most active topics for research and discussion at FM conferences.

We often use the terms 'workplace management' or 'space management' for the activities in facilities management that are related to the planning, provision, management and evaluation of workplaces (Blakstad and Torsvoll, 2010). In workplace management and design, the main focus has been on how one could optimize space in order to support the user's activities and the organization's efficiency and effectiveness as well as the end-user's satisfaction. This is often referred to as the usability of workplaces (Alexander, 2005).

As a result of the growing body of literature, as well as the growing professional discipline, a focus on how workplaces may be used to add value for the user organization has emerged (Arge and De Paoli, 2000; Blakstad and Andersen, 2013; De Paoli et al., 2013). In order to use space strategically, you have to express clear goals and objectives. In the literature, one talks about 'strategic alignment' between the goals for the user organization and for the workplace (Haynes and Nunnington, 2010).

But the strategic position of the workplace is not concerned with the physical workplace only. In workplace management, one usually focuses on value creation as a result of the interplay between social, virtual and physical space (Gjersvik and Blakstad, 2004; Nenonen, 2005; Vartiainen et al., 2007). One argues that the workplace must be understood holistically by looking at the whole system, the physical workplace, the ICT that enables work and is necessary to the work that is being done, how space is managed and the policies and practices at the workplace. Three different dimensions must be integrated to support work:

- The social, made up by people and their organization. Work, what people do, their activities, and their work processes.
- The virtual. Technology and technical infrastructure. Technology facilitates cooperation across geographical boundaries.
- The physical (for example, the interiors, the workplace concept, buildings, cities).

Workplace management's purpose is to support the organization through the provision of and integration between social, virtual and physical dimensions. In the more mobile and fluctuating organization, De Paoli et al. (2013) suggest that the triangle should be transformed into a rectangle, in order to bring leadership and organizational issues into the equation. This development poses new demands for workplace managers, as they will be expected to have knowledge of strategy and leadership, and be able to discuss with top management the strategies needed to develop workplace concepts that are truly a part of corporate strategy and are seen as a means to the development of the business.

THE SOCIAL INFRASTRUCTURE FOR WORK

The modern office is a network of places for interaction, where people are linked by physical and virtual infrastructures. These places for interaction construct the frame in which the social infrastructure of work enfolds. The network model for workplaces implies that work can be done from many different locations and types of space. Important meeting places, 'nodes', in this network may either be in office buildings with open-plan workplaces, meeting rooms, the growing portion of informal places for interaction, or at geographically dispersed places for interaction and work, the second and third places. Thanks to technology, work can also be performed while moving from one of the nodes to the other, working 'on the go'. The resulting focus on openness, places for interaction, serendipity and the possibilities for chance encounters, as well as the integration of places with different use and ownership all affect leadership.

Openness and Transparency

The trend in office design has been towards more openness. For businesses that have deliberately implemented open-plan and activity-based offices, such as Telenor, there is an underlying hypothesis that this will enhance innovation, communication and learning. But the visibility of leadership and the 'Telenor way of working' (Blakstad, 2014) are just as important. In Telenor, they have seen the open and transparent workplace as an enabler for the business to develop a common, open culture, where leaders are visible to all, and where the top management desks are the same as the desks of the employees (De Paoli et al., 2013). Space does not imply status. In many cases open-plan offices take away the employee's private territory (Vischer, 2005); in Telenor's model, neither leaders nor employees have private territory. In open environments employees see their leaders, and the way leaders behave and solve problems will be observed and may shape the culture and work practices. For leaders this means that they are visible and 'always on stage'.

But in open, transparent environments, leaders also see their employees. Leaders in an open office have access to 'rich information' about the organizational environment. And perceptive leaders get a lot of information: Who talks to whom? Does the pattern change? How do people behave, are they optimistic and happy or do they avoid other people? Which clients visit us – and who do they visit? How do we greet them?

In the traditional, hierarchical office, leaders could observe their subordinates, but the spaces were arranged in ways so that the leaders could control to what extent they were observed by the employees. In the modern, transparent open-plan office, the leader is often both observing and being observed.

Open-plan and more transparent workplaces, where leaders and employees work side by side, might create possibilities for richer sensory experiences and felt meanings and thus foster interpretations about the organizational life. Hansen et al. (2007) describe aesthetic leadership as concerned with the aesthetic aspects of social influence processes in leadership. 'Followers and leaders' work together in the same space, which opens up to sensuous experiences from touch, vision, smell, sounds and taste. The openness also affects the possibilities for the inclusion of 'followers' in the leadership processes, as it affects the interaction between leaders and followers. As De Paoli describes in her chapter of this book, the focus is shifting from a traditional view of the leader and his or her personal abilities or leadership style, to leadership as a social relationship and plural collective phenomenon. Leadership is shared and distributed.

Presence and visibility also allows both leaders and employees to experience each other's work and situations. You know 'what it is like' if you have been part of the experience. Bodily leadership knowledge comes from tacit knowledge acquired through experience and social interaction over time (Ropo and Parviainen, 2001).

The Nodes: Formal and Informal Places for Interaction

With the more distributed way of working, where you can work from 'anyplace', places to meet seem to be more necessary than ever. The mobile worker needs space that supports conversations, teamwork, meetings and learning, and a social arena where colleagues meet and build social and organizational ties. With a more mobile work style, there is more need for meaningful spaces for interaction. The spaces for interaction are a network of geographically dispersed 'nodes'. The 'nodes' may be in the central office building, as well as in the second and third places for work.

In a traditional office, the individual work desk is seen as the main function, whether it is in an open-plan or a cellular office. In the modern office, there is more focus on the place where people work together. The main reason to go to the office is to meet with your colleagues. As more and more work requires input from different areas of competence, and cooperation between many stakeholders, accomplishing work relies heavily on working together. When we study how people spend their time at the office, we typically find that they work with other people half the time, and that they divide the time they spend working with others evenly between formal and informal meetings (Becker and Sims, 2001; Brill et al., 2001).

Traditional meeting rooms are well suited for traditional meetings, with one chairperson, formal agendas and structured discussions. They are, however, less effective for alternative ways of working together: brainstorms, workshops, scrum meetings or creative sessions to solve specific problems or as a common workspace for project teams.

The individual work desk and the formal meeting room are often part of the traditional brief for new offices. Informal places to meet and work together are often not as clearly defined in the requirements. This means that both the user organization and workplace designers and managers must pay special attention to places for informal meetings, and carefully plan how they form nodes in the 'Net Work', the social infrastructure for work.

Another difference between formal meetings and informal cooperation is that the latter is less planned. Sometimes the need for spaces to work together occurs ad hoc; the teamwork evolves from a chance discussion or from a challenge that the team suddenly faces. This means that the spaces for cooperation and working together must be easily available, and close to natural meeting places, common workspaces and individual work desks. Places for interaction shouldn't need booking beforehand. They must be available on demand.

With less formal and individual work and more cooperation and inter-action, the tendency towards shared and participative leadership may be strengthened. Leadership in complex systems becomes more relational and more collective (Uhl-Bien et al., 2007).

Serendipity

Informal places to meet can be project rooms, social meeting places, res-taurants, or coffee shops, but not all meetings are planned. Coincidental meetings may be as important for work as planned and formal meetings. Coincidental meetings typically happen in the 'space between' (Harrison and Hutton, 2013), where people meet when they move between different activities. People also typically meet in a communication space, such as by the coffee machine or in the printer room. By consciously designing these spaces with possibilities for informal talks, unplanned and informal meet-ings may occur (Duffy, 2008). Carefully planned spaces for 'bumping into each other' may be important for social interactions in the organization.

In most organizations, there is a hierarchical organizational structure, from the smallest units to departments and to the organization at large. Informal and coincidental places to meet can be used strategically to create spaces for meetings that tie different organizational units together. Meeting places can also be organized hierarchically, from 'local' to 'central'. For top management, central meeting places, such as a restau-rant, the reception area or the coffee machine, may be important places where they can see, meet and be seen by the whole organization. In this way, places for interaction may add an important social meaning to the office. The main 'town square' is where you go to see and be seen, and be part of the social group that inhabits your 'city'. A common social meeting place may, at best, create new connections between organizational units that need to know each other. It can create an 'overview' of the social group to which you belong. In a larger office complex, there is much to be gained by creating meeting places consciously to maximize the effect of chance encounters.

Your Place or Mine?

Mobility creates new opportunities for workplace design management. It also means that you can work effectively from the workplaces of partners, customers or other relations. The network of places for work opens up possibilities for the integration of places with different uses and ownership.

Potentially, this can break down organizational boundaries. More organizations create meeting places into which they invite partners and visitors. Others create common spaces in which employees from different firms can work together in a shared space and with shared services. The nodes in the 'Net Work' do not have to be owned or used by the business alone. People can work from partner offices, rented space, co-working offices, or their own offices. Used consciously by an organization that wants to bring their customers and partners closer to them, open, shared and inviting places to meet and work may create commitment to and identification with the organization not only from their own employees, but from all users that utilize the place.

IMPLICATIONS FOR WORKPLACE MANAGERS AND LEADERS

In a more mobile way of working, the role of workplace management is, in many ways, shifting from focusing mainly on space and buildings into taking responsibility for the total provisioning of what is needed to support work, along with the physical, virtual and social dimensions. This means that the process of defining needs and discussing different ways of working becomes more important. The workplace managers must be able to assist the user organization in the strategic process of defining their main ambitions and strategy related to their workplace and ways of working. This process usually starts by aligning the user organization's goals and objectives, and by seeking to answer the question: 'What do we want to achieve with our workplace?' This requires new skills for workplace managers:

- working together with the user organization's leadership to define the appropriate workplace strategy (social, virtual, physical strategies);
- providing diversified work settings, support spaces and spaces for interaction;
- providing meaningful spaces and supporting the narrative image of the organization: 'telling the organization's story';
- planning for spatial and virtual interaction;
- designing the organization's 'home base' in the network of places for mobile work.

To provide spaces for mobile work means more focus on the social infrastructure of work, to create meaningful places to meet. This means that one has to pay specific attention to:

- providing spaces for projects and project work;
- making sure that the infrastructure supports working from multiple locations, also third places;
- providing spaces for informal cooperation using video to enhance informal and easy cooperation between different locations;
- providing spaces for 'alternative meetings', for example, scrum meetings, brainstorming areas, and so on.

One implication for leaders of the 'Net Work' is that to take advantage of the possibilities of workplaces as a strategic tool, leaders need to make decisions about strategic choices in workplace management. This is usually not one of the core competencies of corporate leaders. Still, important decisions about workplace design and management are usually made by the leadership of the organizations. In real cases, we have seen top managers dive surprisingly deep into detailed decisions and solutions. We don't know much from research on what grounds and knowledge these decisions are made, or the motives and rationales of leaders in cases where their organization's workplace is being changed dramatically.

The challenge for leaders of mobile and dispersed organizations is that the new 'Net Work' workplace might create a strange dichotomy in leadership. On the one hand, there is a push for more openness, cooperation, interaction and transparency, which in many ways nurtures aesthetic, bodily and shared leadership. On the other hand, many leaders have to lead people they cannot see. This means that they will lose some of the information and the possibilities of impacting others that they would have by being in the same room. This can be compensated for with corporate standards, information systems, communication platforms, policies and standardized procedures. Video meetings add a feeling of co-presence to a meeting but will never be the same as being in the same room together. All this might result in virtual leaders losing some of their closeness with their subordinates, leading to less information (or at least less informal information), possibly weaker relationships and inhibited possibilities for nuanced and face-to-face, real-time feedback. This might possibly lead to more direct (authoritarian) ways of leading. To compensate for the lack of richness in the information in a virtual organization, most virtual teams have meetings, or gatherings, face to face. These meetings are usually set in informal environments where the goal is as much to meet (face to face) and create common experiences as to discuss the issues on the agenda. Another way of strengthening the relationships is to create meaningful 'home bases', usually at the main office, in which there is a growing focus on identity and meaning as part of a 'group territory'.

This dichotomy might favour leaders with dual competencies: structural, organizational or even authoritarian leadership as well as shared, dispersed leadership. There is a need for more research on how leaders combine these very different situations: the presence of co-location and the lack of presence of virtual work.

I leave the regional office, and head for the airport. I will be home before dark. But I still have two hours before the plane lifts off. Hopefully, I will be able to get some writing done in the lounge. These days have been important, and recent events created the urgency that we spend some time together. The team and the local leaders needed to see me and talk to me – and I needed to see them and understand what was going on in the team. I am glad I came. It will probably make the rest of the process easier.

The writing of my book chapter is almost done now, and with another two hours in the lounge I will be able to conclude. I have been writing in the café by the ski slope in winter, in numerous airport lounges, on the plane. . . But most of the work has been done at home, at the dining table, in the evenings and even some nights. The final touches will have to be done next weekend in my traditional office, where I keep all of my books. I put on my headphones, as always when travelling. Elvis Costello's voice: 'Home isn't where it used to be. . .' I have to smile. 'No – home is home! But work isn't where it used to be'.

NOTE

* This chapter is based on many years of practice and research in close cooperation with colleagues and clients. I am in great debt to the many people I have worked with and learned from. I especially want to thank Donatella De Paoli for her wise, patient, supporting and yet demanding input into this chapter. Most of all, I would like to thank the late Kirsten Arge. We started this journey together, and although we miss you enormously, we will do our best to carry on your work. Thank you!

REFERENCES

Albrecht, D. and C.B. Broikos (2001), *On the Job: Design and the American Office*, New York: Princeton Architectural Press.

Alexander, K. (ed.) (2005), *Usability of Workplaces: Report on Case Studies*, Rotterdam: International Council for Research and Innovation in Building and Construction (CIB).

Appel-Meulenbroek, R. (2010), 'Knowledge sharing through co-presence: Added value of facilities', *Facilities*, **28** (3/4), 189–205.

Arge, K. and D. De Paoli (2000), 'Strategic workplace design', in B. Nutt and P. McLennan (eds), *Facilities Management Risks and Opportunities*, Oxford: Blackwell Science.

Arge, K. and K. Landstad (2004), *Arbeidsmiljøundersøkelse for Telenor på Fornebu* [Work Environment Study for Telenor at Fornebu], Oslo: Norges Byggforskningsinstitutt.

Becker, F. (2004), *Offices at Work: Uncommon Workspace Strategies that Add Value and Improve Performance*, San Francisco, CA: Jossey-Bass.

Becker, F. and W. Sims (2001), *Offices that Work: Balancing Communication, Flexibility and Cost*, Ithaca, NY: Cornell University, International Workplace Studies Program.

Bedoire, F. (1979), 'Trällhav, landskap och celler' [The sea of slaves, the landscape and the cell], *Arkitektur SV 1979*, No. 1, 16–26.

Blakstad, S.H. (2014), 'Workplaces the Telenor way', information leaflet from Telenor Real Estate.

Blakstad, S.H. and I.Å. Andersen (2013), 'Added value from workplace design, management and use? A case study', *Corporate Real Estate Journal*, **2** (4), 340–53.

Blakstad, S.H. and M. Torsvoll (2010), 'Tools for improvements in workplace management', 9th EuroFM Research Symposium, Madrid.

Blakstad, S.H., M. Hatling and A. Bygdås (2009), 'The knowledge workplace – searching for data on use of open-plan offices', paper for the European Facility Management Conference 2009, Amsterdam.

Brill, M., S. Weidemann and the BOSTI Associates (2001), *Disproving Widespread Myths about Workplace Design*, Jasper, IN: Kimball International.

Dale, K. and G. Burrell (2008), *Spaces of Organization and the Organization of Space*, Basingstoke, UK: Palgrave Macmillan.

Danielsson, C.B. (2010), 'The office – an explorative study: Architectural design's impact on health, job satisfaction and well-being', PhD dissertation, Stockholm: KTH School of Architecture and Built Environment.

Danielsson, C.B. and L. Bodin (2008), 'Office type in relation to health, well-being, and job satisfaction among employees', *Environment and Behavior*, **40** (5), 636–68.

Danielsson, C.B., C. Wulff and H. Westerlund (2013), 'Is perception of leadership influenced by office environment?' *Journal of Corporate Real Estate*, **15** (3/4), 194–212.

De Croon, E., J. Sluiter, P.P. Kuijer and M. Frings-Dresen (2005), 'The effect of office concepts on worker health and performance: A systematic review of the literature', *Ergonomics*, **48** (2), 119–34.

De Paoli, D., K. Arge and S.H. Blakstad (2013), 'Creating business value with open space flexible offices', *Journal of Corporate Real Estate*, **15** (3/4), 181–93.

Doxtater, D. (1994), *Architecture, Ritual Practice and Co-Determination in the Swedish Office*, Aldershot, UK: Avebury.

Duffy, F. (1992), *The Changing Workplace*, London: Phaidon Press Limited.

Duffy, F. (1997), *The New Office*, London: Conran Octopus Ltd.

Duffy, F. (2008), *Work and the City*, London: Black Dog Publishing.

Fayol, H. ([1919] 1949), *General and Industrial Management*, trans. C. Storrs, London: Pitman.

Flagstad, S.M. and S. Laustsen (1983), *Kontormiljøets historiske udvikling* [The Office History], SBI rapport 140, Statens Copenhagen: Byggeforskningsinstitut.

Gjersvik, R. and S.H. Blakstad (2004), 'Towards typologies of knowledge work and workplaces', in K. Alexander, B. Atkin, J. Bröchner and T. Haugen (eds), *Facilities Management: Innovation and Performance*, London: Spon Press, pp. 137–54.

Grenness, T. (2003), 'Scandinavian managers on Scandinavian management', *International Journal of Value-Based Management*, **16** (1), 9–21.

Hansen, H., A. Ropo and E. Sauer (2007), 'Aesthetic leadership', *The Leadership Quarterly*, **18** (6), 544–60.

Harrison, A. and L. Hutton (2013), *Design for the Changing Educational Landscape: Space, Place and the Future of Learning*, London: Routledge.

Harrison, A., P. Wheeler and C. Whitehead (2004), *The Distributed Workplace*, London: Spon Press.

Hastings, C. (1996), *The New Organization: Growing the Culture of Organizational Networking*, London: McGraw-Hill.

Haynes, B. and N. Nunnington (2010), *Corporate Real Estate Asset Management: Strategy and Implementation*, London and New York: Routledge.

Heerwagen, J.H., K. Kampschroer, K.M. Powell and V. Loftness (2004), 'Collaborative knowledge work environments', *Building Research & Information*, **32** (6), 510–52.

Joroff, M., S. Louargand and F. Becker (1993), *CRE 2000: Strategic Management of the Fifth Resource: Corporate Real Estate*, Industrial Development Research Foundation (IDRF).

Kampschroer, K. and J. Heerwagen (2005), 'The strategic workplace: development and evaluation', *Building Research & Information*, **33** (4), 326–37.

Maarleveld, M., L. Volker and T. van der Voordt (2009), 'Measuring employee satisfaction in new offices – the WODI toolkit', *Journal of Facilities Management*, **7** (3) 181–97.

Mayo, E. (1949), *The Social Problems of an Industrialized Civilization*, Boston, MA: Graduate School of Business Administration, Harvard University.

Nenonen, S. (2005), 'The nature of the workplace for knowledge creation', *Turku Polytechnic Research Reports*, No. 19.

O'Mara, M.A. (1999), *Strategy and Place: Managing Corporate Real Estate and Facilities for Competitive Advantage*, New York: Simon and Schuster.

Peters, T. (1994), *Liberation Management: Necessary Disorganization for the Nanosecond Nineties*, New York: A.A. Knopf.

Pevsner, N. (1970), *A History of Buildings Types. The A.W. Mellon Lectures in the Fine Arts*, Princeton, NJ: Princeton University Press.

Ropo, A. and J. Parviainen (2001), 'Leadership and bodily knowledge in expert organisations: Epistemological rethinking', *Scandinavian Journal of Management*, **17** (1), 1–18.

Taylor, F.W. (1947), *Scientific Management*, New York: Harper & Brothers.

Trachtenberg, M. and I. Hyman (1986), *Architecture, from Prehistory to Post-Modernism*, New York: Harry N. Abrams Inc.

Uhl-Bien, M., R. Marion and B. McKelvey (2007), 'Complexity leadership theory: Shifting leadership from the industrial age to the knowledge era', *The Leadership Quarterly*, **18** (4), 298–318.

Van Meel, J. (2011), 'The origins of new ways of working. Office concepts in the 1970s', *Facilities*, **29** (9/10), 357–67.

Van Meel, J., Y. Martens and J. van Ree Hermen (2010), *Planning Office Spaces: A Practical Guide for Managers and Designers*, London: Laurence King.

Vartiainen, M., M. Kakonen, S. Koivisto, P. Mannonen, M.P. Nieminen, V. Ruohomäki and A. Vartola (2007), *Distributed and Mobile Work: Places, People and Technology*, Heidelberg: Springer.

Vischer, J.C. (2005), *Space Meets Status: Designing Workplace Performance*, Abingdon, UK: Routledge.

Weber, M. (1947), *The Theory of Economic and Social Organization*, trans. A.M. Henderson and T. Parsons, New York: Oxford University Press.

Yttri, B. and J.W. Bakke (2003), 'Hybrid infrastructures for knowledge work', accessed 21 January 2015 at http://www.spacesyntax.net/symposia-archive/SSS4/fullpapers/42Bakke-Yttripaper.pdf.

PART II

Open office spaces

3. A spatial perspective to leadership in knowledge-intensive projects

Anne Live Vaagaasar

INTRODUCTION

Interviews detailing positive responses from project participants and managers about being co-located in open office zones (often labelled open-plan settings) are best understood against the backdrop of the mixed results of previous studies addressing the topic. For example, two project managers at a multinational telecommunications company stated the following (Vaagaasar et al., under review):

> I spend most of my time as manager in the open, flexible office space, and I'm very conscious about being there and how to be there. It helps develop the glue in the project. (Tor)

> It is a great advantage to sit in an open zone, because I catch a lot of things. Things I would not have captured elsewhere as leader. It can be concrete things or things that do not work. It can be about bad moods or things happening, the unofficial chat. (Endre)

The typical rationale for selecting the open office plan is the presumed economic benefits of reducing the area needed for employees, despite the adverse working conditions this creates such as loss of belonging and workplace-related identity (Elsbach, 2003), being annoyed by the smells, sounds, look and the mere general presence of others. Though some studies have shown how productivity often decreases as people move from personal offices to open office zones (Becker, 2003; Maher and Von Hippel, 2005; Panayiotou and Kafiris, 2010; Värlander, 2012), interviews conducted with project managers in 2013 about their perceptions and emotions related to the open office revealed a positive attitude. This surprised me at first, but reflecting on it for some time, I no longer find it that surprising. Comments regarding how project work is highly knowledge intensive (Brady and Davies, 2004; Sydow et al., 2004) reveal that a core challenge of contemporary project leadership is to deal with knowledge integration and learning, as well as with inherent uncertainty. Co-location in open office zones can direct learning-related leadership under these conditions, in projects as well as other similar work processes.

Because project organizing has become widespread and requires efficient knowledge sharing and integration, this chapter takes a spatial perspective to leadership in knowledge-intensive projects and reflects on why and how open office zones are suitable for project work.

PROJECTS ARE KNOWLEDGE-INTENSIVE SETTINGS

Projects are everywhere and most of us take part in a number of large and small projects. Since World War II, this form of organizing work has penetrated business life such that Western society has been labelled 'projectified society' (Cicmil and Hodgson, 2006). As projects have become the main strategy-implementation and entrepreneurial-process context, they have converted the central management focus in many organizations. Projects are social arrangements established to coordinate and integrate multiple activities and competencies to solve a specific task, hence, they are often demarcated by the following four characteristics (see, for example, Lundin and Söderholm, 1995): time, task, team and transition. They are temporary organizations in the sense that they are established to solve a task, that is, create some deliveries within a certain time frame and then be dissolved. The task is the raison d'être of the project and to solve the task a team is put together. This team often encompasses a variety of competencies, values and interests (Müller and Turner, 2010). Cross-functionality is seen as an asset in project work as the nature of tasks tends to be relatively unique due to their being established to create deliveries that, when implemented, can create change(s). The transition can relate to almost anything, for example, knowledge, technologies, organizational structures, as well as all kinds of products and infrastructures.

Traditionally, extensive attention has been paid to how projects can be completed within certain specifications such as the time frame and cost, as well as product quality. This occupation is accompanied by the emergence of a substantive body of project management research and a rational, universal, deterministic model for understanding project management (Winter et al., 2006). Over time, this view has become heavily critiqued (see, for example, Kreiner, 1995; Engwall, 2003; Cicmil and Hodgson, 2006) and project processes have come to be understood more as complex, nested and ongoing problem-solving (Packendorff, 1995; Söderlund, 2011), and as dynamic processes of learning by trial and error (Vaagaasar, 2011).

Project work is often described by practitioners as processes of insights gradually emerging and changing over time. Researchers have come to see it as 'a generative dance of knowledge integration that evoke novel associations, collective reflections, and connections and clues, which lead to new meanings and insights about the realities in and actuality of the project' (Söderlund et al., 2008, p. 532, drawing on Cook and Brown's thinking of knowledge work [Cook and Brown, 1999]). Others have also emphasized how project work involves experience accumulation, observations and imitation, informal encounters, and person-to-person communication (Ayas and Zeniuck, 2001), including brainstorming sessions, debriefing, ad hoc meetings, and lessons-learned sessions (Prencipe and Tell, 2001) – all related to learning.

Projects may vary in terms of their particulars, but in general they are widely denoted with uncertainty (risk and opportunities), which requires knowledge work to assemble information that can help reduce uncertainty and to sort out and make sense of ambiguity (Weick, 1995). Therefore, projects obviously merit the most competent available team. Sharing and integrating is a major project leadership challenge since, while project teams are often highly competent, they are often not able to exploit skills and theoretical knowledge.

OPEN-PLAN OFFICES/OPEN ZONES

The spatial perspective is usually not taken into account in discussions of projects in general. Increased awareness of how space can enable efficient knowledge work in projects can enhance the capability to successfully complete projects. The rest of this chapter explores how space matters in project knowledge work.

It is strange that issues of space have not yet gained more attention in discussions of project organizing and work, as the first thing considered about an organization is its materiality. The construction of walls and boundaries include and exclude, integrate and segregate people by defining those who are inside and those who are not (Hernes, 2004). One such discussion addresses how the characteristics of open office zones and traditional settings affect various aspects of work-life. Open office zones include both territorial features, that is, where employees have their personal desk, and non-territorial features, that is, where employees have to reserve a desk on a daily basis ('hot desking'). Open office zone use has increased substantially during the past four decades and is now widely used. The trend is mainly based on a rationale of cost reduction, increased employee satisfaction, or just the wish to create a positive and modern image. It aligns the organization with the general tendency of seeking more dynamic structures, for example, through the application of the project work form. It enables moving employees around within the organization and putting together new work teams more quickly.

Though research has found that open office zones can increase work efficiency and communication and that they have lower operating costs, these findings are not necessarily verified when work satisfaction, motivation and work involvement is taken into account (Panayiotou and Kafiris, 2010), and many descriptions show them to be the area of faceless, interchangeable, and powerless workers, with enclosed spaces such as personal offices being often described as the area of those with power. It is therefore interesting to reflect on what kind of values open and closed office zones present to individuals and organizations (Krekhovetsky, 2003). It is often claimed that more open office arrangements increase the free flow of information (Hatch, 1987), yet research shows mixed and somehow contradictory results related to this (Maher and von Hippel, 2005; Värlander, 2012). Still, generally speaking, open office zones are found to increase the communication among the employees inhabiting the zone (Hundert and Greenfield, 1969; Allen and Gerstberger, 1973; Zhan, 1991), as well as increase interaction, which contributes to an increase in information sharing, coordination, satisfaction and productivity (Oldham, 1988; Okhuysen and Bechky, 2009).

One exciting path has emerged through the application of the identity lens (for example, Elsbach, 2003; Elsbach and Pratt, 2008), which addresses how an enclosed office, when compared to an open-plan setting, reduces task personalization. Personalization of the office space increases the ability to affirm identity, but also nurtures the attributions of others. It might also be interpreted as a controlling of space.

A number of contributions have looked at how different artefacts, for example office decor, signify the distinctiveness and status of a person. In a number of organizations, all employees, including top management, sit in open plans, thereby removing most markers of status and functional group boundaries. Some studies show that this is the case, while others conclude that this is not the case and point to cultural factors that drive or hinder cross-interaction. For example, Elsbach (2003) showed that non-territorial work spaces do not relieve boundaries as employees use portable identity markers such as the way they dress to affirm distinctiveness categories. Other studies have shown that employees sharing an open office zone with managers find them more accessible.

The relationship between flexible office plans and organizational structures such as project-based operations is often scrutinized vis-à-vis individuals and teams thinking and behaving in more flexible ways. Several studies have shown how flexible spatial solutions have been implemented, in combination with efforts to empower employees, to increase flexibility in daily operation (see, for example, Värlander, 2012). However, these efforts have resulted in reduced flexibility due to the emergence of strict peer rules with regard to, for example, the manner and location of conversations, and activities like the use of telephones, perfume, music and laughter. Värlander (2012) argued how peer surveillance can be more repressive than management surveillance.

Open office zones, then, can be challenging in terms of individual work disruption, resulting in the development of rather strict codes of conduct. However, open landscapes are often described as having desirable traits such as sociability and freedom, which facilitate sharing and transfer of tacit knowledge.

OPEN OFFICE PLANS AND KNOWLEDGE-INTENSIVE PROJECT LEADERSHIP

The project member 'Tor', cited at the beginning of this chapter, expressed great satisfaction with open office zones in terms that were partly territorial (within a certain zone) and partly non-territorial (no personal desks within in the zone), which contradicts the mixed research results presented above.

During 2013, interviews exploring leadership were conducted locally in a multinational telecom firm's head office in Norway (by De Paoli and Vaagaasar; Vaagaasar et al., under review). This chapter draws on insights more specifically from interviews conducted with 11 leaders developing telecom projects. As these projects were quite large, many of the project team members worked full-time in the projects, and were located together, sharing one of the open zones in the office building. The interviewees had all been working with the firm for five years or more. Since moving to the new head office in 2002, the employees, including managers (functional and project), mainly inhabited open office zones. Although all the project leaders we spoke to had the opportunity of switching between different office solutions, the general employee situation was co-location in open office plans.

In general, all the project leaders expressed great satisfaction with open office plan settings. Comparing interviews from these managers with interviews from functional managers (representing the same company and inhabiting the same office building), the project leaders tended to be much more positive about a shared and open office space than the other managers:

I spend 70 per cent of my total time in the open project zone because it has to do with the way I like to work, because the persons important to me are there, and because I pay a lot of attention to being physically present for my employees.

There are more emotions in the open zone and it is very visible. Some get easily stressed and that is visible, which creates noise. But the open zone also creates a form of energy where you get things done – it feels like we are able to move faster.

When asked about work location preferences – at home (or holiday home), in cafés or airports, for example, or choice of office (private office or open office plan) – they all pointed to their work-life encompassing a hybrid of places and spaces, meaning that they work in a variety of spatial settings, yet they preferred co-location in open, flexible office plans. They said it gave them an overview of the project, a hands-on feeling, as well as information and knowledge about how the project is developing. All pointed to the importance of the knowledge sharing in the open office zone and related it to efficiency. Several of the leaders spoke of how they obtained information they would not think to ask about. For example, one leader said:

Sitting in the open zone is very important. When I arrive, I say hello to everybody and ask how things are going. The informal communication is very important.

Another leader confirmed this perception:

It is also a lot easier to discuss the things that are not working. It is incredibly efficient to sit in an open project space for both problem-solving, making improvements and operations.

Many of them also pointed to how the zone allowed for a variety of sensory experiences, which again provided valuable information. One said:

I can sense the mood, and feel if there are problems.

Another leader pointed to the 'sound' of the project:

When I can feel the humming, then I know we're on the right track.

All the leaders referred to social aspects when talking about the open plan office, saying things like:

I need to be with my people.
That is where I belong.
Being together gives me and the team energy.

As the citations show, the leaders talk about the energy in the zone and the visibility of emotions, and indirectly the value of seeing others, their work and their sensations. The leaders interviewed also pointed to the feeling of action in the zone (as something positive) and how 'nice it is when it is all humming and buzzing in our project' and they can sense that things are moving forward.

Interestingly, none of the project leaders reported many negative issues in the open zone. When it was not possible to co-locate the project team for the whole work period, several highlighted that it is very important to sit together in the idea and planning stage, when there is an extensive need for discussion and clarification. Several of the interviewees mentioned sitting together as positive for building the team spirit. Also, some leaders pointed out how living with team conflicts is more difficult in the zone than if the members hide in private offices. Therefore, the project leaders and the team members must take responsibility and make an effort to sort out the conflicts, which they perceived as positive for team development.

This positive attitude partly contradicts the insights presented above. Many of these insights, however, have been developed in relation to managers and other employees in functional organizations. Thus, space may affect project work processes differently than functional work processes. One explanation for this is the perception of the zone as space for action and energy, which fits well with the time-based notion of projects. Perceived energy, the observations of others working and 'the action' seem to provide valuable motivation for project work processes. Still, most of the positive attitudes seem to be related to opportunities for ongoing communication and interaction.

The interactive and dynamic character of most project work (Engwall, 2003; Söderlund et al., 2008; Vaagaasar, 2011) seems to lend itself better to co-location in open, operative and flexible office spaces than in the traditional, enclosed cell offices. Even if project members are co-located in cell offices nearby, the barriers of walls and doors limit the project managers' social contact, communication and hands-on control (Allen, 1984). When situated in cell offices, there is a higher need for regular project encounters in formal meeting rooms where the status quo and milestones are reviewed. According to the interviewed project leaders, the challenge in these formal settings is that people often do not report on what the manager really needs to know, and it is difficult for the manager to know what to ask about. Much of the most important project information and competence does not emerge easily in formal meeting rooms and encounters. The link between knowledge processes in projects and open office plans is discussed in the next section.

Within the field of knowledge management and learning, the practice perspective has become widespread, placing emphasis on learning as a process where situated knowledge is developed through participation in activities and relations. Wenger (1998) has pointed out that knowledge is actually knowing and, 'knowing is a matter of participating. . .of active engagement in the world' (p. 4). This means that social life in general is an ongoing production that emerges through recurrent actions, including sociomaterial ensembles of artefacts such as tools, templates, written procedures and ICT (Orlikowski, 2007; Feldman and Orlikowski, 2011). When practitioners can interact frequently, and play around with the same tools, processes of knowing are nurtured. Open office zones provide good opportunities to interact, play with tools, and use verbal and non-verbal cues in their joint sense-making. This is important due to the nature of the task being relatively unique and novel, creating uncertainty. In other words, project task work is plagued with ambiguity, which accelerates the need for sense-making, resembling an orchestra making sense of a composition. As Weick (1995) pointed out: 'What the orchestra members face is not simply the composition placed in front of them, but rather what they do with that composition when they play it through for the first time. The musicians don't react to the environment, they enact the environment' (p. 139).

Studies of project work indicate that bringing the team members together in one zone enables making sense of ambiguity and developing a collective enactment of the task and task-solving process (Okhuysen and Bechky, 2009). These enactment processes require that project members share and integrate knowledge. As indicated, projects often involve iterative processes that call for task enactment frequently during the project. This process might even be requested throughout most of the project duration. Project members sharing an open office zone will mostly increase the amount of informal communication and along with that the development of more personalized trust, which is also interlinked with knowledge sharing and integrating (for example, Nonaka and Takeuchi, 1995; Ayas and Zeniuck, 2001; Koskinen and Pihlanto, 2007).

Acknowledging the importance of knowledge work and learning in projects calls for awareness of how to share and integrate knowledge, the kinds of knowledge that are most valuable in different settings, and how space can lead knowledge processes. Generally speaking, workers are not very good at sharing and harvesting learning in and from projects (Keegan and Turner, 2003; Schindler and Eppler, 2003). One important

Table 3.1   Tacit and explicit knowledge

Tacit knowledge (subjective)	Explicit knowledge (objective)
Knowledge of experience (body)	Knowledge of rationality (mind)
Simultaneous knowledge (here and now)	Sequential knowledge (there and then)
Analogue knowledge (practice)	Digital knowledge (theory)

Source: Nonaka et al. (2001).

reason for this is that much of the knowledge is tacit (Polanyi, 1966), residing in activities, routines and organizational cultures (Koskinen and Vanharanta, 2002). Tacit knowledge is often situated and embodied, and it is often best shared through observations (Nonaka and Takeuchi, 1995), while explicit knowledge can be shared through verbal and written communication, as well as other systems of codification, all of which are easier to store and disseminate. Nonaka et al. (2001) summarized tacit and explicit knowledge, as shown in Table 3.1.

Project work requires both types of knowledge, but the importance of tacit knowledge cannot be overstated (Nonaka and Takeuchi, 1995; Koskinen and Vanharanta, 2002). Still, project management, in line with general management, tends to value more explicit and factual knowledge. Though knowledge is regularly referred to as fairly static, it is actually dynamic in nature. The statement that 'there are no whole truths; all truths are half-truths' (Whitehead [1929] 1978, p. 16) is particularly true in projects as they are created to solve novel tasks; accordingly, dialogues involving tools, symbols, procedures and practitioners in projects need to be quite frequent and in a sense-making mode (that is, trying to interpret the ambiguities they face). Co-location in open office zones facilitates such dialogues as it brings people together, allows for rich perceptions of other members, and facilitates sharing sensory experiences related to objects and tools that feed into the knowledge dialogue. However, sharing space physically is not enough for creating efficient and valuable knowledge dialogues in projects. *Ba* is also needed.

Japanese philosopher Kitaro Nishida first introduced the concept of *ba* and it is extensively used by Nonaka and colleagues (compare Nonaka and Takeuchi, 1995; Nonaka et al., 2001) as the 'place' where knowledge is used and contextualized. *Ba* can be a physical, mental or virtual space – or any combination of these. The concept of *ba* comprises multiple meanings: it can be seen as an interaction among individuals and between individuals and their environment (Nonaka et al., 2001), and as a framework where activation of knowledge as a source can occur. As knowledge is intangible and boundaryless, it cannot be stockpiled; using knowledge requires concentration of resources in time and space. Nonaka et al. (2001, p. 499) put it the following way: 'For example, when knowledge is created, the personnel possessing knowledge and the knowledge base of a company are brought together at a defined space and time, that is, *ba*'. *Ba* is the place where project participants can share not only experiences and mental models, but also feelings and emotions (ibid.), which is important for knowledge production. Where people share feelings and knowledge they can have sympathy and empathy with others, in other words reducing the barriers between the self and the others. Sharing open office zones obviously has the potential for creating *ba* as it allows for the forming of relationships.

Also, project leaders in the zone overhear conversations and see things they did not know to ask about. There is redundancy, in the sense of information that goes beyond the immediate operational requirements, which promotes knowledge production. This is especially important in concept and design phases (Nonaka et al., 2001). Redundancy also helps the project member to see themselves in the project in light of the other members.

Social learning theory as evolved from Bandura (1977) has acknowledged that role-model learning is an important mechanism of producing and sharing knowledge, with a heavy emphasis on management and leadership and 'the leader as a role model' as well as on learning in the project context (see, for example, Ayas and Zeniuck, 2001). The open office zone offers good opportunities for project leaders to lead through their own appearance and action. More importantly, it allows project members to lead and learn from one another through modelling, which is seen as a very efficient way of transferring and integrating knowledge (Nonaka and Takeuchi, 1995; Friedman et al., 2001; Feldman and Orlikowski, 2011). Role-model learning can be inculcated by locating one or more persons in physical proximity to this 'master'. This can also happen through more emergent or unintentional processes, as space has been shown to create warranted and unwarranted learning outcomes. For example, change from enclosed offices to open office zones can facilitate learning and development related to habitual ways of behaving and deciding (Becker, 1981; Becker et al., 2003). The importance of redundancy for knowledge production has already been mentioned. Learning through role modelling is another way of fostering redundancy (Friedman et al., 2001). Role-model learning in shared spaces and knowledge interaction in general also allow for extensive use of shared tools, that is, visual artefacts that can function as important knowledge brokers across spaces (Carlile, 2004).

The above discussions highlight projects as ongoing problem-solving processes that require a great variety of learning, and where the sharing and integrating of tacit knowledge seems particularly salient. Being co-located in the same open-plan office setting enables sharing and integrating both tacit and explicit knowledge, as it offers extensive opportunities for frequent and rich interactions.

Finally, space may also give project tasks priority. It is well acknowledged that project participants often engage in activities in parallel with holding other responsibilities in the organization. Seating project members together in an open office zone can increase the motivation for project tasks and make interdependencies between task, knowledge and people more apparent. The feedback loops may be shortened through daily interaction, which often nurtures motivation (Hackman and Oldham, 1980). Also, shared spaces provide peer control that can facilitate focus on project tasks. Creating an open office zone for all project team members can provide the employees with the opportunity of holistically experiencing what the other members do in the task-solving process, and to see various aspects that comprise the task and its joint enactment. This also includes sharing emotions related to the task, as well as other matters.

Moreover, motivation for project task work is often linked to project identity and the feeling of belonging to a place, a group and a project, as was also pointed to by the interviewed project leaders. Providing members with a group territory through the open office zone may develop group project identity. In the zone, projects can have information, identity signifiers, signifiers of professional project work (such as Gant charts, work breakdown structures and uncertainty matrixes) and their own codes of conduct signal identity (Andersen, 2005). Additionally, the symbolic act of giving the project its own territory may in itself lead to increased legitimacy.

SOME REFLECTIONS AT THE END

In the project-based economy, learning increases the success rate of projects (Ayas and Zeniuck, 2001), and firms' competitive advantage (Kogut and Zander, 1992; Grant, 1996; Spender, 1996; Von Krogh and Roos, 1996) depends on the ability to gather, integrate, use and transfer knowledge into the production of goods and services. We also know from research that knowledge in organizations is often generated through projects (Leonard-Barton, 1995; Nonaka and Takeuchi, 1995), and that important learning processes take place in projects (compare Bourgeon, 2002; Brady and Davies, 2004; Grabher, 2004; Ibert, 2004; Scarbrough et al., 2004; Kim and Wilemon, 2007; Vaagaasar, 2011) and hence the potential for creating competitive advantage by efficiently deriving knowledge from project work is high.

The empirical material and theoretical insights in this chapter point to how space leads knowledge work in the context of projects. This means that project-based firms need to consider how space can affect projects. We have seen how space can lead valuable knowledge processes in projects, yet it is seldom taken into account in discussions of project work.

The ways space leads varies across a number of situation-specific conditions. This chapter has discussed the open office zone in particular, as it seems that this spatial solution in many ways renders positive effects for important leadership aspects of projects, that is, knowledge work and uncertainty management. However, previous research has shown that co-location in open office plans can affect employees and their work processes in negative ways, therefore this chapter ends with reflections on creating knowledge sharing.

Try to co-locate project teams in open office plans when doing projects where most team members only work on one project at a time. If it is not possible to do this throughout the lifespan of a project, give priority to co-location at the beginning of the project. When doing matrix projects, where the team members work on several projects in parallel, try to find certain points in time for co-locating most of the team members. Looking across the project portfolio, if it is not possible to give all projects co-location at a certain point in time, give priority to the projects that are more novel and uncertain than the others.

When co-located, exploit the spatial leadership of knowledge process consciously:

- Encourage information sharing.
- Be aware of how aspects of the learning climate such as trust can be encouraged.
- Emotions and energy are mostly regarded as valuable for information sharing and motivation; encourage that.
- Be aware of how visual tools and shared sociomaterial practices can increase knowledge process potential.
- Be aware of role-model learning possibilities; for example, co-locating those that should specifically learn from one another.
- Be aware of the potential of less constructive learning processes and outcomes. For example, role-model learning can create negative effects such as learned apathy. Social learning theory has provided numerous examples of how actors in a shared setting create one another's apathy through role modelling in the sense that individuals refrain from acting in cases where bad news emerges, even

though they are worried about what is going on. This is explained by each of them observing the inactivity of 'the other', which leads to thinking that they should not act either (often accompanied by an emerging belief in how they initially misinterpreted the situation). In other words, as the actors observe one another's inaction, they create one another's apathy.

- Be aware of potential negative effects of peer control and development of local codes of conduct.
- Be aware of potential loss of work place identity.

REFERENCES

Allen, T.J. (1984), *Managing the Flow of Technology*, Cambridge, MA: Massachusetts Institute of Technology Press.

Allen, T.J. and P.G. Gerstberger (1973), 'A field experiment to improve communications in a product engineering department: The nonterritorial office', *Human Factors*, **15** (5), 488–98.

Andersen, E.S. (2005), *Prosjektledelse – et organisasjonsperspektiv* [Project Management from an Organizational Perspective], Bekkestua: NKI Forlaget.

Ayas, K. and N. Zeniuck (2001), 'Project-based learning: Building communities of reflective practitioners', *Management Learning*, **32** (1), 61–76.

Bandura, A. (1977), *Social Learning Theory*, Englewood Cliffs, NJ: Prentice-Hall.

Becker, F. (1981), *Work Space: Creating Environments in Organizations*, New York: Praeger.

Becker, F., W. Sims and J.H. Schoss (2003), 'Interaction, identity and collocation: What value is a corporate campus?', *Journal of Corporate Real Estate*, **5** (4), 344–65.

Bourgeon, L. (2002), 'Temporal context of organizational learning in new product development projects', *Creativity and Innovation Management*, **11** (3), 175–83.

Brady, T. and A. Davies (2004), 'Building project capabilities: From exploratory to exploitative learning', *Organization Studies*, **25** (9), 1601–20.

Carlile, P. (2004), 'Transferring, translating, and transforming: An integrative framework for managing knowledge across boundaries', *Organization Science*, **15** (5), 555–68.

Cicmil, S. and D. Hodgson (2006), 'Making projects critical: An introduction', in S. Cicmil and D. Hodgson, *Making Projects Critical*, New York: Palgrave Macmillan.

Cook, S.D.N. and J.S. Brown (1999), 'Bridging epistemologies: The generative dance between organizational knowledge and organizational knowing', *Organization Science*, published online, accessed 10 January 2015 at http://pubs online.informs.org/doi/abs/10.1287/orsc.10.4.381.

Elsbach, K.D. (2003), 'Relating physical environment to self categorizations: A study of identity threat affirmation in a non-territorial office space', *Administrative Science Quarterly*, **48** (4), 622–54.

Elsbach, K.D. and M.G. Pratt (2007), 'The physical environment in organizations', *The Academy of Management Annals*, **1** (1), 181–224.

Engwall, M. (2003), 'No project is an island: Linking projects to history and context', *Research Policy*, **32** (5), 789–808.

Feldman, M.S. and W.J. Orlikowski (2011), 'Theorizing practice and practicing theory', *Organization Science*, **22** (5), 1240–53.

Friedman, V., R. Lipshitz and W. Overmeer (2001), 'Creating conditions for organizational learning', in M. Dierkes, A.B. Antal, J. Child and I. Nonaka (eds), *Handbook of Organizational Learning and Knowledge*, Oxford: Oxford University Press.

Grabher, G. (2004), 'Temporary architectures of learning: Knowledge governance in project ecologies', *Organization Studies*, **25** (9), 1491–514.

Grant, R.M. (1996), 'Toward a knowledge-based theory of the firm', *Strategic Management Journal*, **17** (7), 109–22.

Hackman, J.R. and G.R. Oldham (1980), *Work Redesign*, Reading, MA: Addison-Wesley.

Hatch, M.J. (1987), 'Physical barriers, task characteristics and interaction activity in research and development firms', *Administrative Science Quarterly*, **32** (3), 387–99.

Hernes, T. (2004), *The Spatial Construction of Organization*, Amsterdam: John Benjamins.

Hundert, A.J. and N. Greenfield (1969), 'Physical space and organizational behavior: A study of an office landscape', *Proceedings of the 77th Annual Convention of the American Psychological Association*, **1**, 601–2.

Ibert, O. (2004), 'Projects and firms as discordant complements: Organisational learning in the Munich software ecology', *Research Policy*, **33** (10), 1529–46.

Keegan, A. and J.R. Turner (2003), 'Managing human resources in the project-based organization', in J.R. Turner (ed.), *People in Project Management*, Aldershot, UK: Gower, pp. 1–12.

Kim, J. and D. Wilemon (2007), 'Sources and assessment of complexity in NPD projects', *R&D Management*, **33** (1), 16–30.

Kogut, B. and U. Zander (1992), 'Knowledge of the firm, combinative capabilities, and the replication of technology', *Organization Science*, **3** (3), 383–97.

Koskinen, K.U. and P. Pihlanto (2007), 'Trust in a knowledge related project work environment', *International Journal of Management and Decision Making*, **8** (1), 75–88.

Koskinen, K.U. and H. Vanharanta (2002), 'The role of tacit knowledge in innovation processes of small technology companies', *International Journal of Production Economics*, **80** (1), 57–64.

Kreiner, K. (1995), 'In search of relevance: Project management in drifting environments', *Scandinavian Journal of Management*, **11** (4), 335–46.

Krekhovetsky, L. (2003), 'Trading spaces', *Canadian Business*, **76**, 22.

Leonard-Barton, D. (1995), *Wellsprings of Knowledge: Building and Sustaining the Sources of Innovation*, Boston, MA: Harvard Business School Press.

Lundin, R.A. and A. Söderholm (1995), 'A theory of the temporary organization', *Scandinavian Journal of Management*, **11** (4), 437–55.

Maher, A. and C. von Hippel (2005), 'The influence of inhibitory ability, stimulus screening, perceived privacy and task complexity on employee reactions to open-plan offices', *Journal of Environmental Psychology*, **25** (2), 219–29.

Müller, R. and J.R. Turner (2010), 'Leadership competency profiles of successful project managers', *International Journal of Project Management*, **28** (5), 437–48.

Nonaka, I. and H. Takeuchi (1995), *The Knowledge-creating Company*, Oxford: Oxford University Press.

Nonaka, I., R. Toyama and P.A. Byosière (2001), 'Theory of organizational knowledge creation: Understanding the dynamic processes of creating knowledge', in M. Dierkes, A.B. Antal, J. Child and I. Nonaka (eds), *Handbook of Organizational Learning and Knowledge*, Oxford: Oxford University Press.

Okhuysen, G.A. and B.A. Bechky (2009), 'Coordination in organizations', *The Academy Management Annals*, **3** (1) 463–502.

Oldham, G.R. (1988), 'Effects of changes in workspace partitions and spatial density on employee reactions. A quasi-experiment', *Journal of Applied Psychology*, **73** (2), 253–8.

Orlikowski, W.J. (2007), 'Sociomaterial practices: Exploring technology at work', *Organization Studies*, **28** (9), 1435–48.

Packendorff, J. (1995), 'Inquiring into the temporary organization: New directions for project management research', *Scandinavian Journal of Management*, **11** (4), 319–24.

Panayiotou, A. and K. Kafiris (2010), 'Firms in film: Representations of organizational space, gender and power', in A. van Marrewijk and D. Yanow (eds), *Organizational Spaces: Rematerializing the Workaday World*, Cheltenham, UK and Northampton, MA, USA: Edward Elgar Publishing.

Polanyi, M. (1966), *The Tacit Dimension*, New York: Doubleday & Co.

Prencipe, A. and F. Tell (2001), 'Inter-project learning: Processes and outcomes of knowledge codification in project-based firms', *Research Policy*, **30** (9), pp. 1373–94.

Scarbrough, H., M. Bresnen, L.F. Edelman, S. Laurent, S. Newell and J. Swan (2004), 'The processes of project-based learning: An exploratory study', *Management Learning*, **35** (4), 491–506.

Schindler, M. and M.J. Eppler (2003), 'Harvesting project knowledge: a review of project learning methods and success factors', *International Journal of Project Management*, **21** (3), 219–28.

Spender, J.C. (1996), 'Making knowledge the bases of a dynamic theory of the firm', *Strategic Management Journal*, **17** (S2), 45–62.

Söderlund, J. (2011), 'Pluralism in project management: Navigating the crossroads of specialization and fragmentation', *International Journal of Management Reviews*, **13** (2), 153–76.

Söderlund, J., A.L. Vaagaasar and E.S. Andersen (2008), 'Relating, relating, routinizing. Developing project management competence', *International Journal of Project Management*, **26** (5), 517–26.

Sydow, J., L. Lindkvist and R. DeFillippi (2004), 'Project-based organizations, embeddedness and repositories of knowledge: Editorial', *Organization Studies*, **25** (9), 1475–89.

Vaagaasar, A.L. (2011), 'Development of relationships and relationship competencies in complex projects', *International Journal of Managing Projects in Business*, **4** (2), 294–307.

Vaagaasar, A.L., D. DePaoli and R. Muller (under review), 'Project leadership construction. Project type and space matters', under review by the *Project Management Journal*.

Värlander, S. (2012), 'Individual flexibility in the workplace: A spatial perspective', *Journal of Applied Behavioral Science*, **48** (1), 33–61.

Von Krogh, G. and J. Roos (1996), 'A tale of the unfinished', *Strategic Management Journal*, **17** (9), 729–39.

Weick, K.E. (1995), *Sensemaking in Organizations*, Thousand Oaks, CA: Sage.

Wenger, E. (1998), *Communities of Practice: Learning, Meaning and Identity*, Cambridge, UK: Cambridge University Press.

Whitehead ([1929] 1978), *Process and Reality: An Essay in Cosmology*, London: Macmillan.

Winter, M., C. Smith, P. Morris and S. Cicmil (2006), 'Directions for future research in project management', *International Journal of Project Management*, **24** (8), 638–49.

Zhan, L.G. (1991), 'Face to face communication in an office setting: The effects of position, proximity and exposure', *Communication Research*, **18** (6), 737–54.

4. Leading employee wellbeing by workspace experiences

Niina Uolamo and Arja Ropo

This chapter (re)narrates the story of the spatial wellbeing of employees. The current literature tells one, quite unanimous narrative on employee wellbeing and its relationship to the built work environment. This narrative has undeniably been very useful as it offers many easy-to-implement guidelines for architects and facility managers. The narrative is about numbers, statistically significant correlations and causal relationships of the architectural elements, such as layout and lighting, in terms of employee wellbeing. In research lierature wellbeing is typically understood as a set of measurable constructs, such as motivation, stress and job satisfaction (for example, Oldham and Brass, 1979; Sundström et al., 1980; Evans and McCoy, 1998; Vischer, 2007; Danielson and Bodin, 2008; Aries et al., 2010).

We argue, however, that the narrative constructed by many researchers during the last decades falls solely into one of the three spatial categories suggested by Taylor and Spicer (2007), namely 'planned' space. They suggest that spaces can be planned, practised and imagined. By limiting the narrative to just one of these categories other aspects of the phenomenon are left untouched. We believe that an understanding of space and employee wellbeing through people's subjective experiences of using and sensing the spaces provides a broader picture of how the built environment, leadership and employee wellbeing are related to each other. Our view on leadership builds on a constructionist, relational, embodied and post-heroic approach to leadership (for example, Crevani et al., 2007; Taylor and Karanian, 2008; Denis et al., 2012; Ropo et al., 2013) that deviates from the mainstream leader-centric, cognitive and objective leadership theory.

As shown later in this chapter, our observations suggest that there is something messy, subjective and less manageable and controllable about how people feel about their workspace and how they talk about it. In this chapter we wish to shed light on the less discussed, socially constructed and aesthetic nature of the spatial wellbeing of employees. We will tell a different narrative – a narrative in which the subjective, aesthetic spatial experiences play the leading role, not the architectural or the managerial agency. We will look for inspiration and justification for our narrative from the recent, more critical theorizing on the multidimensional and socially constructed nature of organizational space (for example, Lefebvre, 1991; Kornberger and Clegg, 2004; Clegg and Kornberger, 2006; Taylor and Spicer, 2007; Dale and Burrell, 2008).

We illustrate our view with empirical data collected by the first author in a service centre of a major Finnish technology company where she also worked. We will start with a description of the company's spatial arrangements that we call 'the stage'. After that we explain the research process and how the data were gathered followed by the subjective narratives of the informants. We point out the fragmented nature of the narratives and their internal tensions. Toward the end of the chapter, we discuss our findings with two sets of literature, one representing the managerial approach and the other the more recent literature that emphasizes the socially constructed, lived experiences of organizational spaces. Finally, we outline some connections between leadership, space and employee wellbeing.

THE 'STAGE' WHERE THE SHOW TAKES PLACE

All the informants worked at the time of the study for a Finnish technology corporation in the same building. The building was originally built in the late 1960s and was planned for industrial production. During the past decades the building has gone through several changes. One massive change took place at the turn of the millennium when most of the spaces were completely renovated and considerably extended. The workspaces were divided into so-called office modules. Each module consisted of an open-plan office space, negotiating rooms and some separate workrooms. A long, wide, tall entrance hall goes through the whole building. Beginning at the front door a slope leads people from the second floor down to the first floor, where most of the office modules are located. Scattered around the building are some coffee oases for recreation. In the centre of the massive entrance hall is a round testing hall that represents the building's history as a factory.

The entrance hall has its own negotiation rooms into which visitors are usually led. The informants referred to these rooms as the better, presentable side of the building, whereas the internal meetings are held in the rooms within the office modules at a lower level. To us, this spatial arrangement represents a hierarchical nuance of leadership toward the employees versus the visitors. All the office modules are separated from their surroundings with glass walls. As one of the most recent changes in the office modules, some phone boxes have been brought into the open-plan offices in order to provide the employees some privacy for making phone calls.

The floor plans communicate the architectural and managerial plan of how the spaces are supposed to work. The floor plans emphasize the physical dimensions of the space: how different spaces are related to each other, the order and size of the modules and the locations of desks. One can imagine that the floor plans entail the idea that the occupant of the space works effectively in an open-plan office and moves from time to time to the interactional and spacious entrance hall or to the coffee oases to meet colleagues, to network and to refresh. The supervisors and the managers work in their private offices next to the open-plan workspace. The roof windows of the entrance hall and the glass walls of the office modules create a spacious and airy feel. The open-space arrangement enables people to effortlessly meet and communicate with each other.

DATA COLLECTION AND MATERIALS

The first author, Niina, gathered the empirical materials, interviews, pictures and building layouts. She conducted the empirical study with a narrative approach. The informants told their stories of spatial wellbeing as subjective and personal experiences, but also as a dialogue with each other.

The narrative approach turned out to be fruitful, yet challenging, in studying subjective spatial experiences. Fourteen narratives, which comprise part of the overall research data, were gathered through narrative interviews in summer 2012. The informants represent different levels and functions of two separate business units within the same organization. All the interviews took place in the spaces of the organization – most of them in the negotiation rooms and some in the private offices. The informants were asked open questions, such as 'Would you tell me about working in these spaces?' and 'How do you feel about these spaces?' The informants were invited to tell stories about their feelings in the workspaces.

The biggest challenge was the spoken language – or its limitations. At the early stage of the data collection, Niina had planned to collect only spoken narratives, constructed in narrative interviews. However, while starting the very first interview, it became evident that the spoken narratives would not give the informants a sufficient media to express their experiences on the workspaces. The first respondent found it hard to build his narrative behind closed doors in a negotiating room; he would have preferred walking in the space and talking about it while he showed it to her. After understanding the limits of relying on the spoken narratives, Niina decided to combine them with visual ones (Warren, 2008). She asked the informants to take pictures that would capture some hints of their sensuous experiences of the spaces. They were asked to take pictures of the spaces that they found meaningful to their wellbeing.

As per Mitchell's (1994) suggestion on the use of 'image-text', the spoken and visual narratives in this research were juxtaposed without either being reduced to or being placed as superior to the others. They were viewed as being beyond comparison – each offering a valuable contribution to the creation and communication of meanings, different from, but no better or worse, than the other. In this way the spoken and visual materials took part together in the construction of the narratives.

Besides the content of the narratives, the 'what' question, the narrative approach is interested in how and why events and experiences are told (Riessman, 2008). This study tries to capture all these three questions. Two narrative themes were identified. The first theme concerns how the informants 'live' the spaces through their subjective experiences and constructions of wellbeing. The second theme concerns a specific episode that took place about two years before the interviews: another business unit's move to the same building. We will next describe how the informants described their experiences in the open-plan office space and how these experiences influenced their actions and feelings about wellbeing.

'THE HUSTLE AND BUSTLE' IN THE OPEN-PLAN OFFICE SPACE

> If there is a lot of hustle and bustle and phones ringing, it is hard to concentrate . . .and when I sit at my desk, hands on the keyboard, if someone passes by, one usually always takes a look at the person as the screens [separating the desks] are so low. . . This was not the case in the former office as the screens were so high that you did not even notice if someone passed your desk. (B1)

Here the informant describes the noises and distractions, such as phones ringing and people walking by taking notice of you, as experiences inherent to the open-plan office modules. In the narratives the 'hustle and bustle' is seen as an essential part of the experience of the space – even so essential that some informants describe the occasional lack of this as 'weird and feeling idle'. With careful reading one can notice that there are also other spatial experiences in this excerpt. The past spatial experiences in the previous workspaces take part in the narration. The echoes of the past – similar or totally different spatial experiences and sensations connected to them – are included in the current narratives and in the process of giving meaning to the experiences.

The experience of the open-plan office is not, however, the same for all the informants. This can be most distinctively seen when comparing the above excerpt with the narrative told by a supervisor sitting in a private office next to the open-plan office. She sees the open-plan office through the glass wall of her office and describes the open-plan space from a managerial perspective. For her 'the open-plan office enables employees to easily communicate with each other, and it offers a peaceful environment' for productive work. From her perspective the open space 'leads' on her behalf in enhancing communication.

Different experiences of space give rise to radically different spaces, and therefore, at the end, there are as many lived spaces as there are users of the space. Moreover, the previous research has demonstrated individual differences when it comes to the relationship between employee wellbeing and the built work environment (for example, Oldham and Brass, 1979). Researchers have, however, passed these findings by, briefly referring to genetic and cultural factors, beliefs and individual adaptability from a cognitive perspective without discussing the experiential nature of the phenomenon.

The narratives are not only about the subjectively experienced, lived space; they are woven together with the other dimensions of the space. One informant, for instance, describes the space as a 'practice'. She tells of how she and her colleague unintentionally developed a habit – they started to regularly talk to each other in the open-plan office, both sitting at their own desks. According to her narrative, the empty desks next to her and her colleague encouraged this habit:

> Then one student working on his thesis came to sit next to me. I was embarrassed once as I realized that he's always sitting there and wearing a headset. . .that we hadn't been able to change our habits. . .that we probably distracted his work. . . You don't always understand that. . . We had developed this habit where I could say 'John [name changed], have you already done this?' and then we would start to talk. . . We didn't even bother to move from our own place to the other. . . It wasn't yelling, but it's. . . We have been instructed to move to the other person's work desk and to sit down and talk there. (A2)

The experience of space may support, hinder or reject certain kinds of social practices of the space, such as leadership. The physical space directs its user to a certain practice or habit – for example, choosing specific routes through the space. The low screens of the open-plan offices are described in the narratives as directing the users of the space to talk and gesture to each other in the space without leaving their desks. Similarly, the low screen-height directs the users of the space to 'hang out on the screens', by which the informants refer to people's habit of staying at their colleague's desk talking and leaning against the screen. The spaces planned by the architects and commissioned by the managers are understood to be the culprit for the 'hustle and bustle' of the open-plan office space in the narratives. The way the informants described their relationship to the open office space supports the view that the materiality of workspaces have a way of influencing and directing people's actions and feelings through sensuous experiences: it is not only the humans that lead – so do spaces (for example, Van Marrewijk and Yanow, 2010; Pullen and Vachani, 2013; Ropo et al., 2013).

Under 'Big Brother's Surveillance'

Besides the experience of the 'hustle and bustle', the informants describe their life in the open space through experiences of lost privacy. Privacy is an aspect that has been of interest to previous researchers studying the relationship between employee wellbeing and the built work environment (for example, Oldham and Brass, 1979; Sundström et al., 1980; Elsbach and Pratt, 2007; Veitch et al., 2007). In this discussion privacy has been understood as an objectively measurable characteristic of the workspace, such as the height of the partitions, individual offices, noises and so on. The excerpt below demonstrates that privacy can also be understood as a subjectively felt, aesthetic experience that leads and constructs the employee's wellbeing:

> When you walk along the slope you check who is at work and keep track of. . . And at the same time you have to accept the fact that the groups of visitors that climb the stairs [Photo 4.1] will see you and. . .you can wave them if you want to. . . But it is that kind of a. . .I don't know. . . You get used to everything. . . It's just work. . . But I don't. . . At first it felt very awkward. . . But when you block it out of your mind you can sit there. (B3)

The informant describes her own painful spatial experience of lost privacy. She illustrates the experience by also talking about the feeling of being under 'Big Brother's surveillance'. In the process of narrating her experiences of the open space, adaptation and acceptance appear vital from the employee's wellbeing point of view. The nature of this process is also demonstrated by the informants' comments, such as 'not until now, that we have been sitting here for several months, have I learned not to look at the people walking along the corridor' or 'I was totally confused when I once visited their [the other team's] space – goodness, people were sitting in big rooms, and I was thinking what a strange space'. The informants

Source: All photographs supplied by the informants; with permission.

Photo 4.1   To see and to be seen on the stairs

seem to be engaged in an energy-consuming process of adaptation to and acceptance of the workspace. As a result they learn to overlook or forget other, hypothetical and different spatial arrangements.

Besides their own experiences, the informants describe the (hypothetical) experiences of others. They see themselves causing concentration problems for others in the office space, and at the same time they see themselves as victims of the spatial arrangements. It is also noteworthy that all the hypothetical experiences of others are not seen as equal, as demonstrated by this excerpt: 'On the other side of the corridor there is this cubicle of one manager. . . During the spring it was freezing. . . If we were cold in the open-plan office, it really was freezing there. . .so. . .even the managers don't have it better'. This excerpt leads us to ask whose experience is important in the process of constructing wellbeing at work. The users of the space tell multiple stories, some of them their own and some of them the hypothetical narratives of others. In the process of constructing a narrative they engage in weighing these narratives against each other and thus shape the leadership relationships through space.

The modern and spacious organizational spaces that expose the users to the gazes of the others are described as 'sterile' and 'inhumane'. One informant illustrates the experience by reflecting on the idea of a hypothetical space where there is 'a painting, or even graffiti' on the big wall of the open-plan office module. He speaks about his own intention to bring a poster and attach it to the corridor side of the screen next to his desk. As no one else in his module has done anything like this, he ends up dropping the idea. However, he also describes other modules where people have brought a lot of personal items to their desks. This draws attention to the ways in which the informants construct the idea of one's 'own space' and the appropriate way of being in it.

A Grandiose Space or a 'Mink Farm' – Tensions Within the Narratives

The informant narratives give different and even contradictory interpretations and meanings to their experiences (and to the hypothetical experiences of others). By negotiating between these multiple meanings they construct their narratives of spatial employee wellbeing. As Boje (2001) states, narrators in postmodern organizations are constantly chasing after multiple stories. At the same time they are aware of the risks related to the overly high level of determinism in their storytelling (ibid.). This study supports Boje's idea: the informants construct their stories by reflecting on many different interpretations and meanings and leave their narratives full of tensions between these.

First, the tension between everyday work and the workspace can be identified. Work refers here to the everyday work of the informant but also to the work of other users of the space. The informants explain and interpret, for example, their experiences of noise and lost privacy related to their own work and the associated demands and requirements. In addition, they use their own understanding of other people's work to make evaluations on organizational justice and equality. One of the informants describes one team as 'sitting in their module crammed like sardines', when at the same time there are teams 'whose work doesn't require the big desks that they have'. The informants reflect on the question of who deserves the space. Employee wellbeing, as well as space, is evidently a political, power-related issue in organizations (compare Dale and Burrell, 2008).

Second, the informants describe their experience of pride and set it against the experiences of bitterness related to the space provided for them. They describe the building with adjectives like 'grandiose' and 'magnificent' and refer to visitors' complimentary comments on the space. Some informants also describe special moments in the space:

> I was here once in the evening with my son picking up something. . . He stopped there at the door saying 'Wow, are you working in this grand place, Mom?' I started to feel like. . . This is a pretty fancy place. . . After all these years you can sometimes stop there to admire the view. . .if the sun shines from just the perfect point. . .this corridor looks very nice. . . It is a heck of an accomplishment that after all these years. (A3)

The above excerpt demonstrates that the narratives are about moments in the space. They are not coherent, stable or chronological. As Boje (2001) states, in the postmodern world the experience itself is fragmented and full of chaos, which makes the storytelling difficult. Strict models that demand the narrative have a plot, temporality and culmination of events (for example, Labov and Waletsky, 1967; Riessman, 2008) do not seem to fit well with the analysis of spatial narratives of workplace wellbeing and leadership.

The experiences above describe how the feeling of pride is set against 'the other side of the truth'. One informant describes his first impression of the building as 'really fancy'. He continues, however, by describing 'how the truth was revealed' – how he realized that the magnificent, spacious entrance hall 'deceives the visitor' and that the workspaces are actually not that spacious. In his narrative he walks along the slope and sees on the left-hand side – 'situated in the best place to be seen' – the spacious modules that give the general impression of lightness and wideness. He uses the metaphor of a 'mink farm' (Photo 4.2) and refers to the experience of the efficiently planned space with limited workspace for the employees.

NARRATIVES ON MOVING TO A NEW WORKSPACE – GIVING WAY AND ADAPTING

About two years before the research interviews, the office space had gone through significant changes as the number of occupants of the space doubled. Before that one business unit of the corporation had occupied the building. The employees of the business unit, called Unit A, had experienced layoffs that had resulted in a significantly reduced number of employees working in the building. Another business unit of the same corporation, called Unit B, moved into the building two years before this study took place. At the time of the study, Unit A occupied the office modules located on the right-hand side of the slope, and the employees of the Unit B worked in the modules on the left-hand side. In addition to these business units, there are also some employees from a service unit working in the same building.

Photo 4.2   The 'mink farm'

As one can expect, the narratives concerning the moving in of Unit B turned out to be quite different depending on which unit the narrator came from. We will first discuss the narratives of the Unit B informants. We wish to emphasize that even though these two narrative categories can be identified, it does not mean that the narratives within one category are univocal; on the contrary, the categories are actually rich and multivoiced.

Estranged in an Industrial Era's Tin Hall

The informants from the business-oriented Unit B ponder giving way and adapting to the situation. The move to the new space is typically described as a positive, exciting experience. One informant, for instance, looks back on his first day in the building and describes the memory by referring to the shared experience of 'going to school for the first time'. For him it was like 'a new era had begun'. He describes the feeling in the new space as 'positively titillating' as he (and the other people) did not 'quite know how to be there' in the new space.

On the other hand, the serenity described in the above narrative does not tell the whole story. The narratives are riddled with breaches originating from the previous experiences of the narrators. The employees of Unit B moved into the new office spaces from an old property located downtown. The informants describe their former workspaces as 'worn out'. According to the narratives, the previous workspaces were outdated – the air conditioning and plumbing did not always function properly. On the other hand, the informants referred to the previous building as 'historical' and as 'a mentally nice place to go to'. The juxtaposition of the old and the new spaces was in one narrative highlighted through the metaphor of 'the Industrial Era's tin hall', which was used to refer to the new office building.

As one of the essential experiences in the new workspace, the Unit B informants talked about 'the lost sense of community'. One informant talked about the kitchen and the rest room that the employees used to have in the previous workspace. For him, it was their 'own little kitchen' where they were able to eat lunch, have coffee breaks and even bring something for the colleagues in order to celebrate birthdays and other special days with each other. The previous office with its break room and kitchen was experienced as providing the users with strong sense of community, whereas the coffee oases in the new spacious entrance hall are felt to be full of hustling and throngs. Some of the informants describe experiences in the new space such as 'getting lost in the space' and 'becoming estranged' from the community they used to have (Photo 4.3). Former close colleagues are now 'scattered all around the building', leading to a tragic sense of alienation created by the space. This was hardly the intention that the managers and architects had in mind, but as De Certeau (1984) points out, the planned space does not always come true in the use of it.

Besides the lost sense of community, the informants talk about the broken promise of employee wellbeing. They describe how, before the move to the new office spaces, they were promised 'settling down rooms' designed for work that requires peace and quiet. The informants refer to separate workrooms in the office modules. In the course of time, after the move to the new office spaces, many of these rooms were, however, occupied by supervisors and managers. The informants describe this loss with a satirical and sad tone. They talk about 'old boys' networks' and refer to 'employees who get bullshit from the organization'.

The cultural context provides the informants with an explanation and justification for these events: space produces power hierarchies by separating the managers in their own rooms (Taylor and Spicer, 2007). The informants sarcastically emphasize themselves as 'understanding the supervisors' need for private offices'. Bosses who have to give up their private offices are seen as 'descending to the mortals'. Here, by introducing multiple interpretations the informants again avoid ending their

Photo 4.3   Getting lost in the space

narrative with an overly high level of determinism between the space and the wellbeing of the people.

As a third theme in the narratives, the Unit B informants describe a 'sense of living in someone else's space'. They see the spatial arrangements as emphasizing the distinction between the two business units:

> Initially the corporation had a great vision to bring about fruitful cooperation and such things by situating all of us in the same building, but. . . They have their own modules there and we have our own modules here. People who know each other say hello to each other, but then strangers don't. . .then it's like you were walking in town and people were passing by but you don't know where someone comes from, where he's going to and what his name is. (B5)

The informants make the distinction between 'us' and 'them'. Additionally, they emphasize the lack of 'real' individual space because Unit A has occupied the building since it was originally built. Many informants find themselves with no power to make decisions concerning their workspace. They end up describing themselves as been forced to settle for the decisions of others, both of the managers and the habits and practices of the people from the other unit.

'A Shotgun Marriage'

> It was tragicomic. . . Oh no, now I spoke directly again. I would call it a shotgun marriage as they didn't want to come here. They were used to being downtown. . . We wouldn't of course have wanted them to come here as we got less space [laugh]. . . I visited some of their intranet pages, and there were questions and. . .it was. . . Maybe it was just a small portion of them. . .but it sounded like they had ended up in the middle of nowhere. . . Of course you don't get here with public transportation as easily, but this isn't in the middle of nowhere. (A2)

The above excerpt demonstrates how the Unit A informants talked about the move of Unit B. They describe the reactions of the Unit B employees as disrespectful and picky as they wrote in the intranet 'trivial' complaints about 'the grouse forum'. One can recognize the hurtfulness of these comments. The comments were about the building that the Unit A employees had worked in for many years, some even for decades. This suggests that the space people occupy over a long period of time becomes personally important – layered with past memories and meaningful spatial experiences. Besides describing the reactions that the complaints of the business unit evoked, the Unit A informants also reflected on the question of 'organizational justice' and 'respect'. Before the move of Unit B, the people of Unit A had to clear the other half of the building. At that time some were told to move to 'cellar' modules that had not been properly renovated during the big renovation at the beginning of the millennium. In this renovation the air conditioning was kept the same as it was during the time when the building was used for industrial production. The informants who had been working in these workspaces for the past two years describe their experiences with a bitter tone:

> We mocked them [Unit B employees] as they were used to getting the best. . .and at the same time there was this bitterness. . . Why are we put into these cramped spaces. . .and as an attempt to reconcile they are given. . .well [sigh]. . . They got our better spaces so that these ladies and gentlemen could come here. . .and we were put there, at the bottom of the building without asking us. . .asking whether we wanted it or not. . . It was an order; that 'you will go'. (A4)

The employees working in these 'cramped spaces' describe their workspaces as a 'cellar vacuum' full of smells of electricity and plastic and noises of air conditioning and banging metal doors. However, their narratives tell about the process of adaptation. They talk about 'the empty promises of a forthcoming renovation and of the temporality of the spatial arrangements' that they were given when they moved to these modules. They describe themselves as 'naive' and 'betrayed'. Furthermore, they

interpret the actions of the company and its managers as an 'undervalua-
tion of employees'.

The above illustrations give clear indications of how employee wellbeing or the lack thereof can be influenced through workspace solutions.
They also show that the narratives of how employees construct their wellbeing in the workspace do not follow a strict structural, plotted model of a
narrative. Riessman (1993) argues that besides chronological stories there
are other important ways of storytelling that do not fit with the chronological narratives. She argues that besides stories there are also habitual
narratives that people typically use to describe a repeating action that
does not reach a climax. The focus of these narratives is not on a specific
moment, but rather they describe what used to be done at a general level.
According to Riessman, there are also hypothetical narratives that deal
with events that did not occur. The data demonstrate that the spatial narratives on employee wellbeing have, indeed, many elements of the habitual
and hypothetical narratives suggested by Riessman.

WORKSPACE, WELLBEING AND LEADERSHIP

To make sense of our observations, it is time to go back to what the
literature says about the spatial environment and employee wellbeing.
Their relationship provides a way to also rethink leadership in a different way (compare Ladkin, 2010). In their comprehensive review, Taylor
and Spicer (2007) argue that the previous research on spaces and places
in organizations can be divided into three categories: planned, practised
and imagined. In each category, the researchers have engaged with specific
ontological and epistemological assumptions concerning the nature of the
organizational space. In consequence, researchers have ended up choosing
distinct research methods and analyses of different type of data.

According to Taylor and Spicer (2007), the first set of literature emphasizes the 'planned' nature of the organizational space and calls attention to
how spaces are designed and managed to reinforce and maintain relations
of power. The second set of research emphasizes 'distance', concentrating
on the physicality of how people and materials move through spaces. This
set of research examines the measurable relationship between furniture,
machines, architectural objects and those who occupy the workplace. The
third set of research space is understood as 'lived' – as subjective experiences and understandings of distances and as meanings given to the space.
This three-dimensional categorization resembles Lefebvre's (1991) influential theory of spatial production where space can be seen as cognitively
conceived/planned, perceived/practised and lived/imagined. Ropo et al.

(2013) suggest that there is a link between an objective architectural and managerial approach to the physical environment and an understanding of the symbolic meaning of physical spaces in terms of social interaction and power relations.

How do these categories of space then inform each other and the understanding of leadership and spatial wellbeing? For many decades scholars in the fields of architecture and environmental psychology (for example, Oldham and Brass, 1979; Sundström et al., 1980; Evans and McCoy, 1998; Vischer, 2007; Danielson and Bodin, 2008; Aries et al., 2010) have been trying to identify the factors of the built work environment that have an influence on employee wellbeing. A lot of attention has been given to factors such as the open-plan office layout and the architectural characteristics of the workspace. The architectural characteristics that have been identified as influencing aspects of employee wellbeing such as job satisfaction, include the following: window view (Aries et al., 2010), office type (Danielson and Bodin, 2008) and natural light (Finnegan and Solomon, 1981). These researchers have traditionally approached the built work environment by measuring different characteristics of the workspace, such as noise, lighting and privacy.

Researchers of environmental psychology have typically focused either on the psychological or the physiological systems of the human being and tried to understand how the built work environment affects wellbeing through these systems (for example, Suresh et al., 2006). In their comprehensive review, Elsbach and Pratt (2007) conclude that the previous work has shown that the most important characteristics of the built work environment from the employee wellbeing perspective are: (1) the degree of enclosure and barriers, (2) the adjustability of the work arrangements, (3) the degree to which the user of the space is allowed to personalize the workspace and (4) the nature-like surroundings.

The body of research on the built work environment and employee wellbeing referred to above seems to fit with the category of 'planned' space by Taylor and Spicer (2007), 'conceived' space by Lefebvre (1991) and 'managerial/architectural' space by Ropo et al. (2013). This rich body of research has made a strong practical contribution by showing how to influence employee wellbeing factors, such as health, safety, motivation and job satisfaction, by making changes to the spatial arrangements of the workspace. This research evidence suggests that providing employees with natural lighting and plants can, for example (with a statistically significant probability), produce positive changes in employee satisfaction and stress levels.

However, the planned/conceived/managerial narrative only describes the objectified dimension of the organizational space and its relationship to employee wellbeing. In this narrative the complex phenomenon has been pruned to measurable factors that imply instrumental manageability. The relationship between employee wellbeing and organizational space is seen as rather deterministic.

Our observations and the more recent research suggest otherwise. In the light of research on multidimensional, socially constructed space (for example, Lefebvre, 1991; Kornberger and Clegg, 2004; Clegg and Kornberger, 2006; Dale and Burrell, 2008; Viljoen, 2010) and organizational aesthetics (for example, Gagliardi, 1990; Strati, 1999; Linstead and Höpfl, 2000; Taylor and Hansen, 2005; Van Marrewijk, 2011), the relationship between the spatial arrangements and employee wellbeing is far more complex. In becoming sensitive to the aesthetic nature of the workspace and the power of subjective, emotional experiences and memories of spaces it is possible to deepen the understanding of the spatial nature of employee wellbeing. In this relationship the leadership conception also acquires a new understanding: not only humans, but also material spaces can lead, not only as concrete material, such as open or closed doors, but also through the aesthetic, sensuous experiences that the spaces evoke. Leadership becomes not only a social phenomenon but also sociomaterial in nature.

CONCLUSIONS

In this chapter our aim has been to (re)narrate the story of spatial employee wellbeing and leadership. As the research focus has traditionally been on the objectively conceived space and its relationship to employee wellbeing, we have striven to widen this perspective to the lived experiences of the organizational space and how those spatial experiences lead people's actions and feelings. Our observations suggest the following.

First, our study points out that the narratives on spatial employee wellbeing are not chronologically constituted, clear and without tensions. Instead, they seem to be multivoiced, filled with internal tensions and constructed through different spatial experiences – past, present and hypothetical ones. The way the informants avoid being deterministic in their narration refers to something that Boje (2001) sees as a postmodern narrative. As the narratives comprise multiple parallel narratives, they do not reach a definite conclusion. Consequently, spatial employee wellbeing can be understood as an evolving narrative constructed over and over again in the course of time (compare Wood, 2005).

Second, to construct spatial narratives, talk-based interviews do not seem to offer the informants sufficient media to express their spatial feelings and experiences. There is something essentially aesthetic in a spatial experience that escapes the textual form. Some of the informants found it rather difficult to talk about these issues. Beyond the spoken narratives, we asked the informants to take pictures of the spaces they felt meaningful for their wellbeing. The pictures provided complementary materials to the told stories. The informants' pictures were able to capture the uniqueness and randomness of the lived space. The visual, the sounds, the feel for materials, even smells in the space, played a role in wellbeing constructions. With the combination of the told narratives and the sensuous narratives it was possible to touch upon the aesthetic relationship between space, wellbeing and leadership.

Third, our study suggests that planning spaces as objective material solutions does not lead to employee wellbeing as such. This observation gives less opportunity to the managerial and architectural influence to manipulate the workspace solutions to improve employee wellbeing. This study suggests that people's subjective, personal and emotional experiences of spaces seem to lead to how they feel about their wellbeing at work. The wellbeing narratives are constructed in mundane interaction and dialogue with others and the spaces.

Finally, the narratives do not seem to have an ending but rather evolve over time. From the spatial leadership perspective it becomes important who listens to these narratives, which meanings are heard and how they are responded to.

REFERENCES

Aries, M., J. Veitch and G. Newsham (2010), 'Windows, view, and office characteristics predict physical and psychological discomfort', *Journal of Environmental Psychology*, **30** (4), 533–41.

Boje, D.M. (2001), *Narrative Methods for Organizational and Communicational Research*, London: Sage.

Clegg, S. and M. Kornberger (2006), *Space, Organizations and Management Theory*, Oslo: Liber.

Crevani, L., M. Lindgren and J. Packendorff (2007), 'Shared leadership: A postheroic perspective on leadership as a collective construction', *International Journal of Leadership Studies*, **3** (1), 40–67.

Dale, K. and G. Burrell (2008), *The Spaces of Organization and the Organization of Space: Power, Identity and Materiality at Work*, Basingstoke, UK: Palgrave Macmillan.

Danielson, C.B. and L. Bodin (2008), 'Office type in relation to health, well-being, and job satisfaction among employees', *Environment and Behavior*, **40** (5), 636–68.

De Certeau, M. (1984), *The Practice of Everyday Life*, Berkeley and Los Angeles, CA: University of California Press.

Denis, J.-L., A. Langley and V. Sergi (2012), 'Leadership in the plural', *The Academy of Management Annals*, **6** (1), 211–83.

Elsbach, K.D. and M.G. Pratt (2007), 'The physical environment in organizations', *Academy of Management Annals*, **1** (1), 181–224.

Evans, G.W. and J.M. McCoy (1998), 'When buildings don't work: The role of architecture in human health', *Journal of Environmental Psychology*, **18** (1), 85–94.

Finnegan, M.C. and L.Z. Solomon (1981), 'Work attitudes in windowed vs. windowless environments', *Journal of Social Psychology*, **115** (2), 291–2.

Gagliardi, P. (1990), *Symbols and Artifacts: Views of Corporate Landscape*, New York: De Gruyter.

Kornberger, M. and S.R. Clegg (2004), 'Bringing space back in: Organizing the generative building', *Organization Studies*, **25** (7), 1095–114.

Labov, W. and J. Waletzky (1967), 'Narrative analysis', in J. Helm (ed.), *Essays on the Verbal and Visual Arts*, Seattle, WA: University of Washington Press, pp. 12–44.

Ladkin, D. (2010), *Rethinking Leadership: A New Look at Old Leadership Questions*, Cheltenham, UK and Northampton, MA, USA: Edward Elgar Publishing.

Lefebvre, H. (1991), *The Production of Space*, Oxford: Basil Blackwell.

Linstead, S. and H. Höpfl (2000), *The Aesthetics of Organization*, London: Sage.

Mitchell, W.J.T. (1994), *Picture Theory: Essays of Verbal and Visual Representation*, Chicago, IL: University of Chicago Press.

Oldham, G.R. and D.J. Brass (1979), 'Employee reactions to an open-plan office: A naturally occurring quasi-experiment', *Administrative Science Quarterly*, **24** (2), 267–84.

Pullen, A. and S. Vacchani (2013), 'The materiality of leadership', *Leadership*, **9** (3), 315–19.

Riessman, C.K. (1993), *Narrative Analysis*, London: Sage.

Riessman, C.K. (2008), *Narrative Methods for Human Sciences*, Thousand Oaks, CA: Sage.

Ropo, A., E. Sauer and P. Salovaara (2013), 'Embodiment of leadership through material place', *Leadership*, **9** (3), 378–95.

Strati, A. (1999), *Organization and Aesthetics*, London: Sage.

Sundström, E., R.E. Burt and D. Kamp (1980), 'Privacy at work: Architectural correlates of job satisfaction and job performance', *The Academy of Management Journal*, **23** (1), 101–17.

Suresh, M., D. Smith and J. Franz (2006), 'Person environment relationship to health and well-being: An integrated approach', *IDEA*, **1**, 87–102.

Taylor, S.S. and H. Hansen (2005), 'Finding form: Looking at the field of organizational aesthetics', *Journal of Management Studies*, **42** (6), 1211–32.

Taylor, S.S. and B. Karanian (2008), 'Working connection: The relational art of leadership', *Aesthesis: International Journal of Art and Aesthetics in Management and Organizational Life*, **2** (2), 15–22.

Taylor, S. and A. Spicer (2007), 'Time for space: A narrative review of research on organizational spaces', *International Journal of Management Reviews*, **9** (4), 325–46.

Van Marrewijk, A. (2011), 'Aesthetic experiences of designed organizational space', *International Journal of Work Organisation and Emotion*, **4** (1), 61–77.

Van Marrewijk, A. and D. Yanow (eds) (2010), *Organizational Spaces: Rematerializing the Workaday World*, Cheltenham, UK and Northampton, MA, USA: Edward Elgar Publishing.

Viljoen, M. (2010), 'Embodiment and the experience of built space: The contributions of Merleau-Ponty and Don Ihde', *South African Journal of Philosophy*, **29** (3), 306–29.

Veitch, J.A., K.E. Charles, K.M.J. Farley and G.R. Newsham (2007), 'A model of satisfaction with open-plan office conditions: COPE field findings', *Journal of Environmental Psychology*, **27** (3), 77–189.

Vischer, J.C. (2007), 'The effects of the physical environment on job performance: Towards a theoretical model of workspace stress', *Stress and Health*, **23** (3), 175–84.

Warren, S. (2008), 'Empirical challenges in organizational aesthetics research: Towards a sensual methodology', *Organization Studies*, **29** (4), 559–80.

Wood, M. (2005), 'The fallacy of misplaced leadership', *Journal of Management Studies*, **42** (6), 1101–21.

PART III

Virtual workspaces

5. Virtual organizations: a call for new leadership

Donatella De Paoli

I am independent of places and can work developing the company from everywhere, a company that works with photo editing and consists of 25 full-time working employees in the Philippines. I have an office in Norway and one in London and work when I want to, where I want to. I practice virtual leadership as I communicate on Skype 95 per cent of the time, but I would not have been able to develop confidence with my employees if I had not spent time with them in the Philippines. It is important for me to be around my employees at least once a year. You are not able to develop the same relations with people if you are not with them physically for some time. I need to go to the Philippines at least once a year, and for a long time, such as one or two weeks. When I am with my employees, we spend time on just bonding, working together in the office, talking and setting the agenda for the coming month or year. It is important for that relation, important to meet the teams and get a mutual understanding. I talk about how important this is, working deeply with them about the vision and values we have. We do not do anything particularly fancy or expensive; we usually just go to a beach because that is what most of my employees prefer to do the most. I am very concerned with letting them decide, being in charge of what we are doing when I visit. I believe in empowering people, especially because they have to lead themselves most of the time.
(Interview with young entrepreneur, Oslo, 26 April 2013)

This quote is illustrative of a new way of leading in digital space, without the regular face-to-face relations in meetings or in the daily office environment. It says a whole lot about the importance of meeting physically, even if only once a year, for the purpose of establishing and developing physical contact when relations are mainly through electronic devices. The quote is also descriptive of a normal situation of many managers today – working and leading people that are elsewhere. Work is undergoing change at a tremendously fast pace. The constantly developing alternatives of communication and internet technology with globalization and new work practices have made the traditional borders between work and private life increasingly disappear. Virtual work seems to dissolve the notion of place and space as the opportunities offered by modern communication technology are to communicate, work and produce without the need to meet face to face. Work is now done everywhere at all times and in all places: at home, during travel in trains or on the plane, in public places, at weekend resorts or elsewhere.

These changes in work and spaces are not reflected sufficiently in the leadership literature, but leading leadership researchers are aware that the practice field is far ahead of research. Al-Ani et al. (2011) have stated that 'there are significant gaps in developing new conceptual understanding of leadership of virtual or distributed groups or teams' (p. 225). Technology is pushing organizations and society forward, while our way of relating to each other and collaboration remains stable, at least for those of us over 40 who have not been brought up with the Internet, communication technology and PCs. Leadership tends to be conceptualized and interpreted traditionally in most studies referred to in this chapter, despite organizations becoming fully digitalized and leadership happening mostly in virtual spaces.

Most solutions proposed for the challenges posed by virtual leadership are also traditional, as the research review will show. The research on leadership in virtual space, from the fields of information management, project management and leadership, as well as those of social psychological research, exists in considerable richness. At the same time, our mental images, our learned behaviour, our habits and traditions tend to remain the same instead of adapting and changing with new technology. Therefore, some claim there is a need for learning to lead differently (Caulat, 2012), using skills such as listening, focusing and engaging with others on another level than face to face, building and nurturing relations in virtual space. In this chapter, new approaches to and ideas about virtual leadership will be described. One way to develop new approaches to leadership is to turn to the digital natives (Tapscott, 2009), such as the young entrepreneur interviewed, enabling us to be inspired and to learn.

LEADERSHIP IN THE DIGITAL ERA – WHAT IS IT REALLY ABOUT?

One may question whether virtual work and leadership is just a new way of communicating or really implies a new way of leadership. Exploring the conceptualizations of this new phenomenon reveals there are different ways of looking at it depending on the perspective taken. The advanced information technology (AIT) developed since the mid-1990s seems to be an important premise for the concepts in use. The first articles found on the subject were mostly based within the information management system field or in the small-group field using the term 'virtual teams' to label the phenomenon. This field of research is very much oriented towards detecting practical challenges working in virtual space and trying to find constructive solutions. Subsequently, the issues discussed were about virtual team leadership (Zigurs, 2003) and related issues such as leader relations (Pauleen, 2004), trust (Aubert and Kelsey, 2003), communication (Jarvenpaa and Leidner, 1999), life-cycle (Furst et al., 2004), conflict (Wakefield et al., 2008) and other issues. Virtual teams, groups or projects were seen as 'groups of geographically and/or organizationally dispersed co-workers that are assembled using a combination of telecommunications and information technologies to accomplish an organizational task' (Townsend et al., 1998, p. 18). A related term covering the same kind of work and leadership is e-leadership: 'We choose the term e-leadership to incorporate the new emerging context for examining leadership' (Avolio et al., 2001, p. 617).

Apparently, other researchers see the term 'virtual' as too general or unclear as they use this name for 'distributed teams or groups' (Kayworth and Leidner, 2001; Muethel and Hoegl, 2010). The geographical aspect is also underlined as many researchers perceive virtual teams to be global virtual teams (Mendenhall et al., 2012; Zander et al., 2012). Physical distance is not necessarily a premise for virtual work anymore, but the global aspect brings new issues to leadership. Research deriving from the fields of cross-cultural management and international business is less interested in the technological aspects and more in the global, researching global teams uniting people from different parts of the world and different cultures (Kerber and Buono, 2004; Joshi and Lazarova, 2005; Mendenhall et al., 2012; Zander et al., 2012).

Characteristics that differentiate distributed or virtual teams from traditional teams may include greater dispersion in structure, culture, language, temporal settings and geographic location (Zigurs, 2003). Recently, there has been increasing recognition that more and more teams fall into a large 'hybrid category'; that is, they are no longer purely distributed or purely face to face, but use technology according to the needs of their task and team structure.

Looking at the Photo 5.1, one may ask what there is about the context that influences leadership. There is so far no single term or concept in the leadership and organizational field that appropriately covers the leadership of relations that takes place through technological devices. It seems like every new field that has entered the arena has given its own new name to this area, such as virtual team leadership, virtual leadership, leadership of distributed teams, leadership of global teams and finally e-leadership. There is an etymological confusion around the phenomenon indicating

Source: All photographs are from a free online source.

Photo 5.1   Group in a video-conference

that the field is new and under-researched but also that researchers do not agree what the phenomenon is. What is it about the new technology that changes or modifies leadership processes and behaviour? Is it the fact that people communicate through technology, with or without a screen? What role do the senses play in a virtual situation? What kind of technology is most influential in shaping new leadership processes and behaviour? And how is the hybrid work situation influencing and combining physical face-to-face meetings with virtual communication? Another element is the fact that technology allows for more simultaneous international cross-cultural cooperation across time zones. For many researchers, the global element is the most influential factor in shaping new leadership relations and leadership, more than the technology per se.

In one of the few books devoted to virtual leadership, Ghislaine Caulat (2012) writes, 'the virtual leader needs to recognize that working virtually will involve working differently' (p. 27). Practitioners are moving at an incredibly fast pace when it comes to applying new technology, steadily improving and giving organizations new opportunities for cost-efficient communication. Still, many continue to work like they have always done, exchanging information and monitoring tasks in a traditional way in virtual space. Ways of communicating and working, habits and traditions, work styles and culture, work methods, and so on, are quite conservative and stable. Technology changes, but people tend to continue working and leading in the same way. Therefore, according to several researchers (Zigurs, 2003; DasGupta, 2011; Caulat, 2012), there is a need to develop new ways of thinking and behaving in virtual space. As the author of one of the most extensive reviews of e-leadership articulated: 'Leadership and technology enjoy a recursive relationship, each affecting and at the same time being affected by the other; each transforming and being transformed by the other' (DasGupta, 2011, p. 2).

Generally, most research about the topic seems to have little interest in leadership, but more about what makes this new phenomenon different from regular face-to-face work. The tendency to fail to define or explain leadership is generally ingrained in both practice and research as an earlier article illustrates very well (Baker, 1997), also in the research on virtual leadership.

LEADERSHIP IN VIRTUAL SPACE – CHALLENGING OR LIBERATING?

Virtual work is really nothing new as it has gone on for at least 20 years. There has been considerable research about the topic, but even after so many years, virtual work remains an unsatisfactory practice and some-thing most managers do when they have to, not because they choose to (Caulat, 2012). Behavioural aspects deriving from new technology are often mystifying and also highlighted as more particular and special than they are in actuality. Our perception of technology influences the way technology is perceived. Face-to-face meetings with people that you can clearly see, smell, feel and touch is perceived differently than communica-tion through a technological device. Virtual space is about communicating through a technological tool or medium stimulating certain senses more than others, requiring new leadership skills such as nurturing virtual rela-tionships, facilitating virtual processes and developing trust in a new way (Photo 5.2).

A good illustration of what the new virtual reality is bringing is found in one of the earliest writings about this theme. Charles Handy makes a point in arguing that trust is one of the biggest challenges virtual space introduces to relations, organizing and leadership (1995). He writes:

> We will be spending time in virtual space – out of sight, if not out of touch. No longer will our colleagues be down the corridor, available for an unscheduled meeting or a quick progress check. Most meetings will have to be scheduled, and will therefore become more infrequent. We will have to learn how to run organizations without meetings. We will also have to get accustomed to working with and managing those whom we do not see, except on rare and prearranged occasions. That is harder than it sounds. (Handy, 1995, p. 41)

Photo 5.2   Leadership in virtual space

Handy's preoccupation with the entrance of new telecommunication in organizations has been largely confirmed by later research. Kayworth and Leidner (2001) were amongst the first to give a thorough overview of the main challenges virtual work brings to leadership. Table 5.1 is inspired by them, but developed further with issues found in other studies and my own research interviewing managers on the issue.

Table 5.1 shows that practitioners experience new kinds of leadership challenges, but also that the existing leadership challenges are altered when communication and leadership are virtual. Several interviews conducted with managers on different levels confirm the existing findings so it is quite apparent that virtual space is both different and unknown for many managers. Here is an illustration of the typical attitude and experience encountered by many managers today:

> I experience that the contact is very good when I have worked with people previously. When I have virtual meetings with people I have not met previously, I do not know who they are and why they are in the meeting; I do relate to them, but only to what they say. There is more room for judgements and reflections when I do know the people. (Interview with project manager in telecommunication, 30 November 2012)

In general, most managers report that the greatest challenges with leading virtual groups or teams arise when some or all of the members do not know each other (Pauleen, 2004). Other barriers or distances such as religion, language, culture and profession just add to the challenge when people have never met (Mendenhall et al., 2012; Zander et al., 2012).

Table 5.1   Challenges of leadership in virtual space

Challenges	
Trust	Difficulties developing trust when participants do not know each other
Communication	Communication process dysfunction (dysfunctional meanings, distortion and misinterpretation)
	Traditional social mechanisms are lost or distorted
	Poorer communication due to lack of facial expressions, vocal inflections, verbal cues and gestures
	Distinctions among members' social and expert status changed
Process	Hindrance in developing relations can lead to decreased motivation, morale and creativity
	Subgroups easily formed with participants spread throughout different facilities, creating more opposition and conflicts
	Head office subgrouping versus subcontractor or client subgrouping creates in-group challenges
Culture	Broader range of misinterpretation due to cultural differences
	Unrealistic cultural expectations
	Communication may be distorted through cultural misunderstandings/biases
	Conflict more difficult to solve due to cultural differences
Physicalities	Multiple time zones make scheduling meetings as well as travel very difficult
	Participants in different time zones are in different states of mind
Technology	Technophobia
	Need for proficiency across a wide range of technologies
	Difference of technological standards and quality creates communication barriers

Subgrouping is also reported as a big challenge by several of the managers interviewed, when there are people feeling outside the core group that is physically present in the head office.

The challenges listed in the table are to a great extent explained by a lower quality of communication due to the lack of informal cues, body language, sensations and emotional contact (Wakefield et al., 2008; Zigurs, 2003), as the manager below expresses:

> The challenge is that you do not get to see the reactions; when people get insulted and stop contributing, then you do not know the reason for it. When you have face-to-face communication you get the signals. It is easier too for participants

to feel shut out when working virtually. Especially when we have project meetings, then the law of gravity works; the more there are in the meeting room
compared to the ones on the telephone, the more people feel left out. (Interview
with project manager in telecommunication, 30 November 2012)

The virtual leadership situation is described and analysed as if it were
devoid of bodies and physicality, which, according to more recent research,
is not the case (Caulat, 2012; De Paoli et al., 2014). Certain senses like listening, focusing and engaging with others are more stimulated in virtual
settings, especially when participants do not see each other. Another issue
in virtual cooperation and leadership is the ability to connect emotionally
and be committed to the cause. People working virtually do not share their
thoughts, reflections and competences face to face. The feeling of common
cause and destiny may easily vanish. Motivating people that you do not
see regularly can be a challenge. Many also report that creativity suffers
as the meetings in virtual space tend to be more structured, more to the
point and time productive (Muethel and Hoegl, 2010). The substance and
factual dimension of communication is often highlighted. When talking
to managers generally, it appears that going virtual means more effective, shorter and more focused meetings. They also report that it is more
convenient to meet virtually when you have a status quo meeting as everybody focuses more on the content and less on getting to know each other.
The chit-chat and informal jokes tend to disappear in virtual meetings.
This makes leadership more task oriented and focused on the most important issues. Some managers claim they have to be more clear-cut, talking
directly without double meanings and irony. This factual and impersonal approach to the virtual space seems to fit in well with the rational
paradigm in which many businesses exist. But I have to ask myself, in line
with the interviewed project manager below, if the reported research of
leadership in virtual space is too negative and pessimistic:

> It seems most of research about virtual communication focuses on the nega-
> tive side of it. Children use technology in a much more creative way – because
> that kind of communication facilitates us using the technology in better ways,
> getting to do things that you would not be able to do otherwise. (Interview with
> project manager in telecommunication, 30 November 2012)

Following up this view, I question whether most up-to-date research is
relevant for the digital natives and if the challenges people experience in
virtual space are generational. These are questions raised after having read
the literature and talking to managers aged 40 years and over. Therefore,
I returned to the entrepreneur, representing the digital natives, trying to
learn something.

DIGITAL NATIVES NAVIGATING AS LEADERS IN VIRTUAL SPACE

When interviewing the entrepreneur, I was very surprised to discover how easy-going he was about managing a company without his physical presence most of the year. In contrast to the reported research, he did not perceive particular challenges to leading a group of employees from another part of the world, even if they were from a continent with different values, religion, language and culture than his. He thought it was great fun running a business this way, but acknowledged that relationships are important and that the yearly meeting was crucial. This made me curious. How is it a young manager sees no limitations with leadership in virtual space while most research so far reveals a concerned attitude? He obviously has an optimistic approach to new technology and is creative about developing trustful, motivating relationships with employees, I thought. He spoke enthusiastically about the people he led, what they were like, what they were concerned about, what they liked to do when they met and so on. To me he was a vivid manifestation of a young person with no inhibitions whatsoever regarding leading and cooperating in virtual space, communicating mainly through the Internet, email, Skype and smart phones (Photo 5.3). The entrepreneur said he had had to develop his own way of leading, as he did not find much relevance in the existing leadership literature. An interesting thing was that he took control over the technology and communicated only at certain established times during the day, to prepare emotionally, mentally and develop an agenda for the meeting.

Photo 5.3   Leader and follower in virtual space

This can also be conceived as 'tuning in' or focusing when communicating virtually (Caulat, 2012), preparing the body, feelings and mental state for the meeting. Compared to the study of managers' daily activities and tasks in the 1970s (Mintzberg, 1973), which reported managers being interrupted constantly by employees, a manager's work day is different today. Virtuality allows shutting people out, being able to plan the day in advance and deciding specific meeting times. The control over communication, task and time is a major difference between virtual leadership and face-to-face encounters.

One is not physically present in virtual leadership, but the young entrepreneur found a solution to this. He wanted his physical presence felt in the Philippines so he installed a big photo of himself on the wall in the offices. Vice versa, he had a picture of his employees in his office. There were also small symbolic traces of him in their offices, as he brought small presents and souvenirs every time he visited his employees. He also wanted the relationship to be good, not suffering from the distance, so he was particularly keen to remember birthdays, weddings and other important days in their lives. The greetings were sent as films of him dressed in a suit addressing them with kind words. He said he wanted very much to be a leader who trusted his employees and encouraged them all the time to do a better job.

To me he is representative of the young generation leading in virtual space as though it were a normal situation, seeing only limitless opportunities in the technology. He is also a good representative of a servant and participative leader, listening and adapting to his employees' needs and feelings. He may also be seen as using an embodied and aesthetic approach to leadership, being conscious of the senses and physical aspects of leading. He talked a lot about how his presence could be felt, even if he was physically not there. He encourages self-leadership since he knows that he is not there for them most of the time.

The nature of relations and leadership moments in virtual space is an interesting and important aspect of virtual leadership. According to Donna Ladkin (2010), leadership arises out of different and specific social constructions. Using that perspective, virtual space is socially constructed and the way it is perceived depends on who is actually using the technology.

According to Tapscott (2006) here are huge generational differences in how communication and leadership through a computer screen is perceived. Experiencing the 'Net Geners' (Tapscott, 2009) locked in their bedrooms communicating with all their friends, feeling both socially popular, included and happy about it, there are many indications that the future organization will look differently. Young people who have grown up with the computer, Internet and smart phones do not perceive the virtual space as less welcoming, safe and trustworthy than the physical face-to-face meeting.

OVERCOMING THE CHALLENGES OF VIRTUAL LEADERSHIP

Having given a glimpse of how leadership in virtual space can be interpreted by a young manager, I will turn to the studies on the subject. There seems to be a profound belief within the research of virtual leadership that technology is the answer to many of the challenges virtual teams and leaders are facing, such as using communication and information technologies that contain a telepresence (Zigurs, 2003). Other researchers have a belief in new management practices such as developing team norms for the use of communication technology, rotating the time of weekly audio-conferences so that everyone experiences the pain of a late night or early morning, making explicit the task progress such as to regularly post work virtually, develop an expertise directory with photos and CVs of team members, virtual brainstorming through audio-conference sessions and so on (Malhotra et al., 2007).

Regarding leadership, the literature takes two overall approaches. The first is the traditional leader-centric approach using both relational and technological tools in developing and shaping team processes and monitoring tasks and performance (Pauleen, 2004; Zhang and Fjermestad, 2006; Wakefield et al., 2008). The second approach is following the newer perspectives within leadership, arguing that leaders need to distribute and delegate leadership functions and responsibilities to team members (Bell and Kozlowski, 2002) using empowering leadership (Kirkman et al., 2004), self-leadership and shared leadership (Davis and Bryant, 2003; Zigurs, 2003; Muethel and Hoegl, 2010) and transformational leadership (Joshi and Lazarova, 2005; Mendenhall et al., 2012). Likewise, there are contributions going even further by introducing physicality in virtual leadership (De Paoli et al., 2014) and a relational, processual and embodied approach (Caulat, 2012). Following up on the newer perspectives on leadership, I will sketch a new map for leadership in virtual space.

REDEFINING THE CONCEPT OF LEADERSHIP IN VIRTUAL SPACE

Contrasting the young entrepreneur with traditional approaches to leadership in virtual space, one has to find new solutions to new challenges. The traditional leader-centric approach using authority or charisma is more difficult when the people you lead are no longer down the corridor but maybe in another city or even on the other side of the world. Many organizations and leaders working internationally and virtually are knowledge based and their employees highly educated, expecting both autonomy and interesting tasks (Pearce and Manz, 2005). Specialized, competent professionals put pressure on the elitist and centralized leadership model. Groups of new professionals entering the workforce, having grown up with the Internet and technology, the Net Geners (Tapscott, 2009), use the new technology in a different way, which will also make its demands on leadership. They are surely not used to being ruled authoritatively in virtual space. Along with several researchers on virtual space, I make a claim for redefining the concept of leadership in virtual space (Zigurs, 2003; Caulat, 2012; Avolio et al., 2013).

FROM ORGANIZATIONAL HIERARCHIES TO VIRTUAL NETWORKS

A recent thorough study of e-leadership (Avolio et al., 2013), together with other studies of social media and the Internet, shows that new technology increases access to information and leaders while providing greater transparency. Everybody can more easily access each other on the web as generational, ethnic, religious and geographical distances seem smaller than when encountered face to face. The study also reveals that new technology may create a more equal and democratic work environment if used in the right way. New technology can empower people on all levels and especially the digital natives who do not think and act according to authority and rules in social media or the Internet.

A prevalent metaphor for the technologically connected organization is the network. People, units and organizations are connected virtually in networks, both technologically and socially. The network metaphor gives associations to relations and relations that are flatter as well as more equal, informal and flexible. Leadership situations in the virtual space are both more network based, more informal, more transparent and more global than in regular, stable, physical organizations. A network model makes a claim for a less hierarchical and less centralized perspective on leadership, which in itself makes the traditional leader-centric approach dysfunctional. Rather than thinking traditionally about the leader as the centre of the unit, raised above in status and power, the network metaphor equalizes and levels the leader as one of several. This 'leaderless' way of thinking is also in accordance with newer perspectives on leadership, as argued in the next section.

FROM LEADER-CENTRICITY TOWARDS LEADERSHIP AS A RELATIONAL PROCESS

There is currently a change of focus in many leadership studies, from a traditional focus on the leader and his or her abilities, competences and styles towards a focus on leadership as the social relation between the leader and followers (Hosking, 2007; Ladkin, 2010; Salovaara, 2011). Conventional leadership approaches often take a person- or leader-centred perspective, which follows a more heroic leadership stereotype (Küpers and Weibler, 2008). The traditional leader-centric approach with a focus on knowledge, skills, abilities and traits of virtual leaders or different leadership styles does not give the necessary opportunities to improve leadership substantially in virtual space. This traditional thinking is limiting, not stimulating for new ways of working and cooperating. The leader-centric approach confirms a leader in control, even if the situation is very much about not having control, because how do you control people by distance and through technology? The traditional modes of influence and control, whether they are social or material, are technologically filtered, creating new distances as well as limiting distances. The ease of using communication technology, contacting people, setting up a meeting and sharing information stimulates mutual and informal relations between leaders and followers, perhaps downplaying the formal imprint of face-to-face encounters. These are all arguments for focusing on the social process between leader and followers, rather than the leaders themselves, in line with the general development of leadership studies:

> Leadership is embedded in the everyday relationally-responsive dialogical practices of leaders. Relational leadership requires a way of engaging with the world in which the leader holds herself/himself as always in relation with, and therefore morally accountable to others; recognizes the inherently polyphonic and heteroglossic nature of life; and engages in relational dialogue. (Cunliffe and Eriksen, 2011, p. 1425)

This may be seen as a leaderless or weak leadership, but this is not how it is meant to be understood. A focus on leadership instead of the leader means to focus on the ongoing daily activities and relations as they evolve in a process. A process approach connects leadership to everyday life, making leadership theorizing more closely connected to practice. It also takes the leader down from the elevated, elitist power position, rendering leadership more democratic and followers more important.

LEADERSHIP AS A PLURAL COLLECTIVE PHENOMENON

Conventional approaches to leadership take a dyadic perspective, oriented towards the leader and the followers. Leadership has not sufficiently been considered as a relational and collective phenomenon (Uhl-Bien, 2006). With this understanding, influence is mainly seen as unidirectional, flowing from the individual leader to the individual follower (Küpers and Weibler, 2008). Leaders are presented as the ones knowing and structuring activities and processes, followers as subordinates of these processes. In a virtual context, the task solving, the communication and the people do have a visible imprint, either through written mail, messages and spoken or visual signs. There is not a clear material distinction regarding who is in command. This is something that needs to be underlined and made explicit. On the other hand, everybody is visible because communication is through screens, by print or through voices. Groupware and software for group processes have long been used to level out status differences and enable group thinking (Zigurs, 2003). There are several indications that technology can support and stimulate a more participative and shared leadership. Status differences get levelled out, but it also becomes more difficult to take a person-centric approach to leadership.

In a virtual context, supported by a shared and equally distributed technology, reciprocal interdependence and mutual influence processes lead easily towards more collective and shared leadership processes. The hierarchical structure with the leader at the top is just not a descriptive and right model for the virtual distributed network model. There is a growing body of organizational research and theorizing that examines leadership not as a property of individuals and their behaviours, but as a collective phenomenon that is distributed or shared among different people (Denis et al., 2012). A diversity of labels is used to identify these forms of leadership, such as 'shared', 'distributed', 'collective', 'collaborative', 'integrative', 'relational' and 'postheroic'. One may also say that these leadership phenomena represent a more collective and plural form of leadership, whereby more people jointly assist, work and support leadership processes. The way leadership gets constituted here is through relations.

A relational perspective gives light to the process between the people collaborating and the leadership relation as it evolves. A focus on the leadership relation also opens up newer and different kinds of leadership theories such as self-leadership (Pearce and Conger, 2003), shared leadership (Pearce and Manz, 2005), servant leadership, embodied leadership (Ropo and Sauer, 2008) and aesthetic leadership. Newer views of leadership posit that all organizational members are capable of leading themselves to some degree. Shared leadership is seen as a particularly useful approach for teams of people, also virtual teams, and considers leadership, as 'a dynamic, interactive influence process among individuals in groups for which the objective is to lead one another to the achievement of group or organizational goals or both' (Pearce and Conger, 2003, p. 21). Shared leadership entails a simultaneous, ongoing, mutual influence process within a team, which involves the serial emergence of official as well as unofficial leaders. In other words, shared leadership could be considered a case of fully developed empowerment in teams.

AN EMBODIED AND AESTHETIC APPROACH TO LEADERSHIP IN VIRTUAL SPACE

An aesthetic worldview seeks to open up possibilities and widen the understanding of leadership by becoming knowledgeable about the hidden and unrecognized sensuous ways of knowing. Aesthetic practices include language skills, listening, gazing, touching and treating emotion and feelings as important sources of knowledge. Aesthetic leadership takes a relational and embodied perspective (Ropo and Sauer, 2008). By aesthetics it is meant that leadership relations contain sensory knowledge and the felt meaning of objects and experiences, which we experience via our senses (Hansen et al., 2007).

Leadership in virtual space is often perceived as communication and relations devoid of bodies, senses and feelings, but even in telephone and Skype meetings, the participant relates to the tone of voices and moments of silence (Caulat, 2012), as well as the face and part of the body appearing on the conference screen or small Skype picture. It may seem from the outside that bodies, senses, feelings and materiality disappear, but in reality one notices the few noticeable cues even more (De Paoli et al., 2014).

An aesthetic and embodied leadership is also illustrated by the young entrepreneur interviewed when he talks about making his physical presence felt through a big photo of himself on the wall in the Philippines, but also when he sends small video films of him greeting an employee. Researchers have already pointed at using telecommunication with a higher 'telepresence' (Zigurs, 2003) to improve leadership relations in virtual teams. Paying attention to and being tuned in to an aesthetic and embodied way of leading in virtual space means also being conscious about where individuals are situated when appearing live in telecommunication. It makes a great deal of difference whether you are sitting in the midst of your family or in the office, when communicating with team members.

THE IMPORTANCE OF MEANINGFUL PLACES AND SPACES

By addressing the role of places and spaces for the leadership of virtual work, this section will highlight a hitherto overlooked or forgotten aspect – that the physical meeting space is the only or one of the few times the virtual group meets. Paradoxically, research on virtual teams and virtual leadership has not paid any attention to where face-to-face meetings should be held and in what format. Talking to project managers leading virtual teams, it appears they are quite conscious about meeting face to face early during a project process, especially when the task is complex and people do not know each other. However, they do not mention the basis on which the selection of places and spaces is made.

The interviewed entrepreneur is particularly oriented towards letting the employees choose their favourite place to meet, which for them is on the beach playing volleyball. Choosing a good place to meet for virtual work groups means finding a place and space that makes team-building processes go fast, letting people feel at their ease, sharing information and knowledge easily and also to develop a common cause and vision for their work. There is no standardized answer to this as the social construction of spaces and places matters. What is familiar and good for someone can be unfriendly and hostile to others. The important thing then is to choose places and spaces that are meaningful for the people involved, which highlights even more the importance of a social constructionist approach.

SUMMING UP

Virtual leadership is a good example of a work setting that needs to focus more on leadership relations and processes than the leader and leadership itself, in line with the newer leadership perspectives and theories suggested above. The leader-centric focus on leadership is for virtual leadership substituted by a shared and empowered leadership approach whereby people lead themselves in accordance with goals and agendas. I have also presented a leadership view as socially constructed and relational. The notion of meaningful places and spaces is introduced, which is based on individually constructed and perceived meaningfulness, not an exogenously defined meaningfulness. What is meaningful varies with each person. As the issues of place and space for leadership are introduced, I also indirectly highlight the aesthetic and embodied dimension of leadership as important. Leadership occurs and is constructed not only in the mind, but also in and through the sensing and experiencing bodies. Material places are here seen as powerful in leading people, and spaces and places can thus function as substitutes for individual leaders.

REFERENCES

Al-Ani, B., A. Horspool and M.C. Bligh (2011), 'Collaborating with "virtual strangers": Towards developing a framework for leadership in distributed teams', *Leadership*, **7** (3), 219–49.

Aubert, B.A. and B.L. Kelsey (2003), 'Further understanding of trust and performance in virtual teams', *Small Group Research*, **34** (5), 575–618.

Avolio, B.J., S.S. Kahai and G.E. Dodge (2001), 'E-leadership: Implications for theory, research, and practice', *The Leadership Quarterly*, 11 (4), 615–68.

Avolio, B.J., J.J. Sosik, S.S. Kahai and B. Baker (2013), 'E-leadership: Re-examining transformations in leadership source and transmission', *The Leadership Quarterly*, **25** (1), 105–31.

Baker, R.A. (1997), 'How can we train leaders if we do not know what leadership is?' *Human Relations*, **50** (4), 343–62.

Bell, B.S. and S.W. Kozlowski (2002), 'A typology of virtual teams: Implications for effective leadership', *Group & Organization Management*, **27** (1), 14–49.

Caulat, G. (2012), *Virtual Leadership – Learning to Lead Differently*, Faringdon, UK: Libri Publishing.

Cunliffe, A.L. and M. Eriksen (2011), 'Relational leadership', *Human Relations*, **64** (11), 1425–49.

DasGupta, P. (2011), 'Literature review: E-leadership', *Emerging Leadership Journeys*, **4** (1), 1–36.

Davis, D.D. and J.L. Bryant (2003), 'Influence at a distance: Leadership in global virtual teams', in J. Osland (ed.), *Advances in Global Leadership, Vol. 3*, Bingley, UK: Emerald Group Publishing, pp. 303–40.

Denis, J.L., A. Langley and V. Sergi (2012), 'Leadership in the plural', *The Academy of Management Annals*, **6** (1), 211–83.

De Paoli, D., E. Sauer and A. Ropo (2014), 'Disappearing bodies in virtual leadership', in D. Ladkin and S. Taylor (eds), *The Physicality of Leadership: Gesture, Entanglement, Taboo, Possibilities*, Bingley, UK: Emerald Group Publishing, pp. 59–81.

Furst, S.A., M. Reeves, B. Rosen and R.S. Blackburn (2004), 'Managing the life cycles of virtual teams', *Academy of Management Executive*, **18** (2), 6–20.

Handy, C. (1995), 'Trust and the virtual organization', *Harvard Business Review*, May–June.

Hansen, H., A. Ropo and E. Sauer (2007), 'Aesthetic leadership', *The Leadership Quarterly*, **18** (6), 544–60.

Hosking, D.M. (2007), 'Not leaders, not followers: A post-modern discourse of leadership processes', in B. Shamir, R. Pillai, M. Bligh and M. Uhl-Bien (eds), *Follower-Centered Perspectives on Leadership: A Tribute to the Memory of James R. Meindl*, Greenwich, CT: Information Age Publishing, pp. 243–64.

Jarvenpaa, S.L. and D.E. Leidner (1999), 'Communication and trust in global virtual teams', *Organization Science*, **10** (6), 791–815.

Joshi, A. and M.B. Lazarova (2005), 'Do global teams need global leaders? Identifying leadership competences in multinational teams', in D.L. Shapiro (ed.), *Managing Multinational Teams: Global Perspectives*, Amsterdam: Elsevier, pp. 281–301.

Kayworth, T.R. and D. Leidner (2001), 'Leadership effectiveness in global distributed teams', *Journal of Management Information Systems*, **18** (3), 7–40.

Kerber, K.W. and A.F. Buono (2004), 'Leadership challenges in global virtual teams: Lessons from the field', *Sam Advanced Management Journal*, **69** (4), 4–10.

Kirkman, B.L., B. Rosen, P.E. Tesluk and C.B. Gibson (2004), 'The impact of team empowerment on virtual team performance: The moderating role of face-to-face interaction', *Academy of Management Journal*, **47** (2), 175–92.

Küpers, W. and J. Weibler (2008), 'Inter-leadership: Why and how should we think of leadership and followership integrally?' *Leadership*, **4** (4), 443–75.

Ladkin, D. (2010), *Rethinking Leadership: A New Look at Old leadership Questions*, Cheltenham, UK and Northampton, MA, USA: Edward Elgar Publishing.

Malhotra, A., A. Majchrzak and R. Benson (2007), 'Leading virtual teams', *Academy of Management Perspectives*, **21** (1), 60–70.

Mendenhall, M.E., B.S. Reiche, A. Bird and J.S. Osland (2012), 'Defining the "global" in global leadership', *Journal of World Business*, **47** (4), 493–503.

Mintzberg, H. (1973), *The Nature of Managerial Work*, New York: Harper & Row.

Muethel, M. and M. Hoegl (2010), 'Cultural and societal influences on shared leadership in globally dispersed teams', *Journal of International Management*, **16** (3), 234–46.

Pauleen, D.J. (2004), 'An inductively derived model of leader-initiated relationship building with virtual team members', *Journal of Management Information Systems*, **20** (3), 227–56.

Pearce, C.I. and J.A. Conger (2003), *Shared Leadership: Reframing the Hows and Whys of Leadership*, Thousand Oaks, CA: Sage Publications.

Pearce, C.L. and C.C. Manz (2005), 'The importance of self- and shared leadership in knowledge work', *Organizational Dynamics*, **34** (2), 130–40.

Ropo, A. and E. Sauer (2008), 'Corporeal leaders', in D. Barry and H. Hansen (eds), *The Sage Handbook of New Approaches in Management and Organization*, London: Sage, pp. 469–78.

Salovaara, P. (2011), *From Leader-Centricity Toward Leadership: A Hermeneutic Narrative Approach*, Tampere: Tampere University Press.

Tapscott, D. (2009), *Grown Up Digital – How the Net Generation is Changing Your World*, New York: McGraw-Hill.

Townsend, A., S. DeMarie and A. Hendrickson (1998), 'Virtual teams: Technology and the workplace of the future', *Academy of Management Executive*, **12** (3), 17–29.

Uhl-Bien, M. (2006), 'Relational leadership theory: Exploring the social processes of leadership and organizing', *The Leadership Quarterly*, **17** (6), 654–76.

Wakefield, R.L., D.E. Leidner and G. Garrison (2008), 'A model of conflict, leadership and performance in virtual teams', *Information Systems Research*, **19** (4), 434–55.

Zander, L., A.I. Mockaitis and C.L. Butler (2012), 'Leading global teams', *Journal of World Business*, **47** (4), 592–603.

Zhang, S. and J. Fjermestad (2006), 'Bridging the gap between traditional leadership theories and virtual team leadership', *International Journal of Technology, Policy and Management*, **6** (3), 274–91.

Zigurs, I. (2003), 'Leadership in virtual teams: Oxymoron or opportunity?' *Organizational Dynamics*, **31** (4), 339–51.

6. Virtual spaces as workplaces: working and leading in virtual worlds

Matti Vartiainen

INTRODUCTION

This chapter concerns virtual worlds as a type of virtual space that enables and shapes leadership by providing a replica of the 'real world' with different affordances as a platform for action that includes tools to interact, collaborate and influence. When characterizing the relationship between space and place, this chapter builds on Harrison and Dourish (1996, p. 69), who suggested that '[s]pace is the opportunity; place is the understood reality. . . We are located in "space", but we act in "place"'.

The chapter begins with an example of collaboration in a virtual world. Then, virtual spaces as places for work, collaboration and leadership are illustrated, and the prerequisites they offer to leadership and the driving forces behind their emergence are discussed. The differences between virtual spaces and other types of spaces (physical, social, mental) are shown next. Then the enablers of leadership are discussed, such as the affordances provided by virtual worlds, social relationships and the characteristics of an avatar. Finally, different types of virtual worlds as workplaces are described and some conclusions are made.

IDEATION IN A VIRTUAL WORLD

The case in Box 6.1 illustrates interaction in a virtual space, avatars as representations of physically dispersed human actors and their behaviour. Our joint task is to solve a problem and participate in decision-making. The space is a digital replica of a physical meeting room, and actors shown as avatars represent the company employees. We do not know each other very well beforehand as all of us live and work in different corners of the globe. Basic trust exists as we are all recognized experts in the same global

BOX 6.1 INTERACTION IN A VIRTUAL SPACE USING AVATARS

Ideation is a creative step towards innovation. On Thursday 20 June, I have to work until 10 pm in California because of a meeting that involves participants in different time zones. After eating my late evening meal, dressed in my pyjamas, I open my tablet on my kitchen table and join the meeting in a virtual space. I wonder if I am convincing enough as I did not have enough time to tailor my appearance, so I selected one of the available avatars from a list; I look like a construction worker. It seems that a colleague from Sweden has made the same decision, maybe because it is early for her, 7 am on a Friday. We look alike to outsiders, and the problem is who is who? Why did she not select a female avatar? A colleague of mine in Finland has just arrived at his office on Friday 8 am appearing as a green balloon. A creative solution? To me, his external appearance is confusing and uninformative. Luckily we can speak with our own voices. An Indian participant looks quite mundane, even conservative. In addition to us, there is also a female avatar – the facilitator of the meeting from the USA [Photo 6.1].

The meeting is important. We have to decide if the idea presented by the Indian colleague is good enough to progress in the company's innovation process. He has had enough time to prepare his presentation; the time in his office is 12 pm. The

Source: Pekka Alahuhta; with permission.

Photo 6.1 *Persons/avatars from left to right: a colleague from Finland ('a balloon'), me in California ('a construction worker'), a meeting facilitator from the USA ('female avatar'), a colleague from Sweden ('a construction worker') and an Indian colleague ('a mundane avatar')*

aim of our meeting is to validate a prototype for a high-technology product and investigate possible technical problems that might be related to its implementation.

We meet in a virtual world environment provided by a new start-up company. As a platform of technological artefacts, the virtual world provides a number of affordances for us. We can co-create together by sketching on the whiteboards and adding pictures and models to talk about. We also have access to documents and webpages. Most importantly, the virtual world allows us to have a digitalized self-representation through our avatars, enabling navigations and negotiations in a meeting room similar to a physical office space at our company.

'We' – in addition to me (a design manager in California) and the US facilitator – refers to a colleague in India (an 'ideator'); an 'expert' from Sweden; and a 'decision-maker' from headquarters in Finland. So, we are participating from four locations and over several time zones. We discuss possible solutions and sketch them visually on virtual whiteboards, concurrently trying to convince others about the excellence of our own ideas. Although some information is transferred via the auditory channel, a lot of information is transmitted via the visual channel in the form of sketches and other representations. The interplay between visual and verbal representations leads to iterations of ideation, explanations and inquiry. This, in turn, increases the chance for a higher-quality outcome. The session ends in a joint positive decision to go forward in the innovation process.

company. During the meeting, we are labourers of a global company digitized as avatars. We are equal in that we are all experts in our own fields. We are also autonomous in making our evaluations and decisions, utilizing the affordances provided by the virtual environment and social cues gained from other participants. I myself am the design manager and am responsible for calling this meeting together. Otherwise we would have to lead ourselves to reach our target.

What Types of Places are Virtual Spaces for Leadership?

Virtual worlds are types of virtual spaces. A 'virtual space' as a concept refers to the global Internet and an organization-wide intranet as a workplace for the digital labourer and as a collaborative working environment (CWE) for members of dispersed teams. As working platforms, virtual spaces provide both simple communication tools such as email and complex collaborative environments. The complex environments integrate many different communication tools, such as email, audio-conferencing, video-conferencing, group calendar, chat, document management and presence-awareness tools, into a collaborative working environment, such as a 3D virtual environment, that is, a virtual world. A virtual workplace is such a place in a virtual space that is used for work and collaboration. The role of virtual spaces as workplaces has grown as mobile information and communication technologies increasingly enable flexible working from multiple physical locations. A whole 'class' of digital labourers has emerged worldwide, working for international employers (Scholz, 2013) and often doing micro-tasks on a freelance basis. Locally, in companies, many knowledgeable workers 'escape' from their main office to their homes or public places where they can do their jobs, concentrating in peace. A virtual space for work is a necessity for them to access knowledge and their clients, as well as to collaborate with colleagues.

Virtual worlds considered here are communication and collaboration environments in which multiple actors share the same three-dimensional digital space despite occupying remote physical locations. It is possible to navigate and manipulate objects there, and communicate with one another via avatars that are flexible and easily transformed digital self-representations in a graphic 3D form (Yee and Bailenson, 2007). They act as digital replicas of actors in a 'real material world'. Virtual world environments differ from other collaborative working environments such as high-fidelity video-conferencing (for example, HALO rooms) due to their cheaper price, enabled by the Internet. One strength of virtual world environments is the ability to use parallel communication tools. For example, a user could chat, talk, write and draw practically at the same time.

In the next sections, I will outline the changes that are altering the previous and current leadership methods. Finally, I will describe the contextual space layers that are used by multilocational knowledge workers, including experts, managers and leaders.

PREREQUISITES OF LEADERSHIP

Leadership usually strives for a good performance and success in any work environment. As stated in the introductory chapter of this book, leadership can be understood as a relational construction between people, issues and the environment rather than as an individual quality. In a virtual world environment, three intertwined and partly embedded factors seem to be critical for individual and team performance and success: the nature of a task to be performed, the affordances provided by a context, and the necessary processes for self-actualization and collaboration.

Assignments and tasks usually vary from routine to creative tasks. In our virtual world meeting, ideation as a joint task was rather complex, requiring a lot of creativity, commitment and argumentation skills from each participant. The contextual affordances arose from the features of physical, virtual, social or organizational and mental spaces we used when collaborating.

The nature of the task and contextual affordances together influence those internal processes that each of us and we as a team needed to manage objects, relations and boundaries in ideation. All these factors influenced our attitudes when working. After an hour and a half, we could decide to move the idea forward to decision-makers in the company.

When working in virtual worlds, the contextual affordances emerge both from the physical and social spaces each participant is in and from the virtual spaces in which they collaborate. To illustrate, in our meeting, each of us participated from a different physical location because we were globally dispersed. Socially, I was alone in my kitchen in an apartment in the USA, the Swedish colleague was at home with her husband and kids, the Indian 'ideator' was at his open office workplace in a Southern Indian harbour town among his coworkers, and my Finnish colleague was at his office's hot desk in the company's headquarters surrounded by other product designers (although I thought he was still at home). We were all communicating through our avatars in a common virtual space, in a virtual world collaboration environment. Our mental states of mind were different; I was a bit drowsy, my Swedish colleague was clearly irritated a couple of times, the Indian 'ideator' was very enthusiastic, and my Finnish colleague sounded somewhat reserved. These contextual features strongly influenced our methods for working in a virtual world environment.

NEW WAYS OF WORKING REQUIRE VIRTUAL WORKPLACES

Traditionally, knowledge workers, that is, white-collar workers, have conducted most of their work on their employer's premises under the close surveillance of their superiors. However, as a result of globalization and as information technologies, communication technologies and digitalization are progressing at an ever-increasing speed, new ways of flexible working have emerged, increasing the autonomy and self-sufficiency of knowledge workers. This has led to the current situation in which employees work in various places during the work day, week or month. New ways of working include both individual telework, that is, mobile work using flexible multiple locations, and distributed teamwork and collaboration from multiple locations. In addition, an unknown number of digital labourers around the world who make a living benefitting from the possibilities that virtual spaces offer find customers and work for them. For these practical reasons, it is justifiable to argue that fundamental changes have occurred in the ways in which people work and lead on both individual and group levels.

On an individual level, new ways of working usually involve telework. Telework is characterized by distance (a spatial and often temporal dispersion) and the use of information and communication technologies (ICT) (Taskin and Devos, 2005). Thus, telework means working outside the conventional office using telecommunication-related technologies to interact with supervisors, coworkers and clients (Baffour and Betsey, 2000). Mobile work is a special type of telework. Mobile workers spend some paid working time away from their home and away from their main place of work, for example, on business trips, in the field, travelling, or at a customer's premises. Lilischkis (2003) called this type of working in many places 'multilocational work' and Halford (2005) uses the term 'hybrid workspace' to describe the combination of organizational (that is, office) and domestic (that is, home) spaces mediated by cyberspace. Hislop and Axtell (2007) added a third dimension of 'locations beyond the home & office' to this concept of 'hybridity' and defined this type of multilocational work as 'mobile telework' or 'multilocation work'. According to Hislop and Axtell (2009), using ICT it is increasingly possible to work not only at home and office but also in public spaces such as airports, hotel lobbies and cafés, sometimes referred to as 'non-places' because of their transience, as well as in mobile locations like cars and planes.

When considered from a team perspective, mobile, multilocational employees collaborate in teams whose members are geographically separated from each other. This type of team refers to a 'distributed team'. A distributed team uses extensively various forms of computer-mediated communication that enable its geographically dispersed members to coordinate their individual efforts and inputs (Peters and Manz, 2007). Distributed teams are not monolithic but can have different forms. For example, physical mobility of group members adds a new feature to distributed work. Mobile teams are always distributed, but not all distributed teams are mobile. Virtuality, as the use of ICT and digital environments for communication and collaboration, makes a team into a distributed virtual team or mobile virtual team. As replicas of the 'real world', virtual worlds provide mobile workers places to work and collaborate with others as remote colleagues.

VIRTUAL AND OTHER SPACES

Flexible use of many physical work locations brings the increased influence of local contextual factors. For example, I participated in the ideation meeting from California, working in my apartment's kitchen using my tablet and its virtual world environment for collaboration. From a social point of view, there was nobody physically present, so my social relationships were limited to the other avatars used in the virtual world and their remote masters in their own physical locations. Each of the five participants in the meeting had their specific local contexts providing different preconditions for their working. The meaning of contextual factors is great because employees use multiple locations during their working days. In each location, the combination of the contextual factors is unique and their outcomes different. When talking about virtual working environments, especially virtual worlds, 'location' has two meanings: where a person physically is and the location of his or her virtual representation, the avatar.

A virtual space and its avatars is a digital layer of an environment in which individuals and groups work and collaborate. Other layers are physical, social and mental spaces. Virtual workplaces are needed when employees move a lot and need to collaborate from afar. However, the domains of social and material worlds are not distinct and independent spheres of organizational life. Decades ago, Lewin (1972) introduced the idea that each individual exists in a psychological force field called the 'life space' that determines and limits his or her behaviour. 'Life space' is a highly subjective environment that characterizes the world as the individual sees it while still remaining embedded in the objective elements of physical and social fields. According to Lewin (1951), behaviour (B) is a function (f) of a person (P) and his or her environment (E): $B = f(P,E)$. Physical and social conditions limit the variety of possible life spaces and create the boundary conditions of the psychological field. 'Subjective' and 'objective' elements are not strictly divided, but the context is blended and layered, as reflected in the concept of '*ba*' (Nonaka et al., 2000). This concept is useful for differentiating the various contexts leading knowledge workers. *Ba* refers to a shared context in which knowledge is shared, created and utilized by those who interact and communicate there. *Ba* does not just refer to a physical space but also to a specific time and space that integrates layers of spaces. *Ba* unifies the physical space (such as an office space), virtual space (such as virtual worlds), the social space (such as colleagues), and the mental space (such as common experiences, ideas, and ideals shared by people with common goals in a working context). Modern workplaces, either for individuals or groups, are combinations of physical, virtual, social and mental spaces or environments offering their affordances to work, collaborate and lead:

- A *physical space* consists of all the material objects and stimuli and their arrangements, for example, an office or a customer site where a remote employee works. The five categories of physical spaces are (Vartiainen et al., 2007): (1) home; (2) the main workplace ('main office'); (3) moving places (cars, trains, planes and ships); (4) premises of customers, partners or other premises of the company ('other workplaces'); and (5) public places such as hotels and cafés ('third workplaces').
- *Virtual spaces*. A wide variety of tools and devices enable individuals that are not in the same working location or are at a great distance from each other and whose interaction is mediated by a computer and Internet to perform collaborative work together. A virtual world is a very specific and powerful collaborative working environment. In virtual worlds, the contextual factors and actors are shown as digital representations of real-world contexts and actors.
- From the *social space* point of view, knowledge work is performed both alone and with others. A knowledge worker's daily life consists of events and episodes in a continuum, varying from working physically alone in solitude, to asynchronous or online collaboration with others via ICT, to face-to-face meetings. Working in solitude does not mean just 'working alone in privacy', as working is affected either by self-initiated virtual outgoing contacts with others via phone and online chat or externally by an incoming flow of requests and questions via email and text messages. This is a transitional stage between deep concentration in flow and fully social polyphonic events, which is referred to here as the stage of 'pseudo-privacy', to take a term from Becker and Sims (2000, p. 15).
- A *mental space* refers to cognitive constructs, thoughts, beliefs, ideas and emotional states of mind that employees perceive, feel, maintain and share. Creating and forming joint mental spaces requires communication and collaboration, such as exchanging ideas in face-to-face or virtual dialogues.

Enablers of Leadership in Virtual Spaces

In the long tradition of leadership research and practice, leadership has been understood as a quality of an individual or a relation between one or more subjects (leader–follower or within a team, for example). As discussed in the introductory chapter, the term leadership is not necessarily limited to human–human relations, as it can be observed to take place between humans and physical materiality. Orlikowski and Scott (2008, p. 434) warn against the assumption that technology, work and organizations should be conceptualized separately, claiming that there is an inherent inseparability between the technical and the social. They suggest that a reconsideration of conventional views of technology may help us more effectively study and understand the multiple, emergent and dynamic sociomaterial configurations that constitute contemporary organizational practices. When analysing leadership in virtual spaces, leadership is a relation that is constructed both between people, between people and materiality (for example, local built environment, place, artefacts) and between people and digital representations (for example, virtual worlds and its visual artefacts), including the characteristics and behaviour of an avatar. Next, leadership in virtual spaces is explored from three perspectives: affordances of virtual worlds, social relationships, and the characteristics of an avatar.

AFFORDANCES OF VIRTUAL WORLDS

Materiality when working in virtual spaces consists of two layers (physical, digital) influencing leadership prerequisites. First, each participant has his or her own local, physical space from which they can participate in collaboration. Usually the local conditions vary greatly in their influence on the quality of collaboration. Second, the participants have a common virtual space as a replica of the 'real world', which has its own features. In real life, dispersed knowledge workers often have many superiors and coworkers as they work in many teams for different purposes. Sometimes they have never seen each other face to face. As virtual world environments are more or less exact replicas of layered spaces in a real world, their affordances influencing working and leadership are discussed next.

Affordances are properties of a virtual space that create consequences for individual behaviour and thus enable leadership in virtual world environments. Virtual worlds as virtual workplaces have certain specific characteristics that separate them from serious games and mirror worlds like Google Earth. A virtual world allows many users to participate at once through a graphical user interface on the Internet. The worlds depict space visually, mostly as realistic 3D environments. They are immediate, for interaction takes place in real time and interactive, allowing users to alter, develop, build and submit customized content. They are also persistent because they continue to exist regardless of whether individual users are logged in and active. They also allow and encourage the formation of in-world social groups such as guilds, clubs, cliques, housemates and neighbourhoods.

Creative activities and an implementation of creative and novel ideas within an organization is the acid test for the affordances of virtual world environments. The proposition is that if you can do creative and innovative tasks in this environment then you can also use it for simple tasks. In their literature review, Alahuhta and his colleagues (2014) revealed the affordances of virtual worlds contributing towards team creativity. The results of the literature review propose eight affordances for fostering team-level activities that are relevant to virtual worlds:

- *Avatars* as digital self-presentations allow the team members to express themselves and their insights and note information to others. Avatars assist users in expressing their feelings in a more convenient and accurate manner to communicate a significant amount of non-verbal social information and their identity to other collaborators both consciously and unconsciously.
- *Changing the users' frame of reference* embraces the virtual world's potential as a context for creative actions. Virtual worlds allow users to interact directly with objects and the world rather than simply describing or displaying those objects.
- Perceived feelings of *co-presence* within the team members. 'Co-presence' is a sense of 'being together' with other remote team members. Virtual worlds offer such a shared three-dimensional place, where virtual team members can interact with each other while seeing the spatial positions and movements of others. This, together with the virtual world's multimodal communication, is likely to foster a sense of co-presence among virtual world users.
- An *experience of immersion* contributes towards engaging creative team collaboration. 'Immersion' is the extent to which the technology is capable of delivering an inclusive, extensive environment and a vivid illusion of reality to the senses of a human participant.
- *Multimodality*. Virtual worlds provide richer communication media than traditional communication mechanisms in collaborative working environments by providing several different communication modalities through simultaneous textual, auditory, visual and graphic channels, or via text-based chat, voice communication, graphical cues and organizational tools.
- *Rich visual information* as virtual worlds offer enhanced possibilities for the presentation of visual content compared to poorer collaboration technologies. Virtual worlds convey the potential to present data and information in unique and compelling ways.
- *Simulation capabilities*. Virtual worlds allow one to modify the collaboration environment to simulate a new type of reality. For

example, the possibility to create virtual objects forms a fertile ground for creative motivation within the virtual environment.

- *Supporting tools utilized in collaboration.* For example, virtual worlds offer the potential for modelling objects within a design team, as well as the possibility of introducing objects to other users. Assimilation to virtual world simulation capabilities while observing different possible solutions and retrieving instantaneous information concerning how these solutions bring about change will be discussed. Finally, built-in interactive tools and in-world information services of virtual worlds could direct the users to interaction; for example, recording and archiving tools enable the persistence of the virtual space and allow the teams to utilize already existing material in their work processes. In addition, artificial agents like avatars can facilitate collaboration between team members who experience co-presence, or haptics could contribute towards user-perceived immersion. Persistent use of the virtual space can enhance collaboration over time. Different virtual world technologies offer different supporting tools for working, and virtual world users can even create such tools by themselves.

These types of contextual affordances influence the ways of working and leadership in virtual world environments.

SOCIAL RELATIONS BETWEEN AVATARS

Leadership is a relational construction between people, issues and the environment rather than an individual quality. Leadership as a socially constructed phenomenon can be distributed and shared among people. Examples of socially constructed products influencing the performance and quality of collaboration in virtual worlds are written and unwritten rules and social codes, signs and symbols that guide avatars on how the virtual space can be used. Construction also appears as beliefs, expectations and attributions towards others' behaviours during social interactions. In this meaning, leadership also emerges in the dynamics of role expectations and adapted roles by actors in virtual worlds. Avatars and their interactions form the social space of virtual worlds and construct leadership there. However, when communication and collaboration take place between avatars, their individual characteristics may influence the quality of interaction and working processes.

Avatars as Leaders

Collaboration in virtual spaces can happen via an interaction of 'equals' without a named power position or status in a hierarchically ordered structure with a named manager and other roles. In traditional academic literature, leadership as a quality of an individual person refers to his or her personal characteristics, traits and behaviours. In virtual world environments, this refers to the characteristics of an avatar. The term 'avatar' as a generic term is used to qualify an infinite number of possible representations of a person. Both employee and leader identities are built based on their most abstract representations (such as geometrical shapes) to those that most resemble the user (anthropomorphic avatars, also referred to as 'clones') (Photo 6.2). Additionally, texts can be used to name the role and task of an avatar. The strength of an avatar is that it (she or he?) can be personalized.

When the ascendancy is set and one of the avatars has the role of a leader, it seems to have a meaning. Nordbäck and Sivunen (2013) show that a designated leader plays a prominent role in coordinating the team towards the group's common goals in a virtual world context. Although leadership functions were to some degree shared, the members wished that the leader had been more determined and that their own roles were more fluid. They concluded that a balance between a leader's control and members' freedoms is a challenge that has to be managed by a virtual team leader. The multiple channels supported by the virtual world were important for both the leader's and members' participation.

Tapie and colleagues (2006) note that, with respect to a group, an

Source: Teemu Surakka; with permission.

Photo 6.2 What is the social influence of an avatar and an individual behind it?

avatar's primary function is to indicate the presence of a user in the environment and make his or her identity known. In addition, avatars should make it possible to differentiate two employees from each other and indicate their social or hierarchical role. In teamwork, an avatar should indicate his or her availability for task execution. Good questions are to what extent gender, profession, role, status, power and hierarchy should be shown in avatars.

Goh and Wasko (2012) studied the role of leadership in virtual world teams in a massively multiplayer online game (MMOG) by using leader–member exchange (LMX) theory. According to them, LMX theory holds that instead of behaving in the same manner towards all of their followers, leaders behave towards and allocate resources differently to members of their workgroup based upon unique dyadic leader–member relationships. By collecting data from 61 guild members in an MMOG in three stages spanning an eight-week time frame, their findings suggest that the leader–member relationship is important. It had a positive influence on allocation of resources, such as higher levels of empowerment and better group assignment, which were also related to higher member performance. In addition, higher-quality leader–member relationships significantly influenced nearly all of the relational capital constructs, such as obligation, norms and identification, with the exception of trust. The higher levels of relational capital were also related to higher performance. Contrary to expectations, trust was not influenced by leadership, nor did trust directly influence performance. The unique nature of collaboration in a virtual world in which one's avatar may be directly observed suggests that trust may not be as vital in virtual teams in which everyone's actions are visible.

WHAT ARE VIRTUAL WORLDS AS WORKPLACES USED FOR?

Virtual worlds and their affordances provide platforms for different purposes. Some of the most common uses are a small business meeting for negotiations and decision-making or meetings for product ideation and design. In his review on using virtual worlds in professional settings, Surakka (2012) divides their use purposes into four types: small collaborative meetings, large events, learning and training, and product development and process simulations. Bosch-Sijtsema and Sivunen (2013) developed similar categories in their study based on 47 interviews with virtual world vendors, researchers and managers who use professional virtual worlds. They concluded that the main uses of professional virtual worlds are small group meetings, training, community building and conferences. Surakka (2012) reviewed approximately 120 virtual environments, technological platforms and solution providers, 50 of which were selected for a more detailed analysis for the purpose of estimating their potentials for meeting differing business needs.

A small collaborative meeting is one of the most common uses of virtual spaces. In these meetings, participants share ideas, discuss and collaborate with a globally distributed group of people. Using virtual environments in such settings can have benefits, such as enhanced communication and a sense of presence provided by participants' avatars, as well as visual cues and sharing the same virtual 3D space. In most cases the minimum requirement for a small collaborative meeting is the ability to present material such as presentations and documents to other participants and to collaborate around that material. Productivity tools such as document integration, brainstorming tools, and shared whiteboards are also important in this use. Communication tools such as voice and text chat were present as integrated functionalities in all of the suitable environments.

Large events organized with the help of virtual environments usually consist of different types of trade shows and conferences. One of the foremost advantages to organizing large events with virtual environments is the inherent benefit of being able to participate from geographically distributed locations. In addition to the reduction in travel costs, virtual environments can offer time savings and even built-in systems for generating leads.

Networking and the opportunity to exchange opinions with other participants are the usual benefits of large events. Certain virtual environments incorporate social networking tools, and many of them include the option to add other participants as friends. This integration of communication and social networking tools provides quick access to other participants for conversation.

Virtual worlds for learning and training vary significantly from case to case (Palomäki and Nordbäck, 2014). For example, the requirements of leadership training compared to training of technical personnel vary a lot. Leadership training might require more from productivity tools in the environment whereas the training of technical personnel might require more from the environment's capabilities in importing custom 3D content.

To create learning that engages participants, the environment should be immersive to create a sense of presence. The sense of presence in virtual environments is something that goes beyond high-quality graphics alone. Being able to work effortlessly, for example, is just as important. In addition, environments used for training and learning purposes may need to include programming capabilities to provide interactive elements for users. Users in training and learning scenarios often require built-in features that make social networking possible. It can be quite useful, from both the learners' and instructors' points of view, to be able to form groups and networks from the people who attend the same training.

Many products are today developed with 3D CAD software, and virtual environments have the potential to support collaboration around 3D content. The use case of product development has certain similarities with the use case of small team collaboration. In both cases, the platforms should include various tools to ease collaboration. Productivity tools like document-sharing support and whiteboards are, therefore, some of the features to look for in virtual environments used for this purpose. In addition to productivity tools, the platform needs to support collaboration by providing reliable communication tools such as voice and text chat.

In process simulation, the possibility to replicate real-life physical environments is essential. In addition to graphic fidelity, replication and simulation may require interactive elements from the environment. The support for programming inside the environment is also, therefore, important.

DISCUSSION AND CONCLUSIONS

As argued in the introductory chapter, future leadership is not only about leaders and followers but is also about opening up to see how other 'things' in our environment lead us. These environments have become complex lately. When working in virtual spaces like virtual worlds, their design, available visual artefacts, interactions with other avatars and individual emotional and sensory experiences construct leadership activities as sociomaterial products. Virtual spaces as workplaces are still in their early phase of development. However, technologies and the willingness to use them progress swiftly. Not much is known about their use for working and collaboration, in particular from the perspective of leadership practices. For example, Sivunen and Hakonen (2011) identified four trends and research opportunities in their literature review on social and group phenomena in virtual worlds: (1) scholars in the field concentrate on demonstrating that real-life behavioural norms of group work also apply in virtual environments, which is not necessarily true; (2) not much is known about these environments as potential platforms for distributed work teams; (3) the scope on groups in current research has a strong focus on micro-level phenomena, such as personal distance or eye gaze; and (4) covering (meta) theories of group processes are mostly missing.

The advantages of virtual worlds are very similar to the advantages of other online collaboration technologies. For example, they have lower travel costs, provide access from anywhere with an Internet connection, and contribute to rather strong feelings of presence and visibility. In addition, they can be tailored to the specific needs of an organization. The disadvantages include the still early maturity of the technology, which results in technological problems and low user friendliness. For example, the interfaces of different worlds are inconsistent, there is no interoperability between worlds, and avatars can seldom capture users' real appearance.

From a leadership viewpoint, virtual worlds as virtual workplaces increase the demands of shared leadership and self-leadership. It is evident that leadership in virtual worlds makes a difference with the Tayloristic principle of dividing planning and goal-setting as a task and a role of a person from its execution and performance.

REFERENCES

Alahuhta, P., E. Nordbäck, A. Sivunen and T. Surakka (2014), 'Fostering team creativity in virtual worlds', *Journal of Virtual Worlds Research*, **7** (3), 1–18, accessed 26 January 2015 at https://journals.tdl.org/jvwr/index.php/jvwr/article/viewFile/7062/6354.

Baffour, G.G. and C.L. Betsey (2000), 'Human resources management and development in the telework environment', paper prepared for US Department of Labor Symposium, 'Telework and the New Workplace of the 21st Century', New Orleans, LA, 16 October.

Becker, F. and W. Sims (2000), *Managing Uncertainty: Integrated Portfolio Strategies for Dynamic Organizations*, Ithaca, NY: Cornell University, International Workplace Studies Program.

Bosch-Sijtsema, P.M. and A. Sivunen (2013), 'Professional virtual worlds supporting computer-mediated communication, collaboration and learning in geographically distributed contexts', *IEEE Transactions on Professional Communication*, **56** (2), 160–75.

Goh, S. and M. Wasko (2012), 'The effects of leader–member exchange on member performance in virtual world teams', *Journal of the Association for Information Systems*, **13** (10), 861–85.

Halford, A. (2005), 'Hybrid workspace: Re-spatialisations of work, organisation and management', *New Technology, Work and Employment*, **20** (1), 19–33.

Harrison, S. and P. Dourish (1996), 'Re-place-ing space: The roles of place and space in collaborative systems', in *Proceedings of the 1996 ACM Conference on Computer Supported Cooperative Work*, New York: ACM Press, pp. 67–76.

Hislop, D. and C. Axtell (2007), 'The neglect of spatial mobility in contemporary studies of work: The case telework', *New Technology, Work and Employment*, **22** (1), 34–51.

Hislop, D. and C. Axtell (2009), 'To infinity and beyond? Workspace and the multi-location worker', *New Technology, Work and Employment*, **24** (1), 60–75.

Lewin, K. (1951), *Field Theory in Social Science: Selected Theoretical Papers*, ed. D. Cartwright, New York: Harper & Row.

Lewin, K. (1972), 'Need, force and valence in psychological fields', in

E.P. Hollander and R.G. Hunt (eds), *Classic Contributions to Social Psychology*, London: Oxford University Press.

Lilischkis, S. (2003), 'More yo-yos, pendulums and nomads: Trends of mobile and multi-location work in the information society', *STAR, Socio-Economic Trends Assessment for the Digital Revolution, Issue Report No. 36*, Germany: Empirica.

Nonaka, I., R. Toyama and N. Konno (2000), 'SECI, Ba and leadership: A unified model of dynamic knowledge creation', *Long Range Planning*, **33** (1), 5–34.

Nordbäck, E. and A. Sivunen (2013), 'Leadership behaviors in virtual team meetings taking place in a 3D virtual world', in *Proceedings of the 46th Hawaii International Conference on System Sciences*, Wailea, HI, 7–10 January, pp. 863–72.

Orlikowski, W.J. and S.V. Scott (2008), 'Sociomateriality: Challenging the separation of technology, work and organization', *The Academy of Management Annals*, **2** (1), 433–74.

Palomäki, E. and E. Nordbäck (2014), 'Bringing playfulness and engagement to language training using virtual worlds: Student experiences, results and best practices from a virtual language course', in C. DeCoursey and G. Garrett (eds), *Teaching and Learning in Virtual Worlds*, Oxford: Inter-Disciplinary Press, pp. 95–116.

Peters, L.M. and C. Manz (2007), 'Identifying antecedents of virtual team collaboration', *Team Performance Management*, **13** (3/4), 117–29.

Scholz, T. (2013), *Digital Labor. The Internet as Playground and Factory*, New York and London: Routledge.

Sivunen, A. and M. Hakonen (2011), 'Review of virtual environment studies on social and group phenomena: Trends and agenda for further research', *Small Group Research*, **42** (4), 405–57.

Surakka, T. (2012), 'Benchmark of 3D virtual environments', accessed 22 March 2014 at http://www.vmwork.net/wp-content/uploads//2012/11/Benchmark_Report_5.pdf.

Tapie, J., P. Terrier, L. Perron and J.-M. Cellier (2006), 'Should remote collaborators be presented by avatars? A matter of common ground for collective medical decision-making', *AI & Society*, **20** (3), 331–50.

Taskin, L. and V. Devos (2005), 'Paradoxes from the individualization of human resource management: The case of telework', *Journal of Business Ethics*, **62** (1), 13–24.

Vartiainen, M., M. Hakonen, S. Koivisto, P. Mannonen, M. Nieminen, V. Ruohomäki and A. Vartola (2007), *Distributed and Mobile Work: Places, People and Technology*, Helsinki: Otatieto.

Yee, N. and J.N. Bailenson (2007), 'The Proteus effect: Self-transformations in virtual reality', *Human Communication Research*, **33** (3), 271–90.

PART IV

Service spaces

7. The symbolic dimension of space and artefacts in a bookstore: leadership without a leader?

Kaisa Greenlees*

INTRODUCTION

This chapter highlights the symbolic meanings attached to space and artefacts, which are usually taken for granted. With examples taken from a Finnish bookstore from a PhD thesis study in progress I will discuss the symbolic meanings attached to some spaces and artefacts from the employees' and managers' perspectives. I concur with Ropo et al. (2013, p. 379) in that '[m]aterial places are powerful in leading people, and spaces and places can thus function as a substitutes for individual leaders'. I will also highlight examples of how the phenomenon of leadership can happen without the presence of the leader through the clues coded into our physical environment.

MEANINGFUL BOOKSTORE

A bookstore holds multiple meanings for individuals. For some people it is a place to drop by when they need, for example, a present for a friend. They enter the bookstore, look around the shelves and quite soon find what they are looking for and then pay for their purchase and leave. There are also people that like to spend time in the bookstore; they walk around, they touch and browse through the books and see what is new. For many individuals the experience of the bookstore as a meaningful place (Tuan, 1977) is important. One salesperson I interviewed explained that customers could even wander around the bookshop for an hour or more. She explained that customers come to a bookstore because it is such a peaceful place to spend time and view the books. According to her

They come to spend time, for example when their wife goes to shop, they come here to look. Then sometimes at the weekends they say that they are only looking when they have arranged to meet here. Where people used to meet in a coffee shop, nowadays many people meet in a bookshop.

But what are the important elements of space that create the peaceful atmosphere in a bookstore? Bookstores stimulate all the senses and the experience of space is most of all sensual (for example, Martin, 2002). Books and other items can be found in all colours, even if the main colour in the shop under study, in the uniforms of the workers, and in the marketing material, is red. In the bookstore there is background music that needs to be neutral and not too loud in order to avoid disturbing the customers. There are also bright lights that help the customers to find the books. According to a salesperson: 'There is a distinctive smell. They [the customers] are used to that smell of dust and printed ink'. 'Relaxed, usually cheerful' is how she described the atmosphere in the bookstore. On the other hand, one interviewee described how the number of stimuli is sometimes hard to handle.

ENTERING THE BOOKSTORE AND COLLECTING THE DATA

I worked in this multisensory environment of the bookstore for two months as a salesperson in autumn 2009. The bookstore was not a totally unfamiliar world to me, since I had previously worked in the same shop as a student. This two-month visit was different; I wasn't just a salesperson, but simultaneously performing ethnographic data collection for my PhD study in management and leadership. The purpose of my study was to bring out different meanings attached to space and artefacts and to investigate how they inform us about organizational culture and socially constructed leadership. The main focus was to approach space as socially produced and to pay attention to the subjective experiences of the users (see also Taylor and Spicer, 2007, p. 333; Ladkin, 2010; Peltonen, 2011; Ropo et al., 2013, p. 380).

I remember the excitement the first day I went to work in the bookshop in autumn 2009. I knew I had to adopt a new working culture, get to know colleagues and managers and to be prepared to perform physically demanding work while serving the customers. Besides being a familiar place for me, the bookstore under study was chosen because it is one of the best-known Finnish brands. I also assumed that a bookstore as space holds multiple meanings for the people that use the space. The research was also facilitated by the fact that the bookshop is a commercial space. This made it much easier to make multiple visits to the field.

The bookstore under study was one outlet of a large and well-known Finnish chain. The company was founded in 1912 and currently there are 56 bookstores in various locations in Finland and two shops that sell paperback books. Since 1999 an Internet bookstore has also formed part of the chain. In the shop where I worked there were six full-time, eight part-time and five temporary staff, the majority of whom were female.

According to Alvesson and Berg, studying organizations from the symbolic perspective means approaching organizations as cultures and paying attention to 'subjective and emotional elements in the meaning which organizational members place on objects and phenomena' (Alvesson and Berg, 1992, p.119). The way space and artefacts are experienced involves tacit knowledge that is difficult to describe verbally due to their sensuous nature (Strati, 1992; Warren, 2002; Hansen et al., 2007, p.552; Ropo et al., 2013). For these reasons I collected data from different sources to support this interpretation. The data include notes, informal conversations, photographs and interviews that were carried out between autumn 2009 and spring 2011. I interviewed the chief executive officer, regional manager, local manager and six sales personnel including the head of the books section and the head of the goods section.

In the interviews I asked the managers about the planning of the spaces and the employees were, for example, asked to describe different places. They also described their work and the norms and routines (organizational culture). One important clue while I was working in the bookshop was how the employees reacted in different situations, how they felt (comfortable, uncomfortable, etc.). Emotion has been acknowledged as an important indicator that reveals the subjective meanings attached to our physical environment. (Rafaeli and Vilnai-Yavetz, 2004). This is why I often asked in the interviews what kind of feelings were evoked in a certain place or situation (see also Warren, 2002).

MEANINGS ATTACHED TO DIFFERENT SPACES IN A BOOKSTORE

The Entrance

According to Tuan (1977, p. 3) '[s]pace and place are basic components of the lived world; we take them for granted. When we think about them, however, they may assume unexpected meanings and raise questions we have not thought to ask'. For example, everybody knows how to behave in a classroom or in a workplace. The clues that physical surroundings and artefacts such as buildings provide us play an important role in this meaning-making

Source: All photographs taken by the author; with permission.

Photo 7.1   The beckoning staircase

(see, for example, Rapoport, 1982; Berg and Kreiner, 1990; Bitner, 1992; Hatch and Cunliffe, 2006). Directly in front of the entrance to the bookstore there was a large and wide staircase (Photo 7.1) and I often found myself walking straight downstairs even if it wasn't my intention. The entrance in the bookstore had a symbolic value; one of the employees described how she took on the role of sales personnel when entering through the door. According to her, '[W]hen I come to the staircase, I look immediately what the store looks like, especially if I haven't done an evening shift, I look very carefully. I always look; sometimes I can even go and straighten something with my coat on'. Another interviewee explained that 'I have to be service minded, when I have entered the store and I meet the customer'. These are examples of how individuals' behaviour can change when entering the workplace, even their mental state.

Upstairs and Downstairs

The field and practices of bookstores have undergone major changes in recent decades. For example, in Finnish bookstores there used to be a large sample collection of books. Since 1975, this was slowly whittled down and the bookstores concentrated on marketing only a few books that sold well. Since 1970 the majority of Finnish bookstore sales have come from items other than books, such as postcards and other paper goods. This development even led the booksellers to call themselves 'book and paper sellers' (Häggman, 2008, p. 487), and can be seen in the bookstore where I collected the data. In the bookshop there were two floors: the upstairs space was called 'the book section' where mainly books were sold, and the downstairs space was called 'the goods section' where other office items and schoolbooks were also sold. Nowadays more than 30 per cent of the sales come from goods other than books, such as calendars, games and office stationary. The bookstore under study was a bookstore with a relatively wide collection of sample books. In the bookshop, in addition to the retail 'book section' and 'goods section' there was the staff changing room and break room downstairs, and the private offices of the regional and local managers and a warehouse. There was a sales desk in both the upstairs and downstairs retail spaces.

While working in the bookshop I noticed rather quickly that different meanings were attached to the different floors. Some of the employees preferred to work upstairs rather than downstairs and vice versa. It was described, for example, that there was a market atmosphere in the downstairs space because of all the other items that were sold besides the books. One interviewee explained: 'What can it be, what can the word be, that atmosphere upstairs. . .it is some kind of calmness'. And another commented: 'Well, there are books upstairs, goods downstairs and schoolbooks. Upstairs is a little bit fancier, because there are only the books. This is a little bit of a confusing space'. One explanation for this can be the cultural and historical appreciation of a book. One interviewee described how the book had symbolic value. It was considered in a way to be 'a sacred item' in her early career and she was advised never to leave it on the floor while wiping the shelves.

The Retail Space

According to the chief executive officer, there is a rational undertone to the bookstore under study. The arrangement of space is made to serve the purpose of the shop from a managerial and planning perspective: for the customers to find the books and other items, and for them to move around easily and to make purchases. In a bookstore there are different groups of people using the space – the customers, employees and manager(s) – and they all attach different meanings to the space. In the space there is also an understanding of the purpose of the space from the planner's perspective.

In retail it is important to regularly redevelop the shop's concept. For example, according to the local manager there was a time when white was the only possible colour for bookshelves in a bookstore. Today, in the newest space concept in the chain under study the main colour is black and there are already several shops with this new concept. Also in the shop under study there had been a rearrangement of space. In the renewed space the stairs were widened, the colours were a warmer red colour and spotlights were added to highlight the items. The new concept of the space was planned to reflect an 'oceanic' atmosphere, explained the regional manager (Photo 7.2). According to him, the concept for the space originated from a picture of a sailing ship that was on the development director's wall. Communality, feeling good and a warm welcome are attached to sailing and these are the elements that the space was planned to express. According to the regional manager, darker colours express more dignity than light colours. Therefore, even if the floor and shelves were a lighter

Photo 7.2   The 'oceanic' atmosphere of the bookstore

colour than earlier, being too light would have decreased the feeling of dignity. 'It's so fine now that we have had a renovation' said one salesperson. Another commented, 'There's more light and it looks more spacious with lighter surfaces and the light is directed more sensibly'.

The symbolic expressions attached to the space were carefully planned at managerial level. According to the chief executive officer, the main philosophy for the bookstore is to be a store for every Finn. 'Warm, close, friendly' was the way the chief executive officer described the images that customers attached to the brand according to research. According to him the surroundings shouldn't express an image that is too high-end or too cheap, therefore the artefacts have been carefully planned and selected so that any particular group of customers is not excluded.

From a symbolic-interpretive standpoint the meaning that symbols convey is created through social action. This means that the symbol itself does not hold an immutable meaning; the meanings change over time, as in the way symbols are used in a particular culture (Hatch and Cunliffe, 2006, pp. 192–194). For example, in the bookstore the colour red was present in different artefacts and it held multiple meanings for the staff and the customers. It was, for example, associated with love, warmth, Christmas and even certain political views. This is an example of how difficult it is to manage the meanings attached to space and artefacts.

According to the chief executive officer there is a need for the bookstore, at some point in the future, to undergo a transformation towards being a more experiential place. For example, the bookstores in Central Europe are quite different to bookstores in the chain under study. They are often places that customers want to spend more time in, with comfortable sofas and cafeterias. Many of the interviewees mentioned their wish to have a cafeteria in the same space as the bookstore. According to them this would make the bookstore a place to meet friends. The sales personnel were pleased that two armchairs were taken upstairs for customers. According to the chief executive officer there should be more elements of comfort in the shop to give the customers more reason to visit the bookshop instead of ordering the books from the Internet. The central focus of this transformation is therefore on the physical space and artefacts in the bookstore.

SALES PERSONNEL'S SPACES

Being a Salesperson: Rules and Routines and a Mental State

Culture is often described as 'shared meanings', especially from the organizational symbolic point of view (Smircich, 1983, p. 342). Physical space and artefacts are important in transmitting these values, roles and rules of organizational culture (for example, Gagliardi, 1990). They are important in leadership, because they are always present and transmit hints or clues as to how to behave (for example, Paalumäki, 2014). In the bookstore the sales personnel performed many daily routines, such as opening the shop and counting the cash, and moving in the space had become somewhat routine. This can also be referred to as embodied knowledge (Seamon, 1980, according to Hatch and Cunliffe, 2006, p. 241; see also Ropo and Parviainen, 2001). An amusing example of this was when one interviewee remembered that after the renovation, all the sales personnel automatically moved from the sales desk towards a place where the warehouse used to be located. Then when they came from the warehouse they always moved to the place where the sales desk used to be, and this lasted for two months. 'It's like when a person learns to walk certain routes. It's amusing that we all went. We were really laughing'.

Performing the role of a salesperson and taking part in everyday tasks, gave me a great deal of understanding about the organizational culture. 'You have to be tidy, friendly and efficient' was the way my colleague described the rules of being a salesperson. The role of sales personnel has changed substantially in recent years. No longer was the salesperson just standing behind the cash desk, but moved around the shop actively selling books and other goods. In the beginning this was especially hard for me because I hadn't been used to standing and already on the second day at work I was wondering if I would ever get used to it. The only time I was able to sit was during the two ten-minute coffee breaks and 30-minute lunch break. Especially during the autumn sales the workdays were really hectic and sometimes standing behind the cash desk was a bit of a relief compared to serving customers in the shop area.

There were both written and unwritten rules as to how personnel should behave in a bookstore. Everybody read the *Handbook for Sales Personnel* when starting the job. The handbook was the official guide that included many details about the salesperson's work. I also held discussions with the local manager about the nature of my work when I started and then weekly about my sales thereafter. An example of an unwritten rule was that in the bookstore the sales personnel were not allowed to discuss personal things too much behind the sales desk or in the retail area. I noticed that when the manager was present I became even more aware of these and other rules, which had an impact on my behaviour.

The break room, in addition to the dressing room, toilet, sales desk, lift and warehouse, were clearly the areas that the customers were not allowed to enter, even though this wasn't signposted physically. Actually, only on the door of the warehouse was there a 'Staff only' sign. The break room was a place where sales personnel discussed things that they could not discuss in the shop, such as different situations with customers, and they generally acted more casually. The break room and the dressing room were the places where sales personnel had some personal items. It was interesting that the unwritten rules of social behaviour also extended to the break room. Some interviewees mentioned that even in the break room there are some issues that shouldn't be discussed, such as politics and religion.

According to Alvesson and Berg (1992, p. 86) 'a symbol always represents something different or something more than itself'. A powerful artefact that often changed individuals' behaviour in a bookstore was the work uniform. Wearing it helped me to adopt the company's rules, common goals and to mentally adapt to the role of a salesperson and orientate towards coworkers and customers (see also Pratt and Rafaeli, 1997; Rafaeli et al., 1997). When I put on the uniform I immediately knew how to behave. I took on a cheerful facial expression and I was ready to serve the customers and to follow the rules of the company (Photo 7.3). This mental role also excluded negative feelings while being in the retail space. As one interviewee put it: 'You cannot show your mood to the customer

Photo 7.3   Smiling behind the desk

and a professional salesperson is able to hide it'. It would actually be inter-esting to know, how would the sales personnel orientate towards work if they were wearing their casual clothes instead of the uniform?

The Sales Desk

The space is not only physical, but is also socially produced (Lefebvre, 1991). For example, it seemed that many of the workers had a favourite place in the bookshop. Some of the sales personnel preferred to work behind the sales desk. I got the impression that this gave them a feeling of control over the situation. This was something I personally preferred, because there was more physical distance from the customers. It was considered to be a safe place compared to the retail area where unexpected questions could be asked. There were some confusing situations when a customer suddenly entered the sales personnel's space, such as the sales desk. According to one interviewee it happens rarely but she finds it unpleasant: 'I would always like to say that "Hi this is our area"'. I also found this kind of situation awkward. I had written in my notes about one incident: 'When I was behind the desk, suddenly a man jumped very close to me, so close I backed off. My heart was beating very fast when he asked me about some book'. This is an example of how some of the meanings, such as ownership of space are emphasized when something unexpected happens and how some of the boundaries are not only physical but also mental. In many cases everyday practices that are taken for granted are often the most interesting and revealing of social structure (Berger and Luckmann, 1966).

As presented earlier, different places evoke different behaviour (Berg and Kreiner, 1990; Elsbach and Pratt, 2007). There was a surveillance camera behind the sales desk and everybody seemed to be aware of it. For example, I noticed while working behind the sales desk that the presence of the camera made me feel as if somebody was watching me and made me feel uncomfortable. This also affected my behaviour even without the pres-ence of the manager. I noticed I felt less relaxed being next to the camera and talked less about personal things with colleagues. This phenomenon can be interpreted through Foucault's power theory (1977): knowing that there is a possibility that somebody is watching you has an impact on your behaviour. According to Taylor and Spicer (2007) approaching space as a manifestation of power has been a useful way to explain spatial arrange-ments in organizations and it is widely used in many branches of science (see also Dale and Burrell, 2008).

Behind the sales desk there was also the Bookstore of the Year trophy and a diploma that had purely symbolic value (Dandridge et al., 1980). They can be seen to symbolize a common goal for the employees to be professional customer servants. According to Alvesson and Berg (1992, p. 103) 'Meaning and values are created, reinforced, maintained and communicated through the artifacts'. The power of symbols is based on their continuous presence and, for example, holding a regular discussion about them (for example, Paalumäki, 2004).

THE MANAGER'S OFFICE

The local manager's office was situated downstairs in a corner and had no window. The regional manager's room (Photo 7.4) was also downstairs and it was smaller than the local manager's room. The location was explained as being for financial reasons: the less valuable space was planned as office space instead of shop space. Some of the employees' interviews were held in the local manager's office while the manager was working at a desk outside the room. I wondered, was the manager's office a neutral enough place to carry out the interviews? It was, however, a practical solution, because I was interviewing the staff during their working hours. Very soon I noticed that at least some of the personnel were a little bit nervous being

Photo 7.4   Regional manager's office

in the manager's room even if they didn't admit it. Sometimes the manager would sit at his desk behind the door. This had a strong impact on at least one person, who constantly glanced at the door and sometimes talked with a lower voice, as if she was worried that the manager might hear her. I got the impression that the manager still held a control over the space, even if he wasn't physically present in the room.

According to the interviews from the bookstore, the manager's room particularly evoked strong feelings amongst many of the employees. They described it as difficult to enter the manager's room when asked to go there and they often had the feeling that they had done something wrong. According to the managers it had actually become a common joke in the workplace that 'the backroom was calling'. I found this interesting because many of the sales personnel described that the manager's door was open most of time, symbolizing the ease of entering the room. The manager's room also lacked the traditional signs of hierarchy, such as paintings on the wall, plants, or pictures of family members (for example, Eräsaari, 1995). The local manager also often worked with the sales personnel in the retail space wearing a similar uniform. I remember one time when the manager was vacuuming the upstairs floor and nobody seemed to pay much attention to it. Also during the interviews with managers a couple of times a member of the staff entered the room to ask something. In those situations they were joking together and seemed to be relaxed. These observations strengthened my impression of a rather relaxed hierarchy.

This fear of entering the manager's room became apparent so often, that I decided to ask about it in the interviews. Somebody thought that maybe it is because of 'the fear of sir'. The regional manager said that it is part of the Finnish leadership culture that correctional feedback is given in a back room and that praise can be given anywhere. From this standpoint the manager's room can appear as a place of punishment. Actually there was one amusing incident that I was told about when one salesperson who had been in the business for over 30 years was asked to a manager's office. Her first thought was 'What have I done?' It was a huge surprise for her to find out that she and her colleague were rewarded for good sales with a bottle of wine and lunch in a nearby restaurant.

DISCUSSION AND CONCLUSIONS

On Symbolic Meanings in a Bookstore

In this chapter I have highlighted the symbolic dimension of space and artefacts and how those meanings are created in everyday practices. In the bookstore there were many symbolically powerful artefacts present all the time in a space where sales personnel and managers worked. These included, for example, colours, the uniform and arrangements of space. These carried non-verbal clues influencing the actions of sales personnel (see Gagliardi, 1990). In this way they had significance in leadership because they had an impact on rules, routines and the mental state of the sales personnel. These are examples of the sociomateriality of leadership and how leadership can happen without the presence of the leader through the clues coded into our physical environment (see the introduction to this book).

As Ropo et al. (2013, p.381) put it: '[m]aterial places lead people through embodied experiences, such as feelings, emotions and memories of the place'. The feelings attached to managers and retail spaces form a part of the leadership. In the bookstore, in particular the manager's room, evoked different feelings amongst the sales personnel. It seemed that they felt that it was easy to approach the local manager, but despite that, felt awkward entering his room when asked to go there. The sales desk area held many meanings: it was considered to be a 'safe' place because the rules of social behaviour were clearer there. There was also physical distance from customers. The presence of the cash desk and other artefacts such as the diploma and a Bookstore of the Year trophy reminded sales personnel of their behaviour in the bookstore. On the other hand, the presence of the surveillance camera was recognized and it had a controlling influence even if the main purpose was for security reasons. Some spaces had clearly become places for the users as they had given them a meaning via the use of the space and the feelings they had attached to them (see, for example, Tuan, 1977). For example, the warehouse and the break room evoked different behaviour than the shop area, where the sales personnel took on the role of a salesperson and followed the rules of the company. On the other hand, some sales personnel mentioned that even in the break room there were things that shouldn't be discussed.

Some of the symbolic meanings are individual and some are shared in the culture. From the data collected in the bookshop, the difference between cultural meaning and individual meaning seemed difficult to extract. It seemed that, for example, the meanings attached to the manager's room were partially cultural because they became obvious from the speech and actions of several individuals. It is only possible to reveal cultural meanings attached to space to some degree; there is no final interpretation. Also in the bookstore there were incoherencies in interpreting the meanings attached to space, for example, in the meanings of upstairs and downstairs and the meanings that the managers' offices held.

On Leadership and Space

Studying how spatial practices can reflect leadership requires an opposite perspective on leadership to the so-called leader-centric approach (see Ropo et al., 2013). As a student of management and leadership I became familiar with numerous leadership theories, but none of them seemed to fit the study of space and material artefacts. For me, reading Donna Ladkin's book *Rethinking Leadership* (2010) was an eye-opening experience; this was just what I had been looking for. Rather than concentrating on the personal characteristics of the leader (leader-centric approach) Ladkin approached the phenomenon of leadership as a wider cultural, historical and social phenomenon where the experience of followers holds a key position to understanding it. Ladkin also used hermeneutics and phenomenology as a background theory (see also Gronn, 2002; Salovaara, 2011). According to her it is essential from a phenomenological standpoint to make a conceptual difference between 'leaders' and 'leadership' and see leadership as a collective process (see also Meindl, 1995; Crevani et al., 2010; Ropo et al., 2013). From this standpoint leadership can occur without the presence of the leader from the clues hidden in our environment and in the space.

In cultural studies there is an idea that even a smaller unit can reflect the features of the entire culture. A bookstore is one example of these cultural meanings attached to space. However, there is a need to study the 'spatial leadership' phenomenon introduced in this book, in different kinds of organizations. As mentioned above, relational leadership theory can provide a suitable framework for this approach to understanding the material dimensions of leadership.

NOTE

* The author wishes to acknowledge the support of the Jenny and Antti Wihuri Foundation and the Foundation for Economic Education.

REFERENCES

Alvesson, M. and P.O. Berg (1992), *Corporate Culture and Organizational Symbolism*, Berlin: Walter de Gruyter.
Berg, P.O. and K. Kreiner (1990), 'Corporate architecture: Turning physical setting into symbolic resources', in P. Gagliardi (ed.), *Symbols and Artifacts: Views of the Corporate Landscape*, Berlin: Walter de Gruyter, pp. 41–67.

Berger, P.L. and T. Luckmann (1966), *Social Construction of Reality: A Treatise in the Sociology of Knowledge*, New York: Garden City.

Bitner, M.J. (1992), 'Servicescapes: The impact of physical surroundings on customers and employees', *Journal of Marketing*, **56** (2), 57–71.

Crevani, L., M. Lindgren and J. Packendorff (2010), 'Leadership, not leaders: On the study of leadership as practices and interactions', *Scandinavian Journal of Management*, **26** (1), 77–86.

Dale, K. and G. Burrell (2008), *The Spaces of Organisation and the Organisation of Space: Power, Identity and Materiality at Work*, New York: Palgrave Macmillan.

Dandridge, T.C., I. Mitroff and W.F. Joyce (1980), 'Organizational symbolism: A topic to expand organizational analysis', *The Academy of Management Review*, **5** (1), 77–82.

Elsbach, K.D. and M.G. Pratt (2007), 'The physical environment in organizations', *The Academy of Management Annals*, **1** (1), 181–224.

Eräsaari, L. (1995), *Kohtaamisia byrokraattisilla näyttämöillä* [Meetings on Bureaucratic Stages], Helsinki: Gaudeamus.

Foucault, M. (1977), *Discipline and Punish: The Birth of the Prison*, London: Penguin Books.

Gagliardi, P. (1990), 'Artifacts as pathways and remains of organizational life', in P. Gagliardi (ed.), *Symbols and Artifacts: Views of the Corporate Landscape*, Berlin: Walter de Gruyter, pp. 3–32.

Gronn, P. (2002), 'Distributed leadership as a unit of analysis', *The Leadership Quarterly*, **13** (4), 423–451.

Häggman, K. (2008), *Paras tawara maailmassa: Suomalainen kustannustoiminta 1800-luvulta 2000 luvulle* [The Best Goods in the World: Finnish Publishing from the 19th to 21st Centuries], Helsinki: Otava.

Hansen, H., A. Ropo and E. Sauer (2007), 'Aesthetic leadership', *The Leadership Quarterly*, **18** (6), 544–560.

Hatch, M.J. and A.L. Cunliffe (2006), *Organization Theory: Modern, Symbolic and Postmodern Perspectives*, 2nd edition, New York: Oxford University Press.

Ladkin, D. (2010), *Rethinking Leadership: A New Look at Old Leadership Questions*, Cheltenham, UK and Northampton, MA, USA: Edward Elgar Publishing.

Lefebvre, H. (1991), *The Production of Space*, Oxford: Blackwell.

Martin, P.Y. (2002), 'Sensations, bodies, and the "spirit of a place": Aesthetics in residential organizations for the elderly', *Human Relations*, **55** (7), 861–885.

Meindl, J.R. (1995), 'The romance of leadership as a follower-centric theory: A social constructionist approach', *Leadership Quarterly*, **6** (3), 329–341.

Paalumäki, A. (2004), 'Keltaisella johdetut: Artefaktit, johtaminen ja organisaation kulttuurinen identiteetti' [Led by yellow: Artifacts, management and the cultural identity of organization], dissertation, Turku School of Economics.

Peltonen, T. (2011), 'Multiple architectures and the production of organizational space in a Finnish University', *Journal of Organizational Change*, **24** (6), 806–821.

Pratt, M.G. and A. Rafaeli (1997), 'Organizational dress as a symbol of multilayered social identities', *Academy of Management Journal*, **40** (4), 862–898.

Rafaeli, A. and I. Vilnai-Yavetz (2004), 'Emotion as a connection of physical artifacts and organizations', *Organization Science*, **15** (6), 671–686.

Rafaeli, A., J. Dutton, C. Harquail and S. Mackie-Lewis (1997), 'Navigating by attire: The use of dress by female administrative employees', *Academy of Management Journal*, **40** (1), 9–45.

Rapoport, A. (1982), *The Meaning of the Built Environment: A Nonverbal Communication Approach*, Beverly Hills, CA: Sage.

Ropo, A. and J. Parviainen (2001), 'Leadership and bodily knowledge in expert organizations: Epistemological rethinking', *Scandinavian Journal of Management*, **17** (1), 1–18.

Ropo, A., E. Sauer and P. Salovaara (2013), 'Embodiment of leadership through material place', *Leadership*, **9** (3), 378–395.

Salovaara, P. (2011), *From Leader-Centricity Toward Leadership. A Hermeneutic Narrative Approach*, Tampere: Tampere University Press.

Seamon, D. (1980), 'Body-subject, time-space routines, and place ballets', in A. Buttimer and D. Seamon (eds), *The Human Experience of Space and Place*, New York: St. Martin's Press, pp. 148–165.

Smircich, L. (1983), 'Concepts of culture and organizational analysis', *Administrative Science Quarterly*, **28** (3), 339–358.

Strati, A. (1992), 'Aesthetic understanding of organizational life', *Academy of Management Review*, **17** (3), 568–581.

Taylor, S and A. Spicer (2007), 'Time for space: A narrative review of research on organizational spaces', *International Journal of Management Reviews*, **9** (4), 325–346.

Tuan, Y.-F. (1977), *Space and Place: The Perspective of Experience*, Minneapolis, MN: University of Minnesota Press.

Warren, S. (2002), '"Show me how to work here": Using photography to research organizational aesthetics', *ephemera*, **2** (3), 224–245.

8. Front stage with no front-stage employees: customer perceptions of self-service hotels

Ritva Höykinpuro

Source: Drawing by Mika Yrjölä; with permission.

Imagine that you enter a theatre to watch a play. Time is passing slowly. Finally, you realize that no actors will show up on the front stage. It is you who are expected to act on the front stage according to a script that you do not know. . .

The question of how a space leads customers to act in a meaningful way is intriguing. The customers are expected to follow a script (a service concept), but there are no front-stage actors to guide, train or inform them about it. The customer's role shifts from being a spectator to an actor or sometimes even to a lead actor on the stage. How does the service space lead the customers, and then how do they perceive the service space as the service?

A service encounter has been a cornerstone in service management. However, a service space with no front-stage employees is a relatively new phenomenon of service management. No front-stage employees on-site means no face-to-face service encounters. A 'face-to-space' service encounter is thus a new phenomenon and a focus of this chapter. Can a service space and technology substitute for service employees on-site, and then where is the leadership hiding in these desolate service spaces?

This chapter sheds light on customers' perceptions and evaluations (criteria) of service in a case when the service space *is* the service. Self-service hotels illustrate this research phenomenon, as do some customers' personal accounts (narratives) of their stay in such an accommodation service concept.

SERVICE SYSTEM AS A THEATRICAL PERFORMANCE

Service is often described metaphorically (Fisk and Grove, 1996; Grove et al., 1998; Tax and Stuart, 2001) as a theatrical performance where actors perform their roles on the front stage. The service system has a script, a scriptwriter, a director, a back stage where supporting personnel carry out their duties, and actors on the front stage who perform their scripted roles. The customers sit as the audience and watch the play taking place on stage.

However, the theatre metaphor is now criticized, since it treats customers like passive actors in the audience who tamely follow the play. Nowadays, customers have an active role in service production, similar to an experimental theatre where customers participate in the play (Williams and Anderson, 2005). In the contemporary scene, customers are increasingly conducting the duties that used to be done by service employees in traditional, face-to-face service encounters. For instance, think of Internet banking services and self-service at gas stations or in fast food restaurants. Due to the increasing popularity of self-service technologies, human contact has been decreasing dramatically in service encounters (for example, Meuter et al., 2000; Froehle and Roth, 2004; Froehle, 2006; Collier and Sherrell, 2012).

Self-service is productive to service providers; moreover, it can even enhance customer satisfaction by increasing customer benefits and decreasing customer sacrifice (Heinonen and Strandvik, 2009). In many self-service concepts, the front-stage employees are scarce or entirely missing. Hence, a service system without front-stage employees needs to be studied. How do customers perceive the service when no front-stage employees are present? What do customers attribute as good service when they are alone

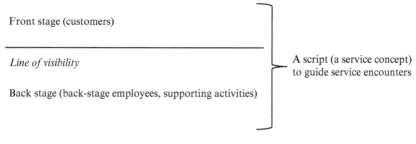

Source: Author's own diagram.

Figure 8.1   A script to guide service encounters in a self-service concept

in a service space? Customers are capable of perceiving and acting above the line of visibility, but they can only imagine what is happening below the line of visibility and how their role is written in the script. Where is the director who is supposed to direct the play? Is there such a director, or is he or she being replaced by a well-designed service space and technology? Figure 8.1 illustrates customers who are alone on the front stage.

A service concept can vary according to the number of customer contacts, labour intensity, interaction and customization (Haywood-Farmer, 1988). Service concepts tend to move toward low labour intensity, minimal number of customer contacts and interaction, and negligible level of customization (ibid.). Such a movement calls for increasing customer participation in service production. It also requires customer willingness to use technology and initiative in service encounters. Additionally, a low degree of customization sets the customers in homogeneous customer groups with minimal differences in expectations and perceptions of the service.

A SELF-SERVICE HOTEL AS A SERVICE CONCEPT

Hotels and restaurants are commonly associated with high-touch services, including human contact and customized face-to-face encounters, such as in à la carte restaurants and five-star hotels. Nowadays, service concepts with the idea of customers as human resources (self-service) are finding their target groups and providing an alternative to traditional high-touch hospitality. These service concepts, with a minimum number of enabling and enhancing services, offer an alternative to customers who prefer the outcome quality to the process quality, and are satisfied when the perceived service is in the zone of tolerance (Grönroos, 1984; Strandvik, 1994).

In a self-service hotel, a customer books a room via the Internet ('face-to-screen' encounter). Thereafter, he or she receives a code to enter the hotel. In the hotel, there is no reception desk or receptionist, just a proper room with the necessary amenities in which to stay overnight and spend

Source: Drawings by Mika Yrjölä; with permission.

Figure 8.2   Images of a self-service hotel

some time (Figure 8.2). The quality of service is the service space and how it succeeds in fulfilling a customer's expectations and needs.

Favourable face-to-space service encounters challenge the traditional service design that is conventionally based on face-to-face, voice-to-voice, or face-to-screen encounters. The following section sheds light on customers' perceptions of service in a case when the space is the service.

CUSTOMER PERCEPTIONS OF SERVICE SPACE AS AN ACCOMMODATION SERVICE

Using a story form for this study, five customers shared their experiences about their stay in a self-service hotel. The researcher's role in the data gathering was to facilitate storytelling by occasionally asking complementary questions. The customers' pseudonyms are Ann, Helen, Mary, Mike and Molly. Customers have different motives for staying or being accommodated in a hotel, specifically when they choose a self-service concept. The five customers had the following motives:

- *Ann* was a student at that time and a member of a student organization that held a conference in another city. The hotel was chosen and booked by the student organization, and four students shared a room.
- *Helen* wanted to spend some time with her husband – go shopping and to the movies. They wanted to stay overnight in a hotel that offered low-priced rooms and was situated in a city centre. The second time, she was alone and needed a place to stay overnight while she was in another city because of her work duties.
- *Mary* had a class meeting in another city and just needed a place to sleep for one night. She thought that a place in the city centre with low prices was good enough, since she was alone and only needed a room for an overnight stay.
- *Molly* was a student who had a course in another city. She was fully occupied with the course all day long, was dining downtown with fellow students, and only needed a place close to the university in which to stay overnight.
- *Mike* had completed his military service some time ago, and the former army guys still kept in touch. They wanted to meet once again and were looking for an inexpensive place to chat and enjoy a sauna room for several hours. One of the guys was the organizer who had booked the place for the whole group.

What did these customers know about the script before entering and staying in a hotel with no front-stage employees – no reception desk or receptionist, no bellboy, no bar or restaurant?

> I had heard that such a new service concept had arrived – it was then totally new and it was inexpensive – it was a kind of concept where there was no reception at all, and you could book it via [the] Internet, then you [would] enter the hotel with a code. You know, it is all right when there is no need for other activities, just go and sleep there. You are not there to enjoy your stay with [some] company. . . There was a monthly calendar [on a web page]. There one could see when there were vacant rooms. Then one had to obtain a code to enter the hotel. It had to be a code that you [would] remember for sure, a PIN code of a bank card or something like that. There was no problem in booking; the only thing was that it was new to enter a hotel with a code. (Mary)

How can the customers be trained to act in a space with no front-stage employees to guide and inform them? There is information on the web page and on-site. The problem is that not all customers read it, especially in advance; they are often the ones in the company of the customer who has a leading role in choosing and booking the hotel:

> I did not really feel myself [as a customer]. Finally, when we were there on-site, I realized that this was the right place. Then I thought that this could be okay as a service concept, if I only knew in advance how I was supposed to act there. I did not know what instructions the group leader had received in advance. (Mike)

Studies related to service productivity highlight the role of customer participation, as well as customer training (Gummesson, 1995; Grönroos and Ojasalo, 2004). Customers can learn to use technology, search for information, show initiative in service encounters, and finally, be satisfied with such a self-service concept. The missing awareness of the script and the customer's role in it can cause dissatisfaction. Moreover, different customers have varying priorities; therefore, service concepts commonly target homogeneous customer groups that have common interests, attitudes and priorities:

> [A self-service hotel is] [e]asy to book through home pages, you can pay it in advance, easy to use. The room is clean; everything is working without any problems. . . And I also think that they can offer low prices, since there is less expense since there are no personnel. Moreover, the hotels are situated in the city centre. It is for the kind of customers who do not need face-to-face services in hotels – I am in that category! I use self-service cashiers, self-service posting since they are easy. . . I am interacting with a machine! As long as the machine works, there is no problem! In the case that the machine does not work, there is a problem, but that has never happened to me. (Molly)

Six themes emerged from these customers' stories. Their first concern involved the lack of front-stage employees and their preference for front-stage employees in accommodation encounters. The second theme was the virtuality of back-stage employees. The third theme concerned the customers' perception of hospitality when no service employees were present on-site. The fourth theme was the customers' sensuous experience in a self-service hotel. The fifth theme referred to the meaning of co-customers in accommodation encounters. Finally, the sixth theme involved the target customers for such a self-service accommodation concept. In the following paragraphs, each theme is discussed and illustrated with quotes from these customers' stories.

Customers' Needs for Front-stage Employees in Accommodation Encounters

What is the front-stage employees' role in accommodation services? The lack of human contact in service concepts or strategies is intriguing, especially in the hospitality sector. Hospitality is defined in the *Oxford Dictionary* as the friendly and generous reception and entertainment of guests, visitors or strangers. Generally, hospitality and hospitableness share a high degree of commonality, especially in their emphasis on the attitudinal and behavioural dimensions of hospitality, notably in relation to those providing hospitality (Brotherton and Wood, 2002, p. 136). Customers, specifically the younger generation, are nowadays used to self-service and do not necessarily expect face-to-face service encounters. However, the customers in this case study felt that the meaning of front-stage employees on-site is a question of emotional and psychological security:

> It is some sort of psychological, peace-of-mind issue. You feel that you are there all alone when no face [human being] is there. You do recall that guy there at the reception, and when you need to call a taxi, you just go there to chat with that guy. Although you [may] never need anything, it is the feeling that you know that there is someone, a person there for you. (Mike)

> I did not think that [there were no service employees], but when I arrived there, I realized that there wasn't any reception desk at all. Well, it worked well, but I felt somehow negative, since there was no one to represent the hotel. Think if something happened. Who to contact then? In an ordinary hotel, you can always go to the reception desk and have a chat there. In this hotel, there was no chance of that. (Helen)

From the perspective of a service provider, the security of a self-service hotel is a concern. There are video cameras and a security service; a guard can arrive when the need arises. However, these customers did not believe that the security in self-service hotels aimed to make them feel secure on-site; rather, it was intended to control them:

> Then at a quarter to midnight, someone first knocked on the door and then opened it with his keys. He was a porter or a security guard; at least he had a body like security guards have. He came to check that we would be out of that place in a quarter of an hour. He was an overseer. The person in our group who had booked the sauna apartment told us that someone might come to ensure that we would check out in time. Most of us had been sure that no one would arrive, and we could stay there a couple of hours later, but that did not happen. It was not an aggressive action to get us out of that place, he checked the facilities and wished us goodnight. (Mike)

Customer-perceived service quality or customer value has been an interest of many service researchers for decades (for example, Grönroos, 2007, p. 71). The authors of these studies agree that customers' perceptions of service or customer value are subjective, relativistic, situational, context dependent, and so on. However, several studies suggest some customer criteria for perceived service quality; the well-known ones are mainly based on human interactions indicated by professionalism and skills, behaviour and attitude, reliability, accessibility and flexibility, service recovery, servicescape and reputation (ibid., p. 90). Specifically, with reference to the behaviour and attitude of front-stage employees, it is argued that 'customers feel that the service employees (contact persons) are concerned about them and interested in solving their problems in a friendly and spontaneous way' (ibid.). Service recovery refers to human interaction, and it is pointed out that 'customers realize that whatever goes wrong or something unpredictable happens the service provider will immediately and actively take action to keep them in control of the situation and find a new, acceptable solution' (ibid.).

Back-stage Employees as Virtual Human Resources

From the service provider's point of view, customers in a self-service hotel are taken care of without any front-stage employees on-site. When a service failure occurs, there is a possibility for service recovery by contacting virtual back-stage employees. However, customers have to take the initiative for a voice-to-voice encounter. Mary had once faced a situation when she was unable to open the door to her room:

> First I felt, 'What shall I do?' I felt that there wasn't anyone to contact! Then I realized that there was a telephone number somewhere. Then I checked whether I had my mobile with me. What if I had no mobile with me?! Or was it that I talked to the wall. . . It felt strange. . .that there you talked to a wall

[laughter]. There was a microphone. It was such a strange system, and I had such a strange feeling. . . I felt that I was chatting to a void, and from there I was being answered. Or was it that I had to wait for a technician to arrive? I had to wait there for a while, and a couple of other people had a problem with a room. There we stood and waited for some time. This is not common in other hotels, since there are employees present there. (Mary)

Security is a concern in self-service hotels. Therefore, video cameras are installed in the facilities. However, the security that is virtually managed does not always convince the customer:

I knew that [there are video cameras there] but I was not thinking of that. . .or I do not trust video cameras. Perhaps someone is really watching them, but you know, it is so easy to escape the cameras. If there is someone who has or knows the code [for the front door], he can enter [the hotel]. That cannot be controlled with the video cameras. I knew [that there are video cameras there], but I think it does not help! (Ann)

It is challenging to replace service employees on-site by virtual human resources back stage. Moreover, so it is to convince the customers about the availability and willingness of virtual human resources to serve them whenever needed.

Customers' Perceptions of Hospitality in a Self-service Hotel

Can the feeling of hospitality and that someone is concerned about a customer's wellbeing and comfort be expressed without a human being on-site?

You can feel [the presence of] human beings with the help of amenities. It [the hotel] can be domestic and easy to enter, and cleanliness is one thing. [How] was [the] hospitality there? My experience was that I felt like we had broken into an industrial facility. It was not domestic; I did not feel cosy; the lights were cold, there were no carpets, it was dirty and dark, the banisters were metallic, [and] there was chewing gum everywhere. [My] fellow customers did not look like they were enjoying their stay there. They looked down, carrying plastic bags – these were my feelings about that experience. (Mike)

Evaluating service quality and a customer's evaluation criteria are difficult to study. Quality is commonly compared to something. An accommodation service can be compared to an experience of sleeping at home as an everyday practice:

In a luxury hotel, there is something luxurious and extra that you cannot experience at home. There are, for instance, soft pillows, a great bathroom with a fancy bath, or a good breakfast. There is something that provides an extraordinary experience for a customer. In [a self-service hotel], everything that is fancy is missing. It is an even worse experience than sleeping at home. (Helen)

Service quality is conventionally defined as customers' assessment between their expectations and perceptions of the service (Zeithaml et al., 1993). For example, customers perceive expectations through a company website, word-of-mouth and fellow customers' experiences. However, customers commonly perceive high satisfaction with the service if their expectations are exceeded:

> Expectations are not exceeded in such a self-service hotel. Somehow, talking to the wall does not make me feel that there is someone who cares and wants everything to be fine. After I had a bad experience. . . I do not know whether or not I am satisfied . . .it is clinical and industrial. . . When you enter a traditional hotel, there is someone there who looks you in the eye and welcomes you; he tells you where to find an elevator. And then, there is that candy on the pillow, and then there is that little bit [of] comical text on the television screen: 'Welcome to the hotel, Mary'. They call you by your first name. The difference is that there is a human being to welcome a human being. (Mary)

In a self-service hotel, the hospitality can be perceived with the help of the interior design and informing the customer about the service mindset of virtual human resources.

Customers' Sensuous Experiences in a Hotel Room

Customers do not commonly encounter any service employees in a self-service hotel. Therefore, it is intriguing to study what customers' service quality experiences are when the space is the service. In such a case, a service experience is more or less sensuous, and a customer evaluates it with his or her senses such as sight, hearing or smell. The following are examples of the customers' sensuous evaluations of their quality experiences:
Sight:

> I was surprised that the room was so large. There was a double bed and then a sofa where I slept with a fellow [student] of mine. It was quite poky, but it was okay when it came to students. It was like a normal hotel room. That time, I was used to overnight [stays] in hostels. I was expecting something similar, but it was a large room, just like a usual hotel room. (Ann)

Hearing:

> Once, the windows were [facing] the main road, and it was really hot. Cars were driving [by], and the noise was loud. I could not choose the room. I'd

have preferred to have windows [facing] the back yard. Cars were driving [by], and there was a lot of noise. I could not sleep. The noise was disturbing me. In a hotel where there are personnel, you can always ask for a room that is quiet and has windows [facing] the back yard. Later I even learned that there were odd and even numbers for the rooms, the odd or even numbers were [facing] the back yard. . .but a one-time customer would not know that. (Mary)

Smell:

And we did stay there for four or five nights. In such a time, a lot of garbage did emerge! We did not have any place to put all that garbage. There was only a small waste basket in the room. It was a students' trip. . .therefore, a lot of beer bottles [and] pizza boxes accumulated. There were yogurt cartons that you wanted to get rid of so that the garbage would not smell there. There weren't any places to put all that stuff. Could we leave them in the corridor? Would the cleaners take them away from the corridor? We stayed there for quite a long time. . .that was not nice at all. . .specifically, there had been a party in one room. They had bought boxes of kebab there; they had not eaten all of them. The next morning, the smell in that room was terrible. The half-eaten kebabs were all over the room, and they were wondering where to throw them; there was no garbage can there. I do remember that we were looking for a garbage can outside the building also, but we did not find any. That was a problem, since there was no one there, and none of us bothered to find out where to call. . . It was all our fault. If we had not brought all those pizza boxes [and] bottles of beer with us. . . I do not remember that they cleaned [while we were] there. . . I have a feeling that they did not. . .they clean there only after the customers have checked out. (Ann)

Studying customers' sense-based experiences calls for redefining their service quality criteria. Sensuous experiences are meaningful in a case when there are no service employees to impact customers' service experiences, for example, in self-service hotels.

The Meaning of Co-customers in an Accommodation Service

Other customers can enhance or detract from customers' service experiences (Grove and Fisk, 1997). Moreover, some services are designed to be experienced in a group (Finsterwalder and Tuzovic, 2010). Think, for instance, of soccer or ice-hockey matches. Part of the extreme experience occurs with fellow customers. Customer needs for hospitality services are partly to meet other people, find some company, or just be with other customers that they would otherwise not meet elsewhere. The other customers can also provide a feeling of security or insecurity:

I have seen few people there. I think that most often, it is quite quiet there, the corridors are empty there, it is almost spooky there. I have felt that I was all alone there. If the other customers do make noise, I feel safer, and it is more natural [to meet other customers]. (Mary)

I think I stayed there then for two nights. I remember that I worked late that night; I was preparing my lectures, and then I brought some packed lunch to that room. Then I just waited for time to pass to have breakfast at the café downstairs. Luckily, there was an Internet connection so that I could check my e-mails. Then I watched the television for some time. . . But it was such a lonely experience. (Helen)

Customer segmentation has been a cornerstone in marketing for decades (for example, Kotler and Armstrong, 2013). Segmenting customers in homogeneous groups with similar service preferences and needs facilitates the service design. However, customers, specifically in hospitality services, prefer to be in a group where they perceive themselves as being one of them. Therefore, they observe one another in ways such as, 'Am I like one of them?' or 'What are they doing here?':

A couple of times, we dropped by the supermarket on the other side of the road. Then we saw people there at the front door. They could open the door with a code. And then we saw some people in the corridor. . . How could I express this. . .well, usually when you meet other people [customers] in a hotel, you presume that they [are staying] overnight there, and they look like tourists or businessmen. I felt conflicted. . .people I met there had a strange profile; we did not exchange any words; we did not look at each other. We took an elevator; they climbed the stairs or stayed there to wait for another elevator. There was no interaction with these other people [customers]. They did not look like [they were] on vacation or businessmen. They had no [extra] clothes, no suitcase; they had some plastic bags, and they were not dressed tidily.

The general appearance of customers in self-service hotels is unknown to the service provider, since booking and entering the hotel occur without any human contact. However, the physical appearance of co-customers seems meaningful for a favourable service experience.

Target Group of a Self-service Hotel

Customers are commonly divided into target groups with the help of demographics (for example, age, gender, profession, income or residence) or behavioural (hobbies, attitudes or values) segmentation criteria. The customers in this case study expressed that being a customer of such a self-service hotel was in fact due to a particular situation, such as needing a place to stay overnight, without the necessity for any enabling or enrichment services. For instance, Molly met demographic and behavioural segmentation criteria. She was in her thirties, a student, married with children, sporty, fond of cats, and so on. She was fully satisfied with her stay in a self-service hotel when she needed nothing more than a proper place to stay for a couple of nights. Nonetheless, she said that she would never stay in such a self-service hotel with her children, since there were no extra services:

> We slept where we slept, and in this case it was [a self-service hotel]. Apparently, if something had happened. . .any noise or something that had disturbed me then. . . If something had happened, then of course. . .the hotel was really quiet that week. I do not remember that I had met anyone. The course was taking place, and we spent a lot of time [attending it], from 9 am to 6 pm. We just slept in the hotel. . . When I stay in a hotel with my children, then I definitely choose a hotel with a playground, and a hotel where they have a babysitting service. With my children, I would not go to a self-service hotel, since it does not offer any babysitting. (Molly)

Choosing a self-service hotel can also be a question of travelling alone or with a group, when all activities are organized outside the accommodation facility:

> Nowadays it is designed in a way that there are three to four customers who share the room. And then, there is no breakfast included. That (breakfast) is an advantage for an ordinary hotel. It is not such a romantic atmosphere. My husband and I used to have some time to spend together. It was rare, since we worked on different shifts, and our child was small. In such a case, I would not have chosen a self-service hotel. When I was alone, it was only a practical solution. (Mary)

Segmentation is not always necessary, specifically when the service is the kind that caters to an everyday practice of people, such as sleeping. However, customers have choices and alternatives in accommodation services. Circumstances vary, and customers have different priorities and preferences, depending on the situation in question.

SERVICE DESIGN IN A CASE WHEN THE SPACE IS THE SERVICE

Designing the service with no front-stage employees is relatively new and rare, specifically in accommodation services. Hence, it is necessary to add to our understanding and study the customer experiences in a case when the space is the service. Service design is a never-ending journey in which the service providers are learning with and from the customers (Matthing et al., 2004).

The idea of offering a space (a facility or a room) as a service entails the

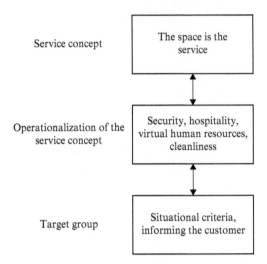

Service concept	The space is the service
Operationalization of the service concept	Security, hospitality, virtual human resources, cleanliness
Target group	Situational criteria, informing the customer

Source: Author's own diagram.

Figure 8.3   Service design when the space is the service

ability to fulfil the customers' needs. There are situations when a customer is satisfied with a proper room to stay overnight; occasionally, there is no need for any extra services:

> I did not have any expectations. . . I had that course there, and I had to find a hotel! We chose this hotel. It did fulfil all our needs in every sense of the word. It did satisfy our needs. (Molly)

However, to operationalize such a service concept calls for studying customer experiences with it. It goes beyond the idea that the customers who are accommodated in self-service hotels are quite heterogeneous; choosing such a service concept is more a situational issue than belonging to a particular target group with some demographic characteristics. Figure 8.3 depicts the service design of a self-service hotel.

It is a challenge to operationalize the service concept of a self-service hotel. The facility should look and be perceived like a hotel, provide hospitality and security, maintain tidiness, and achieve all these goals with no front-stage employees.

The narrated experiences of this case study's customers showed that a self-service hotel's facilities should inform its guests about its hospitality and accommodation services in a way that makes them feel welcomed. Additionally, informing customers where and how to enter the hotel and how to act upon entry is part of the service design. Mike's experience illustrates the importance and meaning of entering the hotel:

> Then we arrived in a dark hall, and I was then quite sure that we had not arrived at any hotel! We took an elevator to the top floor. The lights were off there as well, and we could not turn them on. The group leader was quite sure that we had arrived at the right place. Somehow, we succeeded in getting there. It was such a strange situation; I had reservations, since it did not smell or appear like a hotel at all. I felt all the time like, 'Where have we broken into?' (Mike)

The significance and meaning of security emerged quite evidently from these customers' accounts. Being alone and staying overnight in a hotel with no on-site service employees feeds the customers' imagination. Helen's thoughts about the security in a self-service hotel reveal the customers' fear and ignorance about security issues in such a place:

> As a matter of fact, I stayed there alone that spring. Then I was thinking that a fire could start there. There were those big windows. I cannot remember whether one could open them. . .behind those windows was that street. However, everything there was locked, and you needed a code to every place, and then there was the front door. . .if you panicked, how [would you] get out of there? At the back yard, there was that grating where the cars would drive through, and you needed a code there. You were locked there if something happened. That is the difference. . .in a traditional hotel, you know that there is always someone there (at the reception). (Helen)

Due to the increasing use of self-service technology, customers are now familiar with acting independently without service employees on-site. However, there is a limit to which customers can or are willing to do the job by themselves. Hence, informing them in advance about the security and their role in the case of an untoward incident is part of the service design. Ann's viewpoint about the customers as human resources sheds light on the extent to which customers are willing to act as such:

> There were no personnel there! If something would happen, for example, a flood on the third floor, come and do something about the matter! I am proactive, but I expect to have the possibility of asking someone [service personnel]. I am not the security chief there! There is a limit! (Ann)

CONCLUSIONS AND FUTURE RESEARCH

The service environment is found to be one of the elements that support a customer's positive experience in service processes. Therefore, a number of studies have been conducted to enrich our understanding of service environments and their impacts on customer-perceived service. Due to the different perspectives in the service research, various concepts have been used to frame the service environment, such as servicescape (Bitner, 1992), experience room (Edvardsson et al., 2010), and consumptionscape (Venkatraman and Nelson, 2008). This study supports the social constructionist research approach. Thus, the customer experience is needed in studying service environments. The customer experience is related to the concept that Holbrook (2006) defined as an interactive, relativistic preference experience (p. 212). This study stepped back in time and used the classical theatre metaphor in illustrating a servicescape as a front stage. However, in contrast to traditional studies, this study used an empty front stage as an analogy for a self-service hotel.

The study started from five explorative, narrative interviews. Therefore, its theoretical background is fragmented. However, the study also illustrated the interdisciplinary nature of the research on space. This chapter first presented a service system as a theatrical performance; thereafter, the roles of missing front-stage employees and virtual back-stage employees for customers' service experiences were discussed. Then the customers' perceptions of hospitality and their sensuous service experiences were introduced. Finally, the co-customers' meaning in a service experience and the target groups for such a self-service concept were covered. These discussions were related to service marketing and management, human resources and hospitality management streams of literature. To continue studying this research phenomenon, the theoretical background of the study ought to be more focused. This study stimulates the research in this field and offers several ideas for future research.

First, the customers' experiences in the accommodation service that is provided with a self-service principle require further empirical studies in order to gain an in-depth understanding of the research phenomenon. Suggested suitable research methods for in-depth studies on customer experiences are ethnography and netnography, oral or written narratives, and focus group interviews. Second, customer segmentation, target groups, and segmentation criteria for self-service hotels need to be studied further. A customer's choice of a self-service hotel appears to be more dependent on a situation than on his or her demographic variables. Therefore, situational criteria are more relevant in illustrating the customers (target groups) of self-service hotels. Third, the need for front-stage employees in hospitality services should be studied further. What are the pros and cons of having employees on-site? What is their meaning and value to a customer's service experiences? Fourth, it is necessary to study how customers can be managed as human resources or whether they can be managed and trained as such, since in a way, they replace human resources in self-service hotels. Finally, customers' experiences in service space appear to be of an aesthetic type. Thus, organizational aesthetics seems relevant to apply in the study of customers' sense-based experiences in self-service hotels.

MANAGERIAL IMPLICATIONS

The study provides managerial implications for designing service concepts in which the space *is* the service. Moreover, this study broadens the categorization of service encounters by introducing a face-to-space encounter, when a customer is not interacting face-to-face, voice-to-voice, or face-to-screen, but only with a space such as a facility or a hotel room. How can such a face-to-space encounter be designed in a manner that a customer experiences hospitality, security and satisfaction of his or her senses? Furthermore, how can a customer be trained to be a target client for such a service concept?

REFERENCES

Bitner, M.J. (1992), 'Servicescapes: The impact of physical surroundings on customers and employees', *Journal of Marketing*, **56** (2), 57–71.

Brotherton, B. and R. Wood (2002), 'Hospitality and hospitality management', in C. Lashley and A. Morrison (eds), *In Search of Hospitality – Theoretical Perspectives and Debates*, Oxford: Butterworth-Heinemann, pp. 134–56.

Collier, J.E. and D.L. Sherrell (2012), 'Examining the influence of control and convenience in a self-service setting', *Journal of the Academy of Marketing Science*, **38** (4), 490–590.

Edvardsson, B., B. Enquist and R. Johnston (2010), 'Design dimensions of experience room for service test drives: Case studies in several service contexts', *Managing Service Quality*, **20** (4), 312–27.

Finsterwalder, J. and S. Tuzovic (2010), 'Quality in group service encounters: A theoretical exploration of the concept of a simultaneous multi-customer co-creation process', *Managing Service Quality*, **20** (2), 109–22.

Fisk, R.P. and S.J. Grove (1996), 'Applications of impression management and the drama metaphor in marketing: An introduction', *European Journal of Marketing*, **30** (9), 6–12.

Froehle, C. (2006), 'Service personnel, technology, and their interaction in influencing customer satisfaction', *Decision Sciences*, **37** (1), 5–29.

Froehle, C. and A. Roth (2004), 'New measurement scales for evaluating perceptions of the technology-mediated customer service experience', *Journal of Operations Management*, **22** (1), 1–21.

Grönroos, C. (1984), 'A service quality model and its marketing implications', *European Journal of Marketing*, **18** (4), 36–44.

Grönroos, C. (2007), *Service Management and Marketing – Customer Management in Service Competition*, Chichester, UK: John Wiley & Sons Ltd.

Grönroos, C. and K. Ojasalo (2004), 'Service productivity: Towards a conceptualization of the transformation of inputs into economic results in services', *Journal of Business Research*, **57** (4), 414–23.

Grove, S.J. and R.P. Fisk (1997), 'The impact of other customers on service exchanges: A critical incident examination of "getting along"', *Journal of Retailing*, **73** (1), 63–85.

Grove, S.J., R.P. Fisk and M.J. Dorsch (1998), 'Assessing the theatrical components of the service encounter: A cluster analysis examination', *The Service Industries Journal*, **18** (3), 116–34.

Gummesson, E. (1995), 'Services marketing and the interaction between quality, productivity and profitability', *European Journal of Marketing*, **29** (5), 77–9.

Haywood-Farmer, J. (1988), 'A conceptual model of service quality', *International Journal of Operations & Production Management*, **8** (6), 19–29.

Heinonen, K. and T. Strandvik (2009), 'Monitoring value-in-use of e-service', *Journal of Service Management*, **20** (1), 33–51.

Holbrook, M.B. (2006), 'ROSEPEKICECIVECI versus CCV: The resource-operant, skills-exchanging, performance-experiencing, knowledge-informed, competence-enacting, co-producer-involved, value-emerging, customer-interactive view of marketing versus the concept of customer value: I can get it for you wholesale', in R.F. Lusch and S.L. Vargo (eds), *The Service-dominant Logic of Marketing: Dialog, Debate and Directions*, Armonk, NY: M.B. Sharpe, pp. 208–23.

Kotler, P. and G. Armstrong (2013), *Principles of Marketing*, Upper Saddle River, NJ: Pearson Education Inc.

Matthing, J., B. Sandén and B. Edvardsson (2004), 'New service development: Learning from and with customers', *International Journal of Service Industry Management*, **15** (5), 479–98.

Meuter, M., A. Ostrom, R. Roundtree and M.J. Bitner (2000), 'Self-service technologies: Understanding customer satisfaction with technology-based service encounters', *Journal of Marketing*, **64** (3), 50–64.

Strandvik, T. (1994), *Tolerance Zones in Perceived Service Quality*, Helsinki: Swedish School of Economics, Finland.

Tax, S.S. and F.I. Stuart (2001), 'Designing service performances', *Marketing Management*, **10** (2), 8–9.

Venkatraman, M. and T. Nelson (2008), 'From servicescape to consumption-space: A photo-elicitation study of Starbucks in the new China', *Journal of International Business Studies*, **39** (6), 1010–26.

Williams, J.A. and H.H. Anderson (2005), 'Engaging customers in service creation: A theatre perspective', *Journal of Services Marketing*, **19** (1), 13–23.

Zeithaml, V.A., L.L. Berry and A. Parasuraman (1993), 'The nature of determinants of customer expectations of services', *Journal of the Academy of Marketing Science*, **21** (1), 1–12.

PART V

Cultural spaces

9.   Cities lead

Erika Sauer

By the end of the twenty-first century, ten billion people will inhabit our planet. According to a United Nations study (United Nations, 2014), today more than half of the people in the world live in cities; by the year 2100, 8.5 billion people of the 10.9 billion (78 per cent) will be city dwellers. Cities are hubs of economic and social power, as they represent concentrations of ideas, skills, finance and development (Heyzer, 2014). Cities lead their inhabitants in many ways. Factors such as history, geography, climate, specific weather patterns, traffic, population, urban planning strategies, topography, religion, law, culture and politics all have an effect on how cities' residents live and move around in the city. City residents are driven not only by their own personal needs and daily routines, but also, very mundanely, by the city's grid, traffic arteries and public transport.

Large cities, whether they are political, financial or cultural centres, function as display windows for the outside world. They showcase their nations' culture, aesthetics, development and world view, thus leading the thoughts and emotions of people on a more abstract level.

Cities are rarely planned from scratch. Cities have aspirations and histories. There are places to be avoided and places to be visited. City-dwellers are driven by their dreams, but also by their nightmares. Cities have heroes and villains, domes of worship, places of commerce and sites of pleasure. People develop their cities, sometimes individually without participation of the authorities, sometimes under their control and guidance.

TWO DIFFERENT METROPOLISES

New York and Jakarta, located on opposite sides of the world, do not appear to share much at first glance. New York is a phenomenon; the Big Apple is a strong and alluring brand. Jakarta, by contrast, is a megacity largely unknown outside Southeast Asia. These cities have different climates, different socioeconomic profiles and very different cultures.

New York is often constructed and reconstructed as a magnet, a melting pot, a dynamic metropolis and one of the world's most popular travel destinations. In a way, New York is the city of cities, said to be the capital of the financial world, exemplifying Western democracy and capitalism.

Jakarta is the capital of Indonesia, the world's fourth-largest country according to population (after China, India and USA) and the world's largest Muslim-majority nation. It is a fast-growing megacity suffering from overpopulation, huge environmental and infrastructural challenges, and rapid (perhaps too rapid) economic development. There are many areas of extreme poverty. According to A.T. Kearney Inc. Jakarta has been identified as the emerging city most likely to assume a global role over the next 20 to 30 years (Chen, 2014). However, there are massive challenges to its inevitable growth. Jakarta is often compared to the smelly durian fruit due to its overpowering combination of exhaust fumes, mouth- and sometimes eye-watering kitchen smells and the almost unbearable stink of waste-filled rivers.

Interestingly, Jakarta and New York were founded by the Dutch at about the same time: Jakarta, then called Batavia, in 1619 and New York in 1624. Since then, New York's population has grown to around eight million people. Jakarta is home to roughly 11 million people. As Rukmana (2013) states, estimates of the city's daytime population vary from 13 to 20 million. Jakarta metropolitan area, with its 28 million people, is ranked as the world's second-largest urban area, while New York and its surrounding areas rank eighth.

THEORETICAL UNDERPINNINGS AND METHOD

There is a growing interest in the role that leadership plays in the continuing shaping and re-shaping of place (Stough, 2003; Sotarauta, 2005, 2009; Gibney et al., 2009; Stimson et al., 2009; Collinge and Gibney, 2010). Regional and urban studies researchers often see leadership as a personal, individual phenomenon (asking, for example, 'What does a leader do?'), whereas this chapter argues that the cities themselves exert leadership. Cities lead because space influences organized action. Research on aesthetic leadership and space explores the symbolic meanings and inherent power issues reflected in spaces and places. The relationship between leadership and space is twofold: physical places form and shape leadership constructions, while, simultaneously, leadership produces social, experienced spaces (Ropo et al., 2013). The idea that leadership is a construction and an experience rather than an influence that some individuals exert on others is a very novel approach amongst the mainstream leadership scholars.

We argue that people make subjective judgements of physical places based on their embodied, sensuous experiences. This means that material places have the power to lead people, and that spaces and places can thus function as (substitutes for) individual leaders. While this does not take place objectively, but rather through subjective personal experience, the experience of material places cannot be reduced to managerial or architectural plans and intentions in order to construct a certain kind of leadership. The performative nature of material place occurs through subjective embodied experience (ibid.), meaning that our experience of the space will guide the usage and the function of the space. For example, when walking into a park, we quickly get the idea if walking on the grass is allowed or even encouraged, if the park is safe or to be avoided, or if the park is a botanical masterpiece, made to be admired and watched, not stepped on or touched.

In 1970, Stanley Milgram wrote about the experience of living in cities. His psychological perspective on city life often focused on population density and heterogeneity. While studying the experience of living in the city, Milgram was interested in cities' atmosphere. Through discussions with city inhabitants, he tried to understand what constitutes atmosphere: myths and expectations, weather, visual components, tempo and pace, and so on. He also analysed the population base (residents from overseas or from rural areas nearby) and the specific historic conditions under which urban overload took place, studying the values and the guidelines according to which the city developed (commercial, aristocratic, administrative etc.). The following section will touch upon some of the points that, according to Milgram, constitute city atmosphere and city experience.

Examining the role of material place in understanding embodied aspects of leadership emphasizes the importance of revisiting the ontology of leadership. The concept of materiality in leadership is important from a phenomenological perspective (Alvesson and Sveningsson, 2003; Ladkin, 2010), but what do we mean by material leadership? The material conditions that affect the understanding, creation and maintenance of leadership are social constructions. The discussion of space and place in leading and organizing explores the power of a material place (such as a city) to shape people's actions, interpretations and judgements (Ropo et al., 2013).

The Frankfurt School's critical theorists (notably Horkheimer, Adorno and Marcuse), post-structuralist research on power relations (for example, Foucault's analysis of Panopticon), and the rise of aesthetic epistemology in organization studies (Linstead and Höpfl, 2000) have broadened academic understanding of the relations between physical and social materiality.

To recognize 'the spirit of a place' (Dale, 2005) and to recognize the role of power in organizing aesthetic experiences, research methodology must be sensitive to the studied phenomena. Aesthetic epistemology that legitimizes sense-based data such as emotions, bodily sensations, intuitions and mental representations (Strati, 2007) offers a sound base for recognizing, as well as analysing and reporting, mutually constitutive elements between space and its social impact.

The following discussion of New York and Jakarta illustrates some ways in which these two very different cities lead their inhabitants. The discussion is based on research conducted while producing a documentary film on cities. This research included 16 interviews, each about 40 to 60 minutes long, and about 20 hours of film material related to these cities. The interviewees were asked about culture, work, leadership and life in Jakarta (December 2013) and New York (September 2014). Interviewees included businesspersons, architects, university professors, lawyers, artists, maids, teachers and relocation agents. The discussion is also based on the researcher's personal experience living in both cities.

This research identifies a number of themes: how the scarce space in cities is shared; how the rich and the poor living in the same area divide the space; how city planning and traffic arrangements lead us into, inside and out of cities; how institutions, history and memory guide us; and how the spaces and practices of religion, recreation and relaxation push and pull us. These are mundane, everyday examples of how cities lead us.

HIGHS AND LOWS: CITIES LEADING THE RICH AND THE POOR

In both New York and Jakarta, the most striking urban landmarks are skyscrapers. These tall buildings, each of which seems to strive to reach higher than its neighbours, symbolize growing commercial and industrial power. A New York based architect stated:

> It's crucial for design, and for architecture, to be able to be clear, to present itself, to be able to guide people – along the lines of why they are in a space – what's special about that space, what becomes something they can use or understand. (Architect Alan Barlis, 3 September 2013)

Scarce resources are expensive. In New York and Jakarta, there is a limited amount of land suitable and available for construction. Land prices are soaring, and the calculations of returns on investment are checked and re-checked. In response to the lack of available land, the average building height constantly increases. Most people still live in two- or three-storey houses, but the average height of a high-rise is about

45 floors. The second-largest English daily newspaper in Jakarta, *The Jakarta Globe*, announced in August 2013 that construction had begun on the 113-storey high-rise Signature Tower. When visiting Jakarta city centre, one cannot help but notice that almost all high-rises display signs for banks and corporations. As in New York, the towers are known by their names rather than their street addresses. The builders and architects hope that their creations will become iconic landmarks.

For now most high-rises are office buildings, but more and more of the new constructions in Jakarta are combinations of offices, apartments, shopping centres and hotels, and sometimes even schools, hospitals and kindergartens. They are almost like postmodern villages. In congested areas, these big complexes offer residents the benefit of seldom having to leave the area if they work within the same complex. Those who have the means are willing to pay for the luxury of avoiding a daily commute.

Cities are still commonly divided into areas for work, areas for living and areas for pleasure. In New York, especially Manhattan, certain areas become almost eerily empty at night because of their high concentration of offices and lack of residential buildings. Areas such as the Broadway theatre district, on the other hand, wake up in the evening as the entertainment industry swings into full gear. The division between poor and rich areas is deep and narrow in these two cities. In New York, for example, the townhouses and high-rise apartments of the Upper East Side (east of Central Park) shift suddenly to housing projects and shabbier blocks north of 100th Street. The same trend applies on the West Side, although it is a less affluent and more diverse neighbourhood. Sometimes just one block, or even a single street, marks the dividing line between immense wealth and desperate poverty. These lines blur when gentrification takes place, but gentrification does not eliminate poverty or guarantee that cities become better places to live.

The less glamorous areas outside of Manhattan, for example in Brooklyn, are full of old industrial buildings that have begun to lure artists in need of big spaces. In the words of one restaurant owner, 'I think what attracted people initially were the low rents, and the artistic community' (Ben, 15 September 2013). With artists come restaurants, shops, and avant-garde families with children, who in turn need schools. Rents soar, pushing lower-income residents out of the neighbourhood. This is a classic example of gentrification.

Gentrification often adds to the density problem. In Jakarta, for instance, the nouveau riche are taking over the already upscale houses in Menteng. This results in more built space for fewer people. A higher density of square metres does not necessarily mean a higher density of inhabitants in the same area: the plot of land of 500 m^2 may have had ten small houses for 50 people but when gentrification takes place, the ten houses are torn down and the same 500 m² will have a house of 1000 m² where a family of seven will live. The same is true in the Kemang area. Over the past 20 years, this area has been overtaken by large houses with large gardens. There are fewer people but more cars. A similar pattern has emerged in the Sudirman Central Business District (SCBD), where thousands of families have been displaced over the past 15 years (Kusumawijaya, 2009).

Despite their problems with population size and density, New York and Jakarta remain lucrative places where people want to live. In New York, the cost of living forms a 'natural' barrier for people aspiring to move there. In Jakarta, despite the government's efforts to restrict moving into the capital city, Jakarta is growing uncontrollably. Overpopulation creates congestion and leads to soaring living costs, along with other severe environmental and societal problems. According to the United Nations Human Settlements Programme (United Nations, 2012), an estimated 40 per cent of the population in Asian megacities such as Jakarta live in urban informal settlements, or illegal constructions.

In New York one can easily find neighbourhoods where the average resident's income is far below the national poverty line. Poverty, however, is relative; it looks different in Jakarta than it does in New York. In Jakarta the poor live in informal settlements or illegal constructions that look like temporary huts made of abandoned pieces of wood and cor-rugated iron. Real estate developers have the power to tear down these unlicensed constructions. In New York, on the other hand, low-income settlements known as housing projects are an established part of the city. Subsidized housing maintains the city's heterogeneity. An ethnically and financially heterogeneous population is considered an integral part of the cityscape. New York is not attempting to be a carefree wonderland for the rich. It could be argued that cities need people who are willing to work in low-paying jobs and provide services for the rich. These cities would not function without their poor.

Money is not the only factor that defines city boundaries. Different ethnicities, religious groups, professions or other groups of like-minded people often choose to live close to one another. In Jakarta, ethnic Chinese residents cluster to the north and east of the city centre. Many foreigners choose to live close to other foreigners in areas where there are suitable services and shops. In Manhattan, there have historically been neighbour-hoods dominated by Italians, Chinese, Irish, and so on, but rising housing prices have forced these communities to relocate farther from the city centre. Brooklyn, for instance, is now home to the world's second-largest Hasidic Jewish community. Some New York neighbourhoods are char-acterized by one particular profession. Many residents of the Rockaway area, for example, are firefighters. In Jakarta these divisions are even more visible. Distinct neighbourhoods are dominated by traditional professions such as cloth merchants, furniture makers and iron welders. Shop owners often live in the same area, if not in the same building.

MOVING AROUND THE CITY: TRAFFIC, WATER AND WASTE

'City cultures are defined by their plans. Los Angeles is subdivisions, Paris is broad boulevards, Vienna is the Ringstrasse, and New York is the grid', says Sarah Henry, museum deputy director and chief curator in New York. 'The grid has shaped this vibrant city, imposing an order and controlling its chaos' (Jaffe, 2011). When travelling by road into New York City, traffic flows across bridges and through tunnels towards the city's core: Manhattan. The grid layout in Manhattan is an excellent example of farsighted city planning.

In the early nineteenth century, most of the 96 000 or so residents of New York City were packed into homes near Manhattan's southern tip. The island's principal artery of transportation was not majestic Broadway or sleek Fifth Avenue but a winding dirt route known as the Boston Post Road. The area above what's now Canal Street was divided into large green estates, and someone describing the environment on Manhattan as a whole would have been more likely to use the word bucolic than congested. . . Today the streets and avenues that constitute Manhattan's grid feel like the very bones of the island – no less essential to the city's life than the skeletal system is to our own – but it wasn't until the master plan of 1811 that this scheme came into being (ibid.).

As an example, one of our interviewees, an architect, described the difference between the south part of Manhattan, where there are small curved streets as opposed to the rest of the city where the grid defines the landscape and the experience:

> We tried to understand downtown Manhattan, all grown up on the original city streets, which are very much on a curving tiny small scale – especially as a counterpoint to the grid in the rest of the city, which most of the people are used to – and many people think of when they think of New York, which is rather easy to use and has sky at the end of all the streets. . .one could be standing in that tight construction and see the sky or see the river and have some sense of place markers. (Alan, Architect, 20 September 2013)

In the second half of nineteenth century there were approximately 800 000 people living in Batavia (the Dutch name for Jakarta). During the

Dutch era, city planners concentrated on areas where the Europeans lived. As the result, these areas, which are dominated by government buildings and affluent private housing, resemble European cities.

After the Dutch left, Jakarta's population exploded in the 1950s and has since continued to expand. Family-planning policies and migration limits failed to control population growth. Major decisions about city planning were made in the 1950s, and these decisions continue to affect the city today. President Soekarno, who was in power from 1945 until 1967, had a strong vision to build Jakarta into the greatest city possible (Cybriwsky and Ford, 2001), to symbolize the rise of new independent Indonesia. He wanted Jakarta to have Monas – a 132-metre-high national monument (a very symbolic structure) – modern government buildings, department stores, shopping plazas, luxurious hotels, the sports facilities of Senayan that were used for the 1962 Asian Games, Asia's biggest mosque of Istiqlal, new parliament buildings and the waterfront recreation area at Ancol.

Very little remains of the historical grid. A clear, logical grid facilitates an accurate addressing system, which allows people to find places, deliver post and navigate the city. How does one navigate a place where no such grid or system exists? Jakarta's main roads are often mentioned when giving an address, but these addresses provide only rough guidance for finding small alleys. It is usual that a group of small streets have the same name, but the streets have increasing numbers. In addition to street numbers, there are house numbers. These numbers often refer to the chronological order in which the houses were built rather than the order in which the houses are located on the street. Most importantly, the sheer number of people in Jakarta helps residents and visitors find their way. There are always people to ask.

Jakarta's traffic flows on main roads with four or five lanes, or along narrow lanes sometimes wide enough for only one car at a time. The city's traffic arteries were planned long ago, and today the road system is insufficient. The density of the city centre, along with a general unwillingness to make unpopular decisions such as removing or destroying thousands of homes, has paralyzed long-range transportation development in Jakarta.

Indonesia is a developing country. This is most evident in the sorry state of waste management and water treatment. In Jakarta, less than 3 per cent of the city's buildings are on the sewer system (Diani, 2009). The rich areas can afford effective waste management, but the poor areas cannot. This makes the poor areas difficult to inhabit. Waste leads to unhealthy conditions in some parts of the city, and only the poorest residents live in these areas.

Both Jakarta and New York are coastal cities. Proximity to the sea makes these cities vulnerable to forces of nature. Jakarta floods several times per year, causing casualties, disease and financial loss. Flooding also occurs in New York, but less frequently.

Besides trying to avoid flooding, dirty water, piles of waste or the like, people want to avoid areas where they feel uncomfortable because of other direct threats to their safety. When talking to people in New York, safety was often mentioned as an important factor when choosing in which part of the city to live. The people also talked about the need to have a sense of community around them.

The five boroughs of New York are connected by bridges and tunnels. New York has an extremely efficient public transport system. Its subway is one of the oldest and busiest underground mass rapid transportation systems in the world, with almost 5.5 million rides per weekday. In less than half an hour one can travel more than 21 km from the northern tip of Manhattan to the southernmost station at Battery Park. In addition to the subway system, the Metropolitan Transportation Authority offers bus, ferry and train services. With so many public transportation options, including New York's fleet of yellow taxicabs, it is no wonder that, according to Wikipedia, over half of New York households do not own a car, whereas in the rest of the USA, only 8 per cent of households lack a car (Wikipedia, n.d.).

Besides using mass transportation, New Yorkers walk and bike. Walking is easy, as the walkways are broad and even. More and more bike lanes are being built to accommodate the growing number of cyclists. Jakartans, by contrast, do not walk. Walking is not an option because there are no proper walkways. Jakartans drive motorbikes or take *ojeks* (small moped cars), buses, mini-buses and taxis. Rich people have multiple cars – often at least one car per family member. They spend hours each day commuting to and from work. By the end of 2013, the average vehicle speed in Jakarta had slowed to as low as 10 km per hour (Suhartono and Utami, 2013). The city's excruciating traffic jams, or *macets*, are amongst the worst in the world. The mass transportation system is completely insufficient, making three-hour rides (each way) the norm for people living outside the city. Interviewee Ibrahim notes that 'you see people willing to travel two to three hours one way, so probably four to six hours return from suburb to Jakarta and get back to their house, not seeing their children going to school. Probably when they go home the kids already went to sleep – just to fulfil the basic needs' (Ibrahim, 4 December 2013).

Rush hours influence Jakartans' behaviour. City-dwellers constantly talk about Jakarta's traffic and compare it to traffic in other big cities. Workers who have any say in their schedules try to come into the city as early or late as possible in order to avoid the rush hour traffic from 7.30 to 9.00 am and 3.30 to 7.30 pm. For most workers, however, it is virtually impossible to avoid rush hour travel. Commuters turn their cars into mini offices, or even homes, with drinks, food, television, pillows, as well as clothes and shoes for every occasion. City leaders and politicians attempt to influence traffic flow in different ways in order to lead people's thoughts and achieve political goals. Demonstrations are often organized in places that severely slow down traffic. For example, demonstrations are held almost daily in the traffic circle in the middle of the city.

Jakarta's architecture can be divided into roughly three categories: city centre skyscrapers, villa areas for high-income residents and traditional two- and three-level houses for the middle class and the poor. Most people live in the third category of building. This *kampung* (traditional village) structure has remained unchanged in many areas for decades, if not centuries, not taking into account the modern requirements for sewage, fresh water supply, waste management and car traffic. The *kampung* consists of very narrow lanes better suited to pedestrians and motorcyclists than cars. There are no street names or grid in the *kampung*.

MEMORIES AND MEMORIALS AS LEADERS

In organized space, the political, social and cultural meanings and connotations, and the complex relationships between power and space, are obvious. Since the Enlightenment, there has been a strong ideology regarding architecture as an important part of societal change, recognizing architecture's power to influence people by changing their environment (Saarikangas, 2006). This ideology is not limited to public architecture, but is seen in the use of all space. The wish to control the environment, to leave a mark on history, and to change existing space was exemplified by Baron Haussmann and Napoleon III's efforts to reshape Paris into a modern, strategic space where residents could move around easily while viewing monuments (ibid.).

Political monuments come in many forms. Almost all historical landmarks in Jakarta date back to the Dutch era. The presidential palace, as well as the most highly valued political buildings, were built in the nineteenth and twentieth centuries. Presidents Soekarno (in office 1945–67) and Soeharto (in office 1967–98) built various monuments and statues. Soekarno's national monument, Monas (fondly called the 'last erection of Soekarno'), stands in the middle of a vast field and is a popular gathering place for national celebrations and parades. The military and police have a visible presence in the city in the form of multiple rather pompous build-ings and statues reflecting their tasks. Statues are straightforward monu-ments symbolizing position and prestige.

Jakarta's tumultuous political past is still visible in the city; signs of Dutch colonization are sources of both pride and shame. Many cities have destroyed their symbols of dictatorship, but this is not the case in Jakarta. The monuments built by the first president, Soekarno, as well as the numerous statues erected by the next president and dictator, Soeharto (who loved sculpture, often interfering with the artistic process), are still intact. Signs of the unrest following the 1998 overthrow of the Soeharto regime are still visible in the ruins of burned buildings and battered walls full of bullet holes.

The centre of Jakarta can be divided into constructions that are there to be used (commercial buildings, service buildings), constructions designed to be respected and commemorated (the national monument, president's palace, national museum, statues) and constructions that are ignored (bullet-ridden buildings in Chinatown, mouldy and ruined historical buildings from the Dutch era).

Since New York is not a capital city, national political institutions do not play a big role in the skyline. The Metropolitan Museum, the Museum of Natural History, the Guggenheim and Grand Central Station are important landmarks in New York. They represent an appreciation of history and civilization, and they are good examples of buildings constructed for public use. There is something uplifting in the idea that, through the availability of these public buildings, every individual citizen and visitor is respected. The buildings have a sacred historical quality, partly due to sheer size, but also due to their altruistic function, design, atmosphere and acoustics. In mid-town, skyscrapers bearing the names of industrial conglomerates remind us of the power of the industrialists. The iconic and stylish United Nations building, a symbol of political power, has lost some of its prominence due to taller and glossier high-rises next to it.

New York's architecture proves that something that does not exist anymore can still draw people to where it once was. The twin towers of the World Trade Center, though no longer standing, remain central to people's mental cartography of New York. The memorial site is popular and commercialized. Sometimes things that 'do not exist' still lead people. In Jakarta, as in many places in Indonesia, there are houses, parks, trees and other places that people say are haunted. Even in the congested megacity, these places stay empty.

PLACES OF RELIGION, RECREATION, RELAXATION AND CONSUMERISM

There was a time when church builders made sure that the church tower was the highest structure in the vicinity, majestically ruling the landscape. Those days are long gone in New York, where churches, mosques and synagogues are squeezed between skyscrapers. Congregations gather, almost unnoticeably, in the hustle and bustle of the city. Tourists make an exception as they queue for the gospel services in Harlem on Sundays. In New York, where freedom of religion and separation of church and state are strongly embraced and enforced, religious built monuments are privately funded.

Jakarta's Istiqlal mosque is an example of how religion and politics interact. It is the largest mosque in Southeast Asia, able to host a congregation of 120000 people. President Soekarno, who had the task of uniting the region's 17000 islands, 600 languages and hundreds of cultures, wanted a symbol that would lift the spirits of the Muslim majority and engender pride in Indonesia – a building representing national unity, tolerance and secularism. Across the street from the mosque is the Jakarta Cathedral, and the temples of the Chinese neighbourhoods are nearby.

In Jakarta, religion makes people move. People constantly come and go in mosques and *mushollahs* (small prayer rooms). Mosques are important fixtures in the city. Besides being seen, mosques are also heard. The prayer call, five times a day, is loud and clear. The midday prayer is important, and all men go to mosque for the Friday noon prayer. Everyone is allowed to stop working and attend prayers. Workplaces, malls and all public facilities have a *mushollah* where people gather for prayer. During the fasting month, the Friday prayer is even more important than usual. At noon mosques fill up quickly, forcing many to stay on the street. This is not a problem because the sides of the street are quickly cleared of cars, street vendors and stalls. Carpets are rolled out, making room for all to attend.

If New York is considered a mecca of consumerism and shopping, Jakarta has adopted the same culture. When comparing the purchasing power in New York and in Jakarta, it is unbelievable how Jakarta now has over 173 malls (Trianita, 2013) whereas according to Wikipedia, there are only about 20 malls in New York City (and about 40 within the surrounding area). Malls have become a distinct characteristic of this developing city. Jakarta's malls are not only places for shopping, they are also a way of life and a source of entertainment for citizens. People spend whole days in them, not necessarily buying anything. For most people, the items for sale are beyond their budget. The median monthly income in Jakarta is 5 million rupiah (about 500 US dollars) (Interview with Mr Milne-Davies,

24 April 2014, Chamber of Commerce, Jakarta). However, malls offer food courts, movie theatres, playgrounds and climate-controlled areas for strolling around, meeting friends and people watching. It is as if the old marketplace culture and European café culture had merged with Disney-like displays. Sports, entertainment and food draw people together. In New York, Yankee Stadium and Madison Square Garden attract sports enthusiasts. Broadway, with its theatres and neon lights, attracts enter-tainment seekers. 'I was really drawn to New York City also because of the arts and the culture the film and the theatre and just the excitement of that is you're growing up as a kid, it's New York City. It's the biggest city in the world' (James, screenwriter, 14 September 2013).

In Jakarta, the football stadium is bursting with fans throughout the season. Also, the inexpensive concerts held outside, street festivals and exhibitions draw vast crowds. However, the most popular leisure activity and and most beloved interest of Jakartans is the food. For everyone, it is normal to get a meal from a street-side vendor. For poor people this may be a necessity, as their living quarters often lack options for cooking. The middle class frequent street kitchens because it is quick and easy to grab a meal from these vendors. Sometimes even rich people buy from street vendors. Rumours of exceptionally good food stalls spread quickly, and a small traffic jam in front of a food stall is as sure a sign of quality as a Michelin star. There are very exclusive and expensive restaurants for the gourmands, as well as food courts and more simple restaurants for the middle class. Food attracts people, no matter where you are.

When studying a map of Jakarta, the biggest green areas are golf courses. New York City's largest green space is Central Park, which con-tains a zoo, playgrounds, art exhibits, a rowing pond, a carousel, several jogging tracks, woods and a reservoir. Central Park offers recreation, sports, culture and entertainment for everyone. Establishing and preserv-ing a park of its scale is a remarkable accomplishment, especially from a financial perspective, considering that land is scarce and prices are forever soaring.

In Jakarta, the non-existent city planning, lust for real estate profits, and rampant corruption have left little room for green areas and parks. In theory, everyone agrees that more greenery is needed, not only to improve citizens' quality of life, but also to absorb moisture from the recurrent floods. Additional green spaces are not likely to become a reality however, because land ownership and the rules for government land acquisition are not clear. One could say that the political will or courage just is not there. It seems that people would rather spend their time in shopping malls and food stalls than in Jakarta's scattered green areas. The parks are empty while the malls are full.

THE IDEA OF A BETTER LIFE

The simplest example of how physical spaces lead is the fact that we cannot walk through the wall, but need to look for an opening in it. Cities lead at a concrete level; we have to follow the roads when driving a car. However, we read the city with all of our senses, evaluating our surroundings and letting this knowledge guide us. The city's atmosphere guides us, generating a dialogue between the environment and the people living it.

Cities have 'ready-made' landmarks such as historical buildings and iconic places, statues and towers that function as points of orientation. These places become part of our collective memory: benchmarks of what is valuable, worth preserving and worth observing and admiring. In this way, the inhabitants of the city are in constant 'discussion' with their surroundings, and simultaneously aware of how other people interact with the surroundings.

When asked about their cities, interviewees discussed common themes. Jakarta residents talked about traffic, population density, food and shopping. They also evaluated different areas of the city based on the quality of the buildings, cleanliness, congestion, location and services. In New York, people mentioned the heterogeneity of the population, along with the city's fast pace and dynamism. New Yorkers cherished the abundant stimuli, freedom of choice and the possibility of remaining relatively anonymous. Historical buildings got much more attention in New York than in Jakarta. In New York, people described their search for a safe, welcoming community. In Jakarta, safety or the community were not themes of discussion.

Because cities are dynamic places, it is possible to have multiple interpretations of them that are equally valid. Cities influence our thoughts about what is good, beautiful and worth pursuing. Different cities encourage different lifestyle choices; life in the tropics is different from life above the Arctic Circle, and highly developed infrastructure offers possibilities that are not available in a more challenging environment. Finally, the experiences are subjective and individual: my city leads me differently from yours, even if we are neighbours.

REFERENCES

Alvesson, M. and S. Sveningsson (2003), 'The great disappearing act: Difficulties in doing "leadership"', *Leadership Quarterly*, **14** (3), 359–81.
Chen, S. (2014), 'Jakarta likeliest emerging city to rise, Kearney says', *BloombergBusiness*, 15 April, accessed 30 January 2015 at http://www.

bloomberg.com/news/articles/2014-04-14/jakarta-likeliest-emerging-city-to-rise-kearney-says.

Collinge, C. and J. Gibney (2010), 'Connecting place, policy and leadership', *Policy Studies*, **31** (4), 379–91.

Cybriwsky, R. and L.R. Ford (2001), 'City profile: Jakarta', *Cities*, **18** (3), 199–210.

Dale, K. (2005), 'Building a social materiality', *Organization*, **12** (5), 649–78.

Diani, H. (24.7.2009), 'The sewage: Poor sanitation means illness and high costs', *Jakarta Globe*, accessed 25 May 2014 at http://www.thejakartaglobe.com/archive/the-sewage-poor-sanitation-means-illness-and-high-costs/.

Gibney, J., S. Copeland and A. Murie (2009), 'Toward a "new" strategic leadership of place for the knowledge-based economy', *Leadership*, **5** (1), 5–23.

Heyzer, N. (2014), 'Mastering our urban future', *Project Syndicate*, accessed 25 May 2014 at http://www.project-syndicate.org/commentary/noeleen-heyzer-on-the-six-steps-needed-to-create-livable-and-sustainable-cities.

Jaffe, E. (2011), 'A virtual history of Manhattan's grid', *City Lab*, accessed 30 January 2015 at http://www.citylab.com/design/2011/11/visual-history-manhattans-grid/541/.

Kusumawijaya, M. (2009), 'Density: Myth and reality', *Rujak*, accessed 25 May 2014 at http://rujak.org/2009/08/density-myth-and-reality/.

Ladkin, D. (2010), *Rethinking Leadership: A New Look at Old Leadership Questions*, Cheltenham, UK and Northampton, MA, USA: Edward Elgar Publishing.

Linstead, S. and H. Höpfl (2000), *The Aesthetics of Organization*, London: Sage.

Milgram, S. (1970), 'The experience of living in cities', *Science*, **167** (13), 1461–68.

Ropo, A., E. Sauer and P. Salovaara (2013), 'Embodiment of leadership through material place', *Leadership*, **9** (3), 378–95.

Rukmana, D. (2014), 'The megacity of Jakarta: Problems, challenges and planning efforts', *Indonesia's Urban Studies* [blog], accessed 25 May 2014 at http://indonesiaurbanstudies.blogspot.co.uk/2014/03/the-megacity-of-jakarta-problems.html.

Saarikangas, K. (2006), *Eletyt tilat ja sukupuoli: Asukkaiden ja ympäristön kulttuurisia kohtaamisia* [Lived Spaces and Gender: Cultural Encounters of Inhabitants and Environments], Vaasa: Waasa Graphics Oy.

Sotarauta, M. (2005), 'Shared leadership and dynamic capabilities in regional development', in I. Sagan and H. Halkier (eds), *Regionalism Contested: Institution, Society and Governance*, Aldershot, UK: Ashgate, pp. 53–72.

Sotarauta, M. (2009), 'Social innovations, institutional change and economic performance: Making sense of structural adjustment processes in industrial sectors, regions and societies', *Regional Studies*, **43** (4), 637–8.

Stimson, R., R. Stough and M. Salazar (2009), *Leadership and Institutions in Regional Endogenous Development*, Cheltenham, UK and Northampton, MA, USA: Edward Elgar Publishing.

Stough, R. (2003), 'Strategic management of places and policy', *The Annals of Regional Science*, **37** (2), 179–201.

Strati, A. (2007), 'Sensible knowledge and practice-based learning', *Management Learning*, **38** (1), 61–77.

Suhartono, H. and W. Utami (2013), 'Jakarta traffic jams drive minimart profit jump', *Jakarta Globe*, accessed 25 May 2014 at http://www.thejakartaglobe.com/news/jakarta/jakarta-traffic-jams-drive-minimart-profit-jump/.

Wikipedia (n.d.), 'Transportation in New York City', accessed 30 January 2015 at wikipedia.org/wiki/Transportation_in_New_York_City.

Trianita, L. (2013), 'Jokowi: Too many malls in Jakarta', *TEMPO.CO*, accessed 25 May 2014 at http://en.tempo.co/read/news/2013/09/16/057513745/Jokowi-Too-Many-Malls-in-Jakarta.

United Nations (2012), *State of the World's Cities 2012/2013*, accessed 30 January 2015 at https://sustainabledevelopment.un.org/content/documents/745habitat.pdf.

United Nations (2014), *World Urbanization Prospects: The 2014 Revision, Highlights*, accessed 30 January 2015 at http://esa.un.org/unpd/wup/Highlights/WUP2014-Highlights.pdf.

10. Culture matters: space and leadership in a cross-cultural perspective

Tor Grenness

> But when the manager sits in the same room as the people he is supposed to manage, what is the manager supposed to do then?
> (Russian business professor after having been told that a Norwegian firm decided to choose open-space offices in its new head office building)

INTRODUCTION

The reaction of the Russian professor is not surprising. Traditional office design, in which managers have their own offices that are equipped with a wall-to-wall carpet and are physically distant from the managers' subordinates, definitely signals the relevant status levels, which many still believe is important in organizations that desire such a stratification of the workforce. One may say that the ordering of space in buildings is really about the ordering of relationships between people. The outburst by the Russian professor relates to the fear of managers losing status, respect and power if they have to give up their offices and place themselves among the people they are supposed to manage.

The perspective of this chapter is that of international business and management. Although no authoritative definition of the term 'international business and management' exists, the authors of popular textbooks in the field seem to agree that while international business is about firms engaging in international (cross-border) economic activities, international management is the process of developing strategies, designing and operating systems and working with people around the world to ensure sustained competitive advantage for these firms (see, for example, Bartlett et al., 2008; Peng and Meyer, 2011). All organizations, including those that operate across borders and national cultures, have a set of explicit or implicit corporate values and shared beliefs that greatly influence the way they operate. For managers of multinational corporations (MNCs), it is of particular importance to see to it that the corporate values and the foundations of leadership are accepted and endorsed throughout the firm's international system. Consequently, a critical design problem for top MNC management is how to choose organizational mechanisms that enhance the flow of corporate values and management principles. In spite of this, there is a lack of research on the strategies that MNC headquarters can use to ensure that corporate values and management systems are transferred across various units (Bjørkman et al., 2004). Even in research articles in which these issues are explicitly acknowledged and discussed (see, for example, Gupta and Govindarajan, 2000), the design of office environments is never mentioned when various organizational mechanisms with potential impacts on the flow of values and management systems are discussed.

To my mind, this is somewhat surprising because organizational changes, such as a shift to a less hierarchical management structure, an increase in diversity among employees and an increase in mobile or tele-commuting employees, are creating powerful new ways of working that increase efficiency and productivity, but they are also resulting in a loss of organizational identity and overall cohesion among organizational members. In order to overcome the negative effects of such changes, an MNC developing a workplace design strategy that expresses the corporation's values and philosophies would serve as a consistent message to employees everywhere: 'With us, you have to get used to working in an open-space non-hierarchical physical environment because we think that office space is not a neutral asset but an opportunity to express what this corporation stands for'. For many, choosing open-space office solutions is regarded as a rather radical choice, and, with reference to the Russian professor cited above, open-space offices are indeed creating challenges.

There is little doubt that an open-space office design effectively reduces the power traditionally linked to rank or position in an organization. Organizations are usually designed in ways that ensure that certain structures, which symbolize the various positions occupied by individuals, are brought out. In this way, the physical structure of the organization, that is, the size and location of its offices, underlines the power structure. In structures that are centralized, we typically find that organizations are designed as power hierarchies, with centralized decision-making and tight control over divisions and departments. However, because the structures of organizations are found to mirror to a certain extent those of the socie-ties in which they were created (see, for example, House et al., 2004 for a discussion), it is not surprising that 'organizational pyramids' are most common in societies with a high power distance, which lays the foundation for 'societal pyramids'. The concept of 'power distance' stems from the findings of the Dutch professor and cross-cultural management scholar Geert Hofstede (1980). He argues that the power-distance index measures the extent to which the less powerful members of organizations and institutions accept and expect that power and status will be distributed unequally. Consequently, the index represents inequality (more versus less) as it is defined from below and thus suggests that a society's or an organization's level of inequality is endorsed by the followers as much as by the leaders. Consequently, there is reason to hypothesize that implementing open-space offices in organizations found in high-power-distance societies will lead to more turbulence than doing so in organizations found in societies characterized by equality and a low power distance.

Relationships between people in organizations can take on different forms. Such relationships can be vertical, horizontal or even lateral. In centralized organizations in high-power-distance cultures, vertical relationships will obviously be the dominant form. By 'tearing down the organizational pyramids', which is what actually happens when a flat open-space office solution is implemented, the vertical, top-down relationships between leaders and subordinates will inevitably be replaced by horizontal and even lateral relationships. Hofbauer (2000) has shown that moving from a traditional office design to open-space offices shapes communication, collaboration and interaction. Consequently, the role of the leader, who will no longer be able to benefit from a superior hierarchical position best fitted to a 'command and control' leadership style, will be profoundly affected by the change in architecture. It is probably fair to say that leaders operating in this new context are faced with a range of new and unfamiliar challenges:

> When you are at the same level as the people you are managing and you have no secretary, no status symbol as a manager, you have to convince them even more with your brain and your performance that you are the manager and that you are right to lead them because you have more experience. (An Asian manager who had recently started to work in an open-space office)

WHY THIS TRANSITION IS PARTICULARLY CHALLENGING IN A CROSS-CULTURAL PERSPECTIVE

In the opening chapter of the book *Culture Matters* (Harrison and Huntington, 2000), the authors state that 'culture makes almost all the difference' (p. 2). That culture makes almost *all* the difference may well be debatable, but during the last few decades, I have seen that in order to better understand societies and analyse differences among them, social scientists have increasingly turned to cultural variables to explain differences in areas such as levels of modernization, political development, economic development and performance, gender (in)equality and so forth.

From a management scientist's point of view, the fact that national culture also has a tremendous impact on people's vision and interpretation of leadership has been demonstrated again and again, perhaps most convincingly in the relatively recent GLOBE project (House et al., 2004). This vast cross-national study, which covered more than 60 countries, found that although there are universal aspects of leadership, people from different countries do, in fact, have different criteria for assessing their leaders. What leadership is, as well as what good or bad leadership is, lies in the eye of the beholder. It seems that key cultural differences between nations not only influence employees' perceptions of how they prefer their leaders to lead but will also inevitably influence the leaders' own conception of leadership as well. At the same time, perspectives on leaders and leadership also allow for alternative ways of understanding what leadership is or should be. The ongoing organizational changes described in the introduction of this chapter certainly affect the roles and functions of leaders as well. Leadership as a relational construction between people issues and environment, rather than a distinct role or function, is slowly emerging in the literature (Ladkin, 2010). The traditional leader prototype is, however, still dominating the perception of leadership within Asian cultures (Hofstede, 2007).

Cultural differences across countries can be expressed in many different ways. A number of social scientists have tried to identify the dimensions that constitute a societal culture. The cultural dimensions most frequently referred to are the ones proposed by Hofstede (2001). Power distance, briefly discussed above, is one of them, but GLOBE's cultural dimensions, as well as contributions from Trompenaars (1985) and Schwartz (1994), have all made a substantial impact on our knowledge of cross-cultural organizational behaviour. In an organizational setting, the hierarchy of leaders and subordinates has always been an important and prevalent form of relationship. Hierarchical relationships are characterized by differences in the power, status, dependence and control that the subordinates and their supervisors enjoy. This relationship is, however, moderated by national culture. For example, while 'Brazilians believe that people in positions of authority deserve to be treated with respect and deference' (Javidan et al., 2006, p. 76), Scandinavian subordinates' attitudes to 'the higher ups' are perceived as being non-deferential, and loyalty to the decision-making process may, in many cases, be stronger than loyalty to particular leaders (Schramm-Nielsen et al., 2004).

As has been shown by Hofstede (2007) and House et al. (2004), there is ample evidence that relationships between leaders and followers vary across cultures. In Hofstede's well-known cultural framework, the dimensions 'individualism' and 'collectivism', together with 'power distance', are shown to have the most profound impact on these relationships. While in individual cultures, ties between individuals are loose, individuals in collectivistic countries are integrated into strong, cohesive groups that protect them throughout their lifetimes in exchange for unquestioning loyalty. Given these differences, it is not surprising that the roles and behaviours of leaders also seem to differ across cultures and countries. For example, model leader behaviour patterns differ widely across countries in terms of their emphasis on individualism versus team orientation, particularism versus universalism, performance versus maintenance orientation and reliance on personal abilities, subordinates or rules (see for example, Dorfman and Howell, 1988 and Smith et al., 1996). In line with this reasoning, business leaders from different cultures also tend to perceive their own roles and the power and status vested in them differently. As I have mentioned above, the cultural dimensions of power distance, individualism and collectivism create the most notable differences in organizational behaviour across cultures. The combination of a high power distance and collectivism, which is rather typical of (but not limited to) most Asian and Arab countries, tends to result in a paternalistic leadership style, in which subordinates develop a feeling of obligation, obedience and respect for hierarchical relations. Another consequence of such strong hierarchical structure and power inequality found in high-power-distance/collectivistic cultures is that managers generally enjoy many visual privileges, such as larger offices that are often placed on the top floors, which underpin their rank-based power.

Within the history of organizational studies, not much attention has been paid to the physical environment of organizations, although the physical structuring of organizational action has been an implicit theme in management studies since the early days of Taylorism and the Hawthorne studies (Peltonen, 2008). Still, the majority of studies in organization science describe organizations via concepts such as strategies, charts, structures, culture, norms, behaviours, power and status, with a few exceptions, such as references to the status symbolism of moving into a larger office or the role of the office building as a figurehead for the organization (Bakke and Yttri, 2003). However, in recent years, I have witnessed a growing interest in the physical environment and space in organizations (Kornberger and Clegg, 2006; Elsbach and Pratt, 2007), which has been documented by the growing interest in how the physical environment serves as a symbolic representation of the culture of an organization (Rafaeli and Worline, 1999).

Unfortunately, this growing interest in the consequences of workplace design on organizational behaviour has not yet been adopted by international management scholars. Within the area of international management, particularly international human resource management (IHRM), the questions of how different workplace designs will affect employees' satisfaction and productivity, change the role and function of the leaders and shape the corporate culture deserve to be further investigated. Concern with the effective management of people from different cultural groups is not new. Brewster et al. (2007), for example, cite research in the field of IHRM dating from the 1990s. However, in spite of the growing importance of multinational corporations (MNCs), research in IHRM still tends to centre on traditional topics, such as staffing, performance appraisals and compensation systems. In my opinion, the physical design of subsidiaries' offices deserves to be an integrated part of IHRM studies. At the end of the day, the main objective of HRM is to contribute to the achievement of global competitive advantage through the human resources of the organization. In order to do this, a more strategic approach to HR management seems necessary, and the HRM strategy must be fully integrated with the global strategy of the organization (Goffee and Jones, 1999). It is, however, interesting to note that Walker (1992) states that a strategic approach to HR management implies that opportunities for and barriers to the achievement of business objectives are defined. If the physical layout of the workplace represents an opportunity or a barrier, HR management should consider how this should be handled.

Unfortunately, not many MNCs have given this issue much attention. A notable exception is the Norwegian telecom company Telenor. When Telenor moved to its new head office just outside Oslo in 2001, it decided to design the new workplace so as to create the leading innovative workplace in Scandinavia (Telenor, 2001). The design philosophy was to establish a physical work environment that would be supportive of collaboration and knowledge sharing. Also, Telenor's belief in the Scandinavian way of leading people, that is, a leadership philosophy emphasizing that leaders should be visible, open, accessible and involved, underpins the open-space office solution. Perhaps equally important is the fact that the choice of an open-space office solution supports the central Scandinavian value of equality (Daun, 1986; Grenness, 2011) because this solution means that the majority of status symbols, which historically have been reserved for managers, have been done away with. The indication of rank through office size has been abolished, and managers have no secretaries to take care of many of their day-to-day activities. In short, Telenor exemplifies an ambitious organization development approach in which the physical workplace design is deployed as a truly strategic instrument.

In this connection, it is interesting to note that after more than ten years of experience with the chosen design, in-house surveys of employees including measures of satisfaction and perceptions of the psychosocial work environment have demonstrated that the open-space office design has not impacted the level of job satisfaction of the employees negatively. However, this is Norway. Implementing open-space office solutions in Telenor's subsidiaries in countries that are very culturally distant from Norway could well be a different story.

CULTURE'S CHALLENGES

I'm convinced that architecture has an influence at the social level and that you change the behaviour of people when you change their environment. (Tom Mayne in *NRC Handelsblad*, 1 April 2005)

Ideally, the workplace design strategy of an organization should underpin the corporate strategy. The so-called congruence hypothesis states that the degree to which the strategy, work, people, structure and culture of the organization are aligned will determine the organization's ability to compete and succeed. As I have discussed above, national cultures varies substantially. Culture is composed of certain values that shape one's behaviour and perception of the world (Hofstede and Bond, 1988). Comparative studies of culture show cross-national differences in the values of individuals (Schwartz, 1994; Hofstede, 2001). These differences affect people in business as much as anyone else. The GLOBE research programme (House et al., 2004, p. 19) states that 'societal cultural values and practices also affect organizational form, culture and practice'. No wonder, then, that the shaping of organizations, how decisions are made and what kind of leadership is perceived to be effective differ across nations and cultures.

From a scientific and theoretical perspective, compelling reasons exist for considering the role of societal cultures in influencing leadership and organizational processes. Because the goal of science has traditionally been to develop universally valid theories, there is definitely a need for leadership and organizational theories that transcend cultures. Ever since the American organizational scientists Hair, Ghiselli and Porter asked 'When managers from different countries think about management, do they think about the same thing?' in 1966, we have known that what works in one culture may not work in another. Consequently, Triandis (1993) suggests that leadership researchers will be able to 'fine-tune' theories by investigating cultural variations as parameters of those theories. Also, a focus on cross-cultural issues can help researchers uncover new relationships by including a much broader range of variables that are often not considered in contemporary theories, such as the effects of the physical layout of an organization on leadership and leader–subordinate relationships.

Until recently, a great number of leadership studies have been conducted as if culture was a separate field of study that could be unproblematically left to anthropologists. Fortunately, this is about to change. In an increasingly globalized (business) world, culture – particularly the consequences for organizational and leadership behaviour related to cultural differences – has received more and more attention. Gradually, the recognition that social and organizational life is inherently cultural, that is, inherently shaped and even constituted in part by differences in the ways in which people generate or recognize meaning in social action, has become the norm.

Still, as was briefly mentioned above, studies of international or cross-cultural human resource management have restricted their attention to traditional issues, in which cultural differences are assumed to complicate matters such as compensation practices, management development programmes and so forth. Consequently, theoretical and empirical examples of MNCs that have deliberately changed the physical work environment across their subsidiaries are virtually non-existent. In order to gain more insight, I must therefore rely on the results of more general studies. A typical example is the study of Carlopio and Gardner (1992), who found that removing barriers and enclosures through the use of an open-plan office design reduces satisfaction with the workspace among managers (higher-status workers) but increases satisfaction among lower-status workers. This tells us that eliminating private, enclosed offices, which are recognized as the most widely used physical marker of status in an organization, is obviously difficult for many managers. In line with the above reasoning, I propose that managers from countries characterized by a high power distance, in which the norm is that power and status are unequally distributed, will find this even harder to tackle than managers from low-power-distance, more egalitarian countries.

CASE STUDY – TELENOR

Examples of consequences for leadership taken from global organizations moving from a traditional cell-office solution to an open-space office solution across subsidiaries and cultures are scarce. As we have indicated above, the Norwegian international company Telenor represents one of the rare cases in which a global company has developed a uniform

strategy for the physical layout of its offices across countries and subsidiaries. Based on its experiences with open-space offices in its head office in
Norway, Telenor decided to replicate its office design when it expanded
into Asia a few years ago. Consequently, open-space offices have been
introduced in Telenor's subsidiaries in India, Bangladesh, Thailand,
Pakistan and most recently Myanmar. Interviews with Norwegian Telenor
managers revealed that they did not take any particular notice of cultural
differences between the Norwegian/Scandinavian and Asian cultures
when this decision was made.

However, as I have pointed out above, not only do cultures differ,
but also such differences will affect the central aspects of organizational
behaviour. In particular, such differences will affect the relationship
between managers and subordinates. In order to better understand the
leadership challenges created by the cultural differences between the Asian
and Norwegian cultures, a quick look at typical aspects of the two cultures
is necessary.

Contrasting the Asian and Scandinavian Cultures

A striking example of the difference between the Scandinavian and Asian
cultures was found in the results of a cross-cultural study on business
goals (Hofstede et al., 2002) in which four of India's top five business
goals (family interests, continuity of the business, personal wealth and
power) were among Denmark's bottom five. At the same time, Asia is not
at all a homogeneous entity, so one must be careful in categorizing 'Asian
culture'. Still, across Asian countries and in contrast to the Scandinavian
culture, collectivistic values dominate over individualistic ones. Also, to a
somewhat lesser extent, we find that Asian countries tend to score higher
on power distance than Scandinavian countries (Hofstede, 2007). As I
have discussed above, high-power-distance organizations in high-power-
distance cultures tend to promote vertical relationships. Furthermore,
such relationships promote a top-down hierarchy featuring work situations that are highly structured and in which subordinates are told what to
do (Redding, 1990).

As pointed out above, the combination of high power distance and
collectivism, as is the case in most Asian countries, typically results
in a paternalistic work relationship between superior and subordinate
(Hofstede, 1980). Another way to characterize Asian cultures is to use
the phrase 'dependence of others' (Hofstede, 2007). In an organizational
setting, this dependence is illustrated by the subordinate's dependence on
his or her superior's goodwill. Also, managers generally enjoy many visual
privileges, for example, larger offices that are often placed on the top

floors, separate cafeterias, exclusive parking, and even – as was the case in Thailand before Telenor re-designed the offices – a separate lift, all to underpin their rank-based power.

As for the Scandinavian culture, the classic study by Hofstede (1980) found a rather distinctive cultural profile that was common to the three Scandinavian countries. The Scandinavian countries were categorized as very low in terms of power distance and very high in terms of femininity. Individualism was shown to be moderately high. Scores on uncertainty avoidance varied, but they were generally on the low side. Many reviewers have been sceptical about Hofstede's characterization of the Scandinavian countries as 'feminine'. Much of this is probably due to the confusion caused by the fact that Hofstede's gender-based terms are more often applied to individuals (Smith et al., 2002). Hofstede's conception of a feminine culture, however, is one in which male- and female-gender roles are relatively similar and there is a preference for good working relationships.

In order to focus on a more general value system characterizing the Scandinavian countries, as well as what has recently been called 'the Scandinavian leadership model' (Grenness, 2011), there is one conception or idea that describes the essential value in the Scandinavian culture better than anything else: 'equality' (Kalleberg, 1991; Lindkvist, 1991; Schramm-Nielsen et al., 2004). The value of equality appears to influence all sectors of Scandinavian societies. There seems to be a passion for an equal distribution of economic goods, political influence, regional development, social life chances and cultural experiences. With reference to Hofstede's conception of the 'feminine', a belief in the equality of the sexes is also widespread in Scandinavia. This passion for equality has been documented in several studies (for example, Daun, 1986; Bjerke, 1999). Also, it is important to bear in mind that the common Scandinavian work-life model is in many ways a product of the cultural value of equality (Qvale, 2007). According to the Norwegian Work-Life Forum, the Scandinavian work-life model is described in the following way:

> The way work-life is organized in the Scandinavian countries is different from other regions. In Scandinavia, high productivity is combined with a high standard of living, a high level of employment and a comprehensive social safety net. There is a high level of participation, and equality is strongly expressed. The Scandinavian model has demonstrated its ability to deliver good results. The three Scandinavian countries are at the top of UN measures of quality of life and have a safety net with comprehensive welfare arrangements, such as maternity/paternity leave, sickness benefits and national pension schemes. (Quoted in Qvale, 2007)

The value of equality is also clearly visible in studies of Scandinavian management. Lindkvist (1991) points out that Scandinavian management is characterized by equality, consensus and cooperation: 'The main characteristic of the Nordic alternative is the striving for consensus'. The cooperation between management and employees is emphasized by Bevort et al. (1992), as well as by Schramm-Nielsen et al. (2004). Finally, the value of equality is also reflected in the law. For example, the Norwegian Work Environment Act is regarded as a longstanding attempt to create a more egalitarian society and a more humane social order by improving the total work environment (Kalleberg, 1991).

But Still. . .

In spite of these obvious differences, Telenor decided to choose an open-space office solution when planning its operations in Asia:

> Based on our experiences with the open-office solutions in our head office at Fornebu, we decided to design our new offices abroad likewise. (Norwegian member of Telenor's top management team)

According to what the Telenor managers underscored in the interviews, one important reason for replicating the Fornebu solution abroad was the positive experiences concerning collaboration and knowledge sharing:

> The open workspace actually helps people come together. We have almost no physical barriers, and people can spontaneously make up teams in order to solve problems, share information or whatever.

Likewise, regarding the Scandinavian leadership philosophy:

> As far as I know, the way the building was planned it was an unspoken rule that it was meant to open up the space by bringing down the walls, bringing down the power distance. Leaders should be accessible. It should not be difficult to find your leader, to talk to your leader. This contributes to easier communication.

However, in spite of the firm belief in the positive outcomes of the open-space office solutions, there were also those who were doubtful about how they would be received in Asia:

> I do not know how these open-space flexible offices are working in Asia.

Others, however, did not see this as a problem. According to one of the informants, a Norwegian with several years experience in Telenor's Asian operations, the open-space office solution worked in Asia as well:

> We have created an image of modernity. Asians are actually attracted to our ways of working together.

A side effect of this last statement is – again, according to one of the Norwegian managers responsible for several Asian offices – that the image of modernity also makes employees proud of working for Telenor.

A natural response is obviously to wonder whether Telenor has experienced any differences between the Asian countries in which they operate. As was emphasized above, Asia is not a homogeneous entity. Rather, it consists of many countries in which the religions, histories and languages differ substantially. Was it easier to implement the new office design in India than in Thailand? What about Bangladesh? Based on the interviews, it was fairly obvious that Telenor had not given this issue much thought. Its overall strategy was to copy the design of its head office in Norway (for the reasons given above) and begin its operations in various Asian countries without much further consideration.

What about the Leadership Roles?

Recent theories of leadership underscore the fact that the difficulty in answering the question 'What is leadership?' lies in the different meanings of the construct in different cultures. In other words, leadership means different things to different people. Also, as I have briefly mentioned above, the expectations surrounding the behaviour of successful leaders differs across countries and cultures. Even though the focus concerning expectations has typically been placed on subordinates, there is little doubt that the leaders themselves will have some expectations as to how to perform their roles as leaders as well. For example, Asian leaders expect respect and obedience from their subordinates. Respect and obedience are natural consequences of inequalities in power, status, experience and often age. The unequal levels of status between leaders and subordinates have traditionally been supported by their physical position within organizations. As some of the quotations above demonstrate, tearing down the organizational pyramids obviously has an effect on the role of the leader. Traditionally, Asian leaders benefit from the combination of their physical position in the organization and status symbols such as a large office, a secretary and so forth. Being suddenly deprived of all of this is obviously difficult to tackle for many. As one Asian manager expressed:

> When you are placed in an open-space office, you cannot hide behind your position, and this may come as a shock to managers who are accustomed to working in a more traditional physical work environment.

Obviously, the open-space office design effectively reduces the power usually linked to rank or position in an organization. Being at the same physical level as your subordinates does something to the role and functions of a leader. Also, according to the informants, the consequences of being a leader in an open office space could create a 'culture shock' for some of the Asian managers. The fact that one is both stripped of the visual symbols of a leadership position, as well as a feeling of vulnerability, made it hard for some managers to master their roles. Another effect of the physical layout, according to two of the informants, is that as a leader in this particular context, one must definitely earn the respect of one's subordinates through actions and general behaviour. Respect is therefore no longer something that automatically comes with the position. It is thus not too daring to assert that the effects of open-space offices represent a sort of revolution. While Asian leaders are used to being treated with respect for no other reason than the fact that they are leaders, they must now realize that they have to work hard in order to earn that same respect.

Several Asian managers working for Telenor in Asia had problems coping with this transition. Old managers disappeared, and new ones were hired. In spite of this, one member of Telenor's top leadership team stated the following:

> We will never go back to traditional offices.

However, the same informant also admitted that in hiring new managers:

> We are looking for candidates with the right attitudes, rather than the right skills.

Implicitly, this is an admittance that Asian leaders must go through a radical mental shift in order to feel comfortable in an open-space office environment. An interesting question here is to what extent the educational backgrounds of the managers, that is, whether they had a Western-influenced business education or not, had an effect on their attitudes. Although this was not explicitly discussed in my interviews with Telenor's top managers, their opinion was that age, which is to be taken as an indicator of education in this case, does play a role. The same goes for subordinates. Younger and more educated subordinates found the working environment more stimulating and easier to adapt to than their older coworkers. Still, the effect of education on Asian managers' and employees' abilities to adapt to a new working environment remains somewhat unclear.

It is said that for leaders to get the job done, what matters is how the leaders see and understand the situational and the relevant cultural realities and then capitalize on their own unique personal skills and abilities, including their approaches to leadership. Asian leaders working for Telenor are not, however, allowed to rely on their own approaches to leadership. They have to 'unlearn' their old approaches and relearn new ways of performing their roles as leaders. This is one of the consequences of the fact that Telenor has largely ignored the differences between the Scandinavian and Asian cultures and decided to implement the open-space office solution without any adaptations. Although Telenor informants claim that Asians have few problems adapting to the new physical environment, I still do not know if a more flexible implementation that leaves room for adjustments in order to fit the local culture would have led to fewer leaders resigning, as well as higher levels of effectiveness for their Asian employees.

CONCLUSIONS

The case of Telenor shows us that firms operating internationally should place more emphasis on the values and symbolic meanings attached to spatial solutions, especially their effect on social relationships and organization at work. Today, this perspective is not part of the mainstream international human resources literature. If IHRM is to be a major determinant of international business performance, more research on the effects of spatial solutions is necessary.

REFERENCES

Bakke, J.W. and B. Yttri (2003), 'Hybrid infrastructure and knowledge work', in *Proceedings of the 4th International Space Syntax Symposium*, University College London.

Bartlett, C., S. Ghoshal and P. Beamish (2008), *Transnational Management*, Burr Ridge, IL: Irwin/McGraw-Hill.

Bevort, F., J.S. Pedersen and J. Sundbo (1992), *90'ernes personaleledelse: Et paradigmeskift* [The Personnel Management of the 90s: A Paradigm Shift], Viborg: Systime.

Bjerke, B. (1999), *Business Leadership and Culture*, Cheltenham, UK and Northampton, MA, USA: Edward Elgar Publishing.

Bjørkman, I., W. Barner-Rasmussen and L. Li (2004), 'Managing knowledge transfer in MNCs: The impact of headquarters control mechanisms', *Journal of International Business Studies*, **35** (5), 443–55.

Brewster, C., P.R. Sparrow and G. Vernon (2007), *International Human Resource Management*, 2nd edition, London: Chartered Institute of Personnel and Development.

Carlopio, J.R. and D. Gardener (1992), 'Direct and interactive effects of the physical work environment on attitudes', *Environment and Behavior*, **24** (5), 579–601.

Daun, Å. (1986), 'The Japanese of the north – the Swedes of Asia', *Ethnologia Scandinavica*, **16** (1), 5–15.

Dorfman, P.W. and J.P. Howell (1988), 'Dimensions of national culture and effective leadership patterns', in R.N. Farmer and E.G. McGoun (eds), *Advances in International Comparative Management, Vol. 3*, pp. 127–50.

Elsbach, K. and M. Pratt (2007), 'The physical environment of organizations', *The Academy of Management Annals*, **1** (1), 181–224.

Goffee, R. and G. Jones (1999), 'Organizational culture and international HRM', in P. Joynt and B. Morton (eds), *The Global HR Manager*, London: Institute of Personnel and Development, pp. 39–59.

Grenness, T. (2011), 'Will the Scandinavian leadership model survive the forces of globalization?' *International Journal of Business and Globalization*, **7** (3), 332–50.

Gupta, A.K. and V. Govindarajan (2000), 'Knowledge flows within multinational corporations', *Strategic Management Journal*, **21** (4), 473–96.

Hair, M., E.E. Ghiselli and L. Porter (1966), *Managerial Thinking: An International Study*, New York: John Wiley.

Harrison, L.E. and S.P. Huntington (2000), *Culture Matters: How Values Shape Human Progress*, New York: Basic Books.

Hofbauer, J. (2000), 'Bodies in a landscape: On office design and organization', in J.H.R. Holliday and H. Wilmott (eds), *Body and Organization*, London: Sage, pp. 166–91.

Hofstede, G (1980), *Culture's Consequences*, Newbury Park, CA: Sage.

Hofstede, G. (2001), *Culture's Consequences*, 2nd edition, Newbury Park, CA: Sage.

Hofstede, G. (2007), 'Asian management in the 21st century', *Asia Pacific Journal of Management*, **24** (4), 411–20.

Hofstede, G. and M.H. Bond (1988), 'The Confucius connection: From cultural roots to economic growth', *Organizational Dynamics*, **16** (4), 4–21.

Hofstede, G., C. van Deusen, C. Mueller and T. Charles (2002), 'What goals do business leaders pursue? A study in fifteen countries', *Journal of International Business Studies*, **33** (4), 785–803.

House, R.J., P.J. Hanges, M.P. Javidan, P.W. Dorfman and V. Gupta (eds) (2004), *Culture, Leadership and Organizations: The GLOBE Study of 62 Societies*, Thousand Oaks, CA: Sage.

Javidan, M., P.W. Dorfman, M.S. de Luque and R.J. House (2006), 'In the eye of the beholder: Cross-cultural lessons in leadership from project GLOBE', *Academy of Management Perspective*, **20** (1), 67–90.

Kalleberg, R. (1991), 'Scandinavia in a comparative perspective', Working Paper, Department of Sociology, Oslo: University of Oslo.

Kornberger, M. and S. Clegg (2006), 'Bringing space back in', *Organization Studies*, **25** (7), 1095–14.

Ladkin, D. (2010), *Rethinking Leadership: A New Look at Old Leadership*

Questions, Cheltenham, UK and Northampton, MA, USA: Edward Elgar Publishing.

Lindkvist, L. (1991), 'Management in the Nordic countries – differences and similarities', paper in *Management in Scandinavia: Differences and Similarities* conference proceedings, Copenhagen: Copenhagen Business School Press, pp. 52–62.

Peltonen, T. (2008), 'Architecture and the social structure of organizations', paper presented at the EISAM Workshop 'Architecture and Social Architecture', Brussels, 13–16 May.

Peng, M.W. and K. Meyer (2011), *International Business*, London: Cengage Learning EMEA.

Qvale, T.U. (2007), 'Democratic management, leadership, culture and technology', in G. Szell, C.H. Bosling and U. Szell (eds), *Education, Labour and Science: Perspectives for the 21st Century*, Hamburg: Peter Lang, pp. 447–76.

Rafaeli, A. and M. Worline (1999), 'Symbols in organizational culture', in N.M. Ashkanasy, C.P.M. Wilderom and M.F. Peterson (eds), *Handbook of Organizational Culture and Climate*, London: Sage, pp. 71–84.

Redding, G (1990), *The Spirit of Chinese Capitalism*, New York: Walter de Gruyter.

Schramm-Nielsen, J., P. Lawrence and K.H. Sivesind (2004), *Management in Scandinavia*, Cheltenham, UK and Northampton, MA, USA: Edward Elgar Publishing.

Schwartz, S.H. (1994), 'Beyond individualism/collectivism: New dimensions of values', in V. Kim, H.C. Triandis, C. Kagiticibassi, S.C. Choi and G. Yoom (eds), *Individualism and Collectivism: Theory Application and Methods*, Newbury Park, CA: Sage.

Smith, P.B., S. Dugan and F. Trompenaars (1996), 'National culture and the values of organizational employees: A 43 nations study', *Journal of Cross-Cultural Psychology*, **27** (2), 231–64.

Smith, P.B.J., J.A. Andersen, B. Ekelund, G. Graversen and A. Ropo (2002), 'In search of Nordic management styles', *Scandinavian Journal of Management*, **19** (4), 491–507.

Telenor (2001), *The Telenor Fornebu Project*, brochure, Telenor.

Triandis, H.C. (1993), 'Collectivism and individualism as cultural syndromes', *Cross-Cultural Research*, **27** (3–4), 155–80.

Trompenaars, F. (1985), 'The organization of meaning, and the meaning of organization: A comparative study on the conceptions of organizational structure in different cultures', unpublished doctoral dissertation, University of Pennsylvania.

Walker, J.W. (1992), *Human Resource Strategy*, London: McGraw-Hill.

PART VI

Institutional spaces

11. Leadership and space in 3D: distance, dissent and disembodiment in the case of a new academic building

Karen Dale and Gibson Burrell

In this chapter we seek to show, through the analysis of a single case, that neither architectural spaces nor leadership are 'monolithic'. This term's original meaning refers to a single solitary stone, and it is therefore associated with unity, uniformity and a single dominant figure in a landscape. The 'monolith' is the form predominantly associated with leadership too. As Ford (2010, p. 47) puts it, there is a 'single model of univocal and patriarchal leadership behaviours. . .that is exclusionary and privileged and which constructs a homogeneous and almost superhuman model of leaders and leadership'. The construction of choice for such a framework tends to be the very tall single edifice standing out against its puny surroundings (Parker, 2013). Thus, in the beginning of *1984*, Orwell (1949) captures Big Brother's world of the 'Ministry of Truth' through its monolithic building. Dictatorial leadership is linked with monolithic institutions – hard, impervious, unyielding and dominant. Instead, we wish to present understandings of leadership as a complex set of overlapping fabrics, relatively 'soft' and enfolded, and of different stories and storeys associated with the concept.

The case we examine is that of a new academic building in a UK university. This is a building that one of the authors works in, having experienced the building process and a move into the building three years before this chapter was written. Hence the case presented is one that is personal and subjective, involving the stories, the lived and embodied experience of one author as researcher *and* subject. It is therefore necessarily partial, but also provides an 'insider' account that can be compared to the rhetoric produced by architects, consultants and senior management about new work buildings (for example, those documents on the UK Treasury and Scottish Office new-builds by Allen et al., 2004) or the more abstract academic analysis of workspaces, including those by the current authors

(Hernes, 2004; Clegg and Kornberger, 2006; Taylor and Spicer, 2007; Dale and Burrell, 2008; Yanow and Van Marrewijk, 2010)! Following Strati (1999, p. 67), we believe it is possible to use one's own embodied and sensory experience as a researcher to achieve 'empathic understanding of intentional action'. Martin's (2002) reflections on her aesthetic, sensory and emotional responses to her fieldwork in old people's homes, provokes her to argue for bringing the embodied self of the researcher into our academic work. She refers to Stoller's argument that 'discussions of the sensuous body require sensuous scholarship in which writers tack between the analytical and the sensible, in which embodied form as well as disembodied logic constitute scholarly argument' (1997, p. xv). The individual embodied insider account is supplemented by documents, accounts of other colleagues of consultation meetings and their views of the building, as well as by the account of the architect as given on an architectural tour of the building attended by one of the authors incognito.

THREE STORIES/STOREYS

Moving In

This academic building (Photo 11.1) is constructed on a relatively small footprint between existing buildings on a university campus. It was needed to house a growing and successful faculty, and consists of a ground floor with teaching rooms, and then three floors, each of which houses an academic department that is part of the faculty, which overall consists of eight

Source: All photographs and figures are the authors' own; with permission.

Photo 11.1   The exterior front view

Photo 11.2   The interior showing the atrium

departments and a number of associated research centres. The building is centred around an atrium (Photo 11.2) (which currently seems to be obligatory for new buildings in the UK!). Each of the departmental floors as originally conceived and built consisted of academic offices around the perimeter, with open-plan working space for PhD students between the offices and the atrium.

The design aesthetic of the buildings is a regular 'black box' exterior with precisely spaced windows producing a uniform pattern, a feature that was highly significant to the architect. During his architectural tour of the building he explained the importance of this to him and how he had a particular angle from which he preferred to view the building to maximize the effect of this aesthetic. The architectural firm describes the building as having a 'strong formal presence', its 'monochromatic palette of black brick, glass and aluminium creates simple rhythms in the façade, adding a distinct clarity to the building and emphasizing its pragmatic structure and programming'. The dominance of this exterior design affects the interior of the building: there are 'corridors' that go nowhere but happen to be there because they coincide with the regular arrangement of windows.

The interior is not described in such terms by the architectural firm, but many occupiers and visitors have used the word 'brutalist' as their adjective of choice. In English, this term has two meanings. First is the construction choice of 'raw concrete', which from the French *béton brut* gives us the overall term. But second, of course, is the idea that this architectural 'style' reduces humans to the level of uncivilized 'brutes' diminished of higher ambitions through the anaestheticization of their surroundings (Dale and Burrell, 2003). Certainly the architects have referred to the 'modernist' history of the campus, thus playing upon the former meaning, but the overwhelming experience of the interior is of uninspiring grey concrete, especially the stairways. People liken them to municipal car parks – without the graffiti and stench of urine, but as stark and functional. The implication is that the style choice is devoid of aesthetic opportunities for 'higher' thinking as within the second meaning of 'brutalism' (Banham, 1986). The architect on his tour waxed lyrical about achieving a completely unadorned finish where the metal balustrades enter the concrete of the steps. The disjuncture between his aesthetic interests and the lived experiences (Lefebvre, 1991; Shields, 1997, 1999) of many of those who work in the building is as stark as the concrete itself. However, whether one likes or dislikes the aesthetics of the building is a matter of individual and cultural taste and judgement, and there are both supporters and detractors of the building. The point of this account is not to gripe about the building's appearance, but to understand the lived experience of working in it and what it signifies in terms of leadership as embedded in and experienced through the space.

Our first story happens during the process of moving into the new building. As is often the case with new builds, this one had gone over its deadline, and there was some tension between the university's desire to have the departments move into the building in time for a grand opening by a royal representative and associated publicity on one hand, against the departments' desire not to have to uproot during teaching term time on the other. Thus, the moving process was tightly scheduled, and was starting to occur while the building contractors and subcontractors were still completing their final tasks. The furniture, chosen by a centralized facilities management function, had been placed in the offices, with each room a mirror image of the others. Space in the individual offices is at a premium with little flexibility to move furniture to different positions.

One of the authors of this chapter painstakingly moved a filing cabinet to a preferred position and filled it entirely with documents. This took a great deal of physical effort. When she left the office she felt happier that she had been able to rearrange the furniture in the office to suit her own design of how she wanted to use the space and a bit smug, given the filing cabinet was now entirely full and heavy, so that the workers would never be able to move it back. Not so! She was dismayed to find the next day

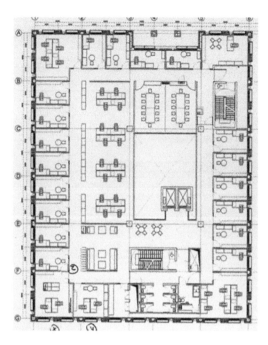

Figure 11.1   The floor plan

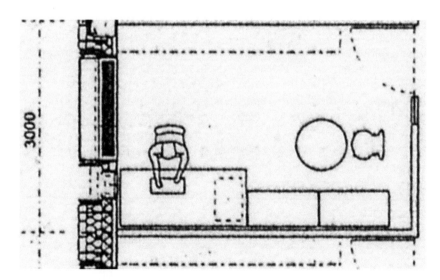

Figure 11.2   The office furniture plan

Photo 11.3　One of the authors' messy but comfortable office

that the cabinet had been returned to its original position. She asked the construction workers why this had been done. One of the men showed her his copy of the design plan (see Figures 11.1 and 11.2) and explained that their job would not be seen as finished and they would not be able to finally sign off the job as completed until everything in the building was *exactly* as it was drawn on the plan. After a couple of months of occupation of the building, the surveillance of the design had become less frequent, and she felt able to both move the filing cabinet to the position she wanted it to be in and to reverse the position of desk and chair so that she no longer had her back to the door (see also Photo 11.3). This gave her a huge degree of satisfaction! Thus, the sociomateriality (Dale, 2005; Yanow and Van Marrewijk, 2010) involved in the interaction of the space with its inhabitants engendered certain possibilities and impossibilities that show the mutual shaping of action and structure: the human and non-human; the material and ideational; choice and determinateness.

Domesticating the Space

The department's communal experience of the building was also one of discomfort, partly through having no collective gathering space, despite a considerable amount of floor space dedicated to open-plan workspace. The rise of open-plan offices as the corporate choice for staff accommodation is associated with the desire to drive down costs, increase staff interaction and create cultures of openness (Duffy, 1980, 1982, 1992; Hofbauer, 2000; Allen et al., 2004). They are widely disliked by many of those who have to work within them. The BBC's self-referential spoof programme *W1A* (Episode 4, BBC, 2014) speaks of the deep desire amongst HQ staff for a 'creative clearing' amidst the concentrated clutter of work stations. For the academic department in this case what had been specifically *disallowed* was the 'luxury' of a dedicated staff room. After moving into the new building, staff experimented with different locations to gather for lunch. The experience of all of these was physical and emotional discomfort. It was rather like Goldilocks and the Three Bears: these sofas were too low to be comfortable, the tables were right by the vertiginous drop to the atrium and felt too high up, the floor-to-ceiling glass wall of the meeting room made lunchtime the equivalent of feeding time at the zoo and all of these places were too open, both visually and auditorily. The embodied experience of being dislocated in these spaces, of having no base, prompted a series of communal activities to remedy this and create a 'home' space within one of the rooms initially designated for postgraduate students. This redesigning of the space required concerted social and collective physical action. First, comfortable sofas from the 'old' building had to be reacquired and surreptitiously brought into the new building. This in itself was a statement of attachment to the old routes and routines of physical being in a previous 'home'. The familiar furniture could not be immediately put into its new home, since this was full of the furniture that had been specially designed and made to fit in the particular space of this room. This consisted of four work stations, which were bolted together in a particular way to form a large square table, with eye-level screens between the desks. It was clear there would be practical difficulties in dismantling these desks, which had been assembled, according to the design master plan, within the office they had been intended for, and reassembling them in a different configuration in a different space. In the meantime, the familiar furniture was placed around the edges of another room, also full of its own brand new furniture.

After an attempt one lunchtime to conduct a conversation between people sat at two sofas with desks and screens between them preventing eye contact, frustration erupted into energy, leading four members of staff to decide there and then to move the furniture to create the staff room. The first challenge was to obtain the necessary tools to dismantle the desks. Luckily one person had an Allen key in their cycle tool kit that fitted. Coordinated physical activity was required to dismantle, move and reassemble furniture from one end of the building to the other. However, the atmosphere was one of enthusiasm, community and achievement, and a frisson of pleasure at foiling the design control of the building. Thereafter

*Photo 11.4   The 'knowledge exchange room', complete with sofas and
colleagues*

the staff room is in use every day. The sofas and soft chairs, now reunited
with their owners, might be a little cramped, but they turn inwards to the
centre of the room, allowing everyone to sit facing and talking with each
other (Photo 11.4). There is both visual and auditory privacy, such that
private conversations about students will not be overheard, and there
is the possibility of being able to get a short time away from the desk
without being under the open gaze available to all who pass. Given that
formally there is no space in the design for a staff room, coupled with the
concern by faculty senior management about shortage of space and that
this is not an appropriate use of space in the new building, members of
the department delight in describing it as the 'knowledge exchange room'.

   Coda: during the writing of this chapter two new members of staff
joined the department. On their first day they were physically and symbolically welcomed by being invited to lunch in the staff room, and being
regaled – as insiders – with the cautionary tale that 'We don't have a staff
room. This is the knowledge exchange room!'

From 'Open Plan' to 'Fish Tank'

The original design of the building had open-plan spaces for doctoral
researchers on every floor of the building. These, as can be seen from
Photo 11.5, were bounded on one side by low cupboards that formed
a 'corridor' between the open-plan space and the academic offices. On
the other side, there was a low wall, to the same height as the cupboards
between the PhD area and the open atrium. This meant the open-plan

Photo 11.5   Open-plan doctoral space

workspaces were open to all the other floors of the building, and to the entrance doors. This design subjected the doctoral researchers to the noise of the whole building, including that of the ground-floor teaching rooms emptying and refilling with students every hour. The other consequence of this design was that they had no control over the temperature of their working area. As the main entrance doors opened automatically every time someone went in or out, the outside air flowed into the building. Given this is a university in the west of the UK, which has a relatively cold and wet climate, it was a common sight to see the few PhD researchers who braved the open-plan area sitting there in their coats and scarves! Not surprisingly, most of the doctoral researchers decided that the space was not conducive to their research or their health, and chose to work at home: 'Its a devaluation of scholarly values. It says its not important to be researching and writing' (quote from a conversation with a PhD student).

The department did what it could in placing as many doctoral researchers as possible in shared corner offices, but there was a constant low-level conflict with the faculty senior management over this, as it was not seen as the use of space that the building had been designed for. Senior managers disliked seeing the empty open-plan space and thought doctoral researchers should not have offices when there was huge pressure on academic space in the faculty as a whole.

The problems of the open-plan space had been communicated to the architects through the design and consultation process, but to no avail. Various arguments were put forward as to why the open-plan areas could not be made into self-contained working areas, including the needs of the heating and ventilation system of the building that (apparently) needed unimpeded flow. As one of the authors joined an architectural tour that the architect was giving to interested (external) visitors to the new building, she was interested to hear him talk about his stated rationale for the design of the open-plan spaces, where he mentioned the British Council for Offices as an influence. This is intriguing, as the British Council for Offices, founded in 1990, is an industry body made up of membership across different areas related to obtaining, designing and usage of offices: architects, designers, financiers, lawyers and surveyors in the commercial property field. Its stated mission is to: 'research, develop and communicate best practice in all aspects of the office sector' (British Council for Offices, n.d.). It provides industry-standard guidelines and specifications for the most efficient offices. But its work is related to 'commercial' office spaces. Although the university building obviously contains offices for academics to work in, its purpose and usage as an educational building is a far cry from that of a commercial office facility. At a very basic practical level, commercial office buildings have controlled entry. Visitors and non-employees cannot just wander in from the streets. Those who occupy the building on a daily basis are involved in the enterprise of the organization as employees, with (at least ostensibly) shared goals and tasks. An educational building, by the nature of its teaching activities, is necessarily open. Students not only have to be able to have access to teaching rooms, but also have to be able to access departments' administrative officers and academics.

The very openness of the building also means that various groups from around campus come into the building to have meetings, sometimes in the bookable meeting rooms and sometimes just in the open-plan seating areas. The potential for disruption of academic work is considerable, especially to the PhD researchers in the open-plan areas. Apart from the noise, the visual distractions of constant churning of people, and the problem of heating, neither their personal belongings nor their research data was secure. This has been made clear to the architect in consultation meetings. It was pointed out that there was an issue of data being insecure in such a layout and this would contravene all existing research ethics codes of practice. For both university and funding agency codes of ethics, which all researchers have to agree to abide by, the building was not fit for purpose. On the other hand, however, the building can be seen to meet those guidelines for office buildings that relates to the commercial sector and it was a definite *non*-interest in ethics that was prioritized in the design of the building. For some staff and students, they were now working within some structure akin to a call centre: 'I saw M. in the morning amid the ghost departments at our end of C Floor and I mentioned how someone had put the wrong sign up [that is "Call Centre"] for the new building; he laughed and speculated that it must have been some student joker!' (extract from an email from a colleague during the process of moving buildings).

From the beginning of occupancy of the building it was clear to everyone on the academic side, from the doctoral researchers themselves to senior academic management, that the open-plan workspaces were not fit for purpose. Facilities management did not concur with this and, indeed, since they themselves work in open-plan areas in a refurbished central university administrative building they used this as a reason why it should not be a problem for academic researchers. Moreover, both financial and practical obstacles were maintained as to why the building could not be altered. In the early period of the new building, the most significant aspects of it for facilities and senior management was that it was accorded a number of prestigious awards (including one by the British architectural professional body, RIBA) and also had the highest rating for its environmental efficiency. These glittering prizes would have been jeopardized by adapting the building in any way.

This situation, of an award-winning building that occupants found of very low utility, probably would have continued if it had not been for the appointment of a new Vice-Chancellor (the highest managerial position in the UK higher education system). He made it a priority to visit each department across the university, and as he visited the departments in the new building he was shown the problems with the open-plan areas. He and the new Deputy Vice-Chancellor insisted that the space needed to be made functional, and after the visit, they made resources available to find a solution to this. The upshot was that over the summer of 2013 interior building works took place to create soundproof glass walls around the open-plan areas and to adapt the heating and ventilation systems to make this possible. The structural changes are indeed successful in terms of complete reduction of noise disturbance and control of heating within the doctoral workspaces. However, they have thrown up problems of their own. The new 'walls' are entirely transparent, as is necessary for the spaces that have no external windows of their own to share the light of the atrium and the rest of the building. But this means that the doctoral researchers – and their data – are continually 'on show', and the potential for visual distraction continues. Indeed, conversations with PhD students show that there are a number of dilemmas related to their visual accessibility – do they wave to or acknowledge other members of the department as they walk around the outside of what has become known as the 'doctoral fish tank' (Photo 11.6), should they just wave or smile the first time in the day they see a colleague or should they ignore them entirely as if they were in a self-contained

Photo 11.6   Doctoral 'fish tank'

office? All the doctoral researchers who formerly occupied shared corner offices have had to move into the fish tank, as per the instructions of senior management. Obviously the money spent on the alterations to the building mean that there is an overwhelming need to show that the changes have been a success and that the space is now fully occupied.

A number of 'discussions' have taken place between faculty senior management and departmental management (Head of Department) and doctoral students to try to have the visual openness of the space ameliorated, but to no avail. One afternoon the three most senior managers within the faculty (Dean, Deputy Dean with responsibility for finance, and Chief Administrator) spent several hours with the Head of Department disputing the problem with the lack of privacy of the space and its effects on academic research. This was a great deal (and cost) of time to spend to disagree over the use of some easily applied plastic panels that would provide some privacy while still allowing light. And the ad hoc putting up of posters was also forbidden! Having outlined some of the basic issues, we now turn to an analysis of the case to see what one single university building might indicate about organizational space and its relation to leadership.

'LEADERSHIP'

The cult of the (male) individual as leader resonates with the Anglo-American tradition of valorizing personality over social structure. In architectural design, for example, creativity is also assumed to be associated with an overarching dominant plan that is the 'brainchild' of a master 'signature architect'. Within the profession, there is the attendant downplaying of the large organizational machine of typical architectural practices with their hierarchical mundanities. Similarly, universities in the Anglo-Saxon world place some emphasis on their 'Presidents' and 'Vice-Chancellors' as leaders who can achieve great things through the power of their personalities. And it is at this point that we should draw attention to the phallogocentric nature of the discourse on leadership as 'heroes'. Jackie Ford (2010) has pointed to the links between patriarchy and leadership in which the leaderly possession of testicles creates a valorization of aggression, manipulation and control-orientated behaviour. She references a number of women writers including Calas and Smircich (1991), Marshall (1995, 2007) and Wajcman (1996) who have indicated this pairing of attributes with supposed leadership – and the disadvantages thereof.

In universities, while the presence of phallogocentrism is undeniable, the widespread absence of heroic exemplars means that there is constant organizational experimentation about how and what should be done within an ever-present tension between centralization and local autonomy. The question has been how to maintain the notion of 'leadership' in higher education when the classic elements do not seem to be much in evidence. Being a case of a building within a university, our material resonates with other knowledge-intensive and professional organizations, where there is not an authoritative hierarchical and leadership structure, and the knowledge and expertise of the whole range of employees is crucial to the effectiveness of the organization. And as academics we do tend to see universities as *by us, for us*. As we shall argue, however, the role of students in this case needs to be remembered in the face of academic staff members' views. Under 'leaderism' (O'Reilly and Reed, 2010), which we discuss below, the students come to have *more* visibility to university senior administrators than the staff do, because they are seen as more germane to corporate success.

Thus, to undertake any analysis of this kind we must assess how we might go about exploring a new university building in the context of changes in British higher education. Within universities, there has been a generalized move away from trade union involvement and committee forms of decision-making to more managerial forms of control. But since universities still resemble organizations based upon 'bureau-professionalism' (Clarke and Newman, 1997; Clarke et al., 2007), this embrace of managerialism has not been completely successful and so the concept of 'distributed leadership' (Spillane et al., 2004; Gosling et al.,

2009) has been utilized to comprehend what has been going on. While the underlying assumptions about leadership continue to coalesce around unity, unidirectional power and influence, such individualistic 'great men' or 'hero' figures are extremely difficult to find. The success of the concept of 'distributed leadership' suggests that universities in Britain do not wish to rely upon a 'heroic' view of their Vice-Chancellors wielding monolithic power.

'Distributed leadership' is the dominant concept of choice that seems to recognize this embracing of 'notions of collegiality and autonomy while addressing the need for management' (Gosling et al., 2009, p. 303). However, Gosling et al. (2009) note that while it does highlight that 'leadership is constructed from the widespread distribution of agency throughout complex organizations' (p. 299), they fundamentally question the actuality of 'distributive leadership' in higher education. They state that in their research in universities, they have observed the rhetoric of 'distributed leadership' alongside 'a steady transition from collegial to more managerial models of administration and the erosion of traditional channels for upwards influence' (p. 300). As Gosling et al. (2009) point out, the discourse of distributed leadership often masks the influence of those who have control over budgets. This and other forms of power can also be observed in this case. It is our argument that the experience of formal leadership within this case was one of distance, dissent and disembodiment. Let us deal with these in turn.

DISTANCE

Our argument is that the building in question shows a process of 'distancing' in a number of ways. First, it demonstrates the social distance that has grown up within universities between senior managers and their staff. It exemplifies that set of issues to do with the 'community' of scholars becoming torn apart by power and income differentials. The salaries of senior managers in British higher education have greatly increased relative to their staff. No longer do British university Senates control the life of their universities for they have been replaced by University Councils as the decision-making bodies (Shattock, 2009). Made up of local worthies from the surrounding areas, Councils have usurped Senates' powers to make academic judgements on the fabric of the university. Academics and students have lost their place in the decision-making processes and have become distant from the resource allocation process.

The budget for the building in question was set by senior management of the university and the school. The building came in on budget, and hence was seen as a successful building project. Indeed, a quotation from the university Director of Facilities on the architects' website describes it as 'a first class educational building at low cost'. Senior management in the school clearly found complaints about the building and its subsequent dysfunctionality as an educational building somewhat irritating. No doubt they also had to deal with a certain amount of politics of envy from those within the school who were still in the 'old' building, but generally their approach seemed to be to expect gratitude for the new building from its 'users' now distanced from the main building.

Second, 'distancing' is in evidence in the role senior managers play in having very little detailed understanding of how the university actually works. The professionalization of management in British universities means that the inhabitants of senior corridors of power seldom leave them to come forth and see what the reality of teaching in lecture theatres or seminar rooms has become. The intensification of workloads is seen by such 'leaders' as necessary to ensure efficient use of resources. They distance themselves from detail in the vain search to be strategic. Therefore the 'distance' is exacerbated in a Tayloristic sense between those who conceive of tasks and those who execute those tasks (Braverman, 1974). The separation of conception from execution creates a distance between planners and process workers.

Third, senior university managers are forced to look for students throughout the world. Funding models have driven them to do this. The belief is then that the university should appear to be global in its welcome, not least in the appearance of its campus. The emphasis on plate glass, open-plan rooms and atriums is redolent of so many corporate buildings one sees across the globe. Senior management wanted a building that was capable of appearing on glossy front covers of its brochures, designed for a global market of international students. The idea that this was a British university in the North West of England with its own place in a Roman-Norman-Georgian civic architecture was lost completely (Massey, 1995) in the desire to make it look like it was consonant with the 'international style'. As such, it was not designed to be a university building AT ALL. It was a piece of corporate architecture designed to be viewed at night from one particular flagstone outside the building with all its lights ablaze but no one in sight. The absence of a single human figure from the architect's conception will be dealt with in a later section as a key example of disembodiment.

To work as an educational building, we have shown that it was in severe need of retro-fitting. Yet it won prizes, often before a single member of staff or student had crossed its threshold. It seems incredibly 'safe' to go for uniform, international styling that would be as at home in Shanghai,

Sydney or Singapore. There is nothing in the chosen design that says 'This is who we have been, and are now, and we are proud of it'. This absence of locality and neighbourhood may actually suggest a lack of confidence in the institution by senior management. This process can be observed in this case in (literally!) concrete form and is linked to the architects' statement that the building is 'based on commercial office design principles'. This is written into their promotional materials, so must be intended as a positive feature of the design. It begs the question, though, as to why these commercial office design principles should be appropriate to an educational building? Why do the designers and senior management in the university believe that the needs and tasks of each are congruent? From what are they distancing the institution?

What is lost in seeking to be 'international' is a regional identity and the use of vernacular styles of architecture and management and those local influences come to be replaced by 'international styles' of architecture and management techniques. In the 1990s, the expansion of the university's buildings, set amongst a city constructed with grey Pennine stone, represented an attempt to create a semblance of an Italian hill village. The Apennines were seen as culturally and aesthetically superior to the Pennines. What is put in the place of localism and what might be cherished (Bachelard [1957] 1994) are globalism and all the attendant debasements that often go with that process of simplification and standardization. What some authors have called McDonaldization (Ritzer, 2001) is also obvious in building design. Seats that are not meant to be comfortable are to be found in a bright decor that is to attract customers in; there is an encouragement to labour oneself at making it work systemically, saving the university costs, so one finds self-clearing of used spaces and an emphasis on speed of throughput. Volume replaces quality. 'Users' replace 'residents' because the notion of 'residency' is politically charged as it implies a lack of centralized control over bourgeois property.

The rhetorical notion of 'user', of course, has significant effects upon how one approaches any monolith. 'User' suggests that one's relationship to a material object is purely functional and transitory. Much of the time one may not be using something, so long-term 'ownership' possibly does not exist. Even a short-term renting of the property by a 'tenant' is not implied by the word 'user'. User is a very low form of engagement. It may well be appropriate as a term for the undergraduate students who wander in and out of the complex for the occasional lecture but for many staff, however, it is totally inappropriate. They feel themselves to be 'residents' with all the cultural and emotional baggage that accompanies that term. This suggests that the architecture seeks to reorientate the building from a 'residence for staff' to a locale for student use, thereby distancing the former.

The fourth meaning of 'distancing' is that while students from abroad are welcomed by the advanced techniques for the suppression of distance, such as air transport (Urry, 2012), they are also kept at a distance from full integration into the society for fear of bringing about unwelcome cultural change. Increasingly in the UK, overseas students are monitored and held in suspicion by the security services about their motivation for studying and 'being here'. There is some emphasis, covertly, on keeping 'overseas students' ghettoized within particular parts of the university, partly because the students like this safety network that accompanies such concentration but also because it distances the 'stranger' students from the host.

Now this focus on students and the 'threats' they offer, ties into the recently developed notion of 'leaderism' (O'Reilly and Reed, 2010, 2011). In seeking to analyse the shifts in British higher education one has to begin from an understanding that from, let us say, 1950–85, universities were run by their Senates, which were made up of academics. Vice-Chancellors (VCs) were usually outstanding academics – without reputations necessarily for managerial skills. They were *primum inter pares* and often returned to an academic life. This situation gave way in the mid-1980s to a system of managerialism where VCs became specialist managers running teams of professional administrators who grew in number and in power. For O'Reilly and Reed, 'leaderism' has recently emerged from 'managerialism' within the dominant rhetorics operating in British universities. The argument is a complex one but may be expressed perhaps in a linear form. The 'cascade of change' that the public sector has been subjected to in the UK since 1997 has had as a key component the notion of rational *consumers* arising as part of 'democratic' or 'militant consumerism'. In the face of this, distributed leadership has arisen to emphasize the importance of getting close to the client and reducing the power of the professional. Thus, in many circumstances, students are listened to more than staff. The university thus becomes 'community driven', involving users and stakeholders seeking to identify their interests as identical interests to those of the organizational elite. In this way, buildings are built that appeal to students and not necessarily to staff! 'Users' replace 'residents' in the organizational rhetoric. The chosen aesthetics are driven by what appeals to the transient and not the domiciled. The local gives way to the global. The building of which we speak was created by a distributive leadership approach to what was assumed students wanted – an educational establishment rather than a faculty office block.

The building has a particular purpose: it provides working space for academics, postgraduate researchers and departmental administrators, as well as teaching space in seminar and lecture rooms. As an educational space, then, it needs to function so that the work of the university can be effectively carried out. If so, it was an abject failure. In profound ways, the change of culture that comes from changed leadership in the university (and other public sector organizations) is embedded in the design of the building and its assumption about its use – most importantly – by students. Some of this, like the control over office space and budgets, the downgrading of the significance of academic staff, the imposition of uniformity, is conscious. So who sought this design control? We identify three sources. First there was senior management of the academic faculty; second, the facilities/estate management section of the university administration; and third, the architectural firm itself. And while there was lip service paid to consultation with 'end users' (that is, academics and administrators who would move into the building), the architect said during the tour that he gave of the building that he had been successful in getting his design implemented *despite* their concerns (Cohen et al., 2005).

In these four ways, our case demonstrates 'distancing' in a multilayered sense as a very active principle within this organizational example of a new building. We now turn to look at 'dissent'.

DISSENT

Before the building was completed, at the level of the school and its decision-making processes, there was a managerial attempt to make it appear as if full participation by staff in the project would be welcome. Resistance to the project and its outcomes would not be necessary (Anderson, 2008). Meetings that were meant to allow the participation of staff did take place and issues of relevance to staff, both administrative and academic, were discussed. However, minutes of these meetings were skeletal and were felt not to represent the strength of feelings that had been expressed by participants. As revealed by the architect in his 'tour' of the building, these meetings were seen by the building's designers to be adversarial in nature with winners and losers. Rather than listen to the voices of the future residents as an aid to design improvement, it appears as if the architect saw it as his mission to get his own way and retain the integrity of the original design. The meetings represented a form of 'pseudo-participation' in which dissent is managed out of the system by the pretence of democratic engagement and the absence of proper minutes of meetings. The professional architect retained control in the face of questions of great relevance to the prospective users. But this absence of real participation engendered more resentment and dissent when the architect had finally left the building, for the aims and objectives of an academic building, facilitating the achievement of a set of university objectives, appear to have given way to the aims and objectives of an architect to win prizes and awards from within his own profession. There had been 'goal displacement'.

There is much literature on the capturing of organizational change by those placed in power, and associatedly, on resistance in relation to this exercise of power (Storey, 1983; Knights and Vurdubakis, 1994). Storey (1983, p. 162) classified forms of 'unorganized' response to changes brought about by the powerful into the following: 'conformity', which implies acceptance of prevailing rules; 'ritualism', which implies people work to rule and refuse to show any initiative; 'withdrawal', which brings with it apathy and resignation, 'rebellion', which is associated with aggression and sabotage and 'innovation', which implies expediency and attempts to modify the regulations. While these are difficult categories to separate in practice, the case of the new university building might reveal forms of resistance more akin to 'innovation' than to anything else. 'Sabotage' is a loaded word but it is difficult to see that the academics in this new building actually threatened property – although they did move it around in anti-managerial fashion. This raises the question of whether it was organized resistance or unorganized resistance, which again problematizes almost all schemas designed to illuminate 'resistance'. It was 'organized' by most of the academics but within one department. It was work group centred rather than involving a collectivity drawn from around the school. And it related to *post facto* resistance to changes that had already occurred.

Much can be observed from the design and lived experience of the building that was *not* deliberately or consciously designed. For example, we described above some of the acts of staff resistance that the design engendered. These points of resistance were not envisaged by the architect but once in place were subject to monitoring by senior management. Room layout changes of any kind that deviated from the master plan needed to be covert. By calling the staff room a 'knowledge exchange room' an attempt was made to evade managerial dictums, always in the awareness of being on borrowed time, such that if the powers-that-be decided, any degree of staff control or discretion over the space could be overturned at any time. So the space and how it is lived demonstrates the embedding of relations of hierarchy and control. And one need not be a Foucauldian (Foucault, 1977) to see that by offering resistance, you point out to senior management that very place where their power ploys next need to be exercised. But as with students and with staff, senior management cannot constantly monitor all forms of resistance. Its attention span declines, it grows weary of its need to maintain the gaze and it moves its monitoring function on to somewhere else. Thus offices may be rearranged for residential use once again. Signs of a non-professional nature can now be replaced on doors and notice boards and staff grew more easy about sitting in a staff room in all but name. Organizational life may well be lived out in these 'spaces in between'. Here in the liminal world where rules and regulations are no longer monitored, we come to find personal and community space, not as users but as residents with perceived rights and privileges. It is clear that human beings were subordinated to the design aesthetic of the 'Other' and sought to reassert their potency within it. Indeed, there was a great sense of the energizing of staff by them taking things into their own hands and being active in reasserting their rights to the control of their lived space. But to do so they needed to reassert their embodiment – their sense of physical domination of the spaces and artefacts in their immediate environment – within an architectural construction that had sought to disembody them from the outset.

DISEMBODIMENT

It is our argument that a conflict of leadership agendas became embodied in the space through the lived experience of the residents (Ropo et al., 2013). The human body has a sensorium that covers the use of sight, sound, taste, touch and smell. The sensorium ensures that the human body is not exposed to prolonged harsh lighting, high decibel levels, excessively high or low temperatures, odious smells and everything else that flesh is heir to. The offices contain gaps between wall and exterior through which cold draughts pour. Electronic fire detectors bleep randomly throughout meetings. Walls are paper thin, meaning that private conversations can be heard by colleagues either side of the relevant office. The draughts coming from the huge atrium make the offices and lecture rooms cold and unwelcoming and equally the atrium produces a noisy atmosphere for all within the building. In other words, the embodied inhabitant of the building had not been considered by the architect at all. The user was a disembodied caricature of a real human being with our feelings, emotions and senses.

Desks were standardized and made stationary. Movement of desks was meant to be prohibited by the location of power points, electronic connector cables, the lighting and so on. In more senses than one, these were meant to be work *stations* in which movement of the human body was to be discouraged. If the academic and administrative staff were not exactly confined to their desk, their desk was meant to be confined to the same spot in the office. The emphasis on tidiness, uniformity and sameness did not recognize the varieties of human body contained within a modern organization. Bodies that were taller, disabled, injured, and out of the ordinary were made to feel excluded by the technologies of the building. The only bodies allowed in a culture of disembodiment were those that made no special claims upon the building whatsoever. They were invisible to the nocturnal aesthetics of the building in its pure, personless architectural form (compare Wasserman, 2011). Aesthetically then the design of this building shows the pressure to keep the 'storeys' (as in different floors of the building) the same, to maintain a design integrity imposed by the architect. Please note that we do not seek to vilify 'design aesthetics' here, for such an approach has many virtues, particularly if it is done democratically or at least participatively. What we wish to question is the predominance of a young architect who imposes his wishes for 'sameness' upon scores of others, with no quarter given to their views.

In a parallel way, metaphors of 'overcoming' continue to be utilized in describing leadership. Some of them can be downright 'violent'! Leaders are 'at the cutting edge', 'branding' their organizations with 'steely' ('Stalinist') intention, seeking 'impact' on the market. To read the leadership material in the popular press, chief executives are very dangerous and violent members of society. They will cut and bludgeon their way through all before them. If harming the human body is often a sign of power and of leadership, buildings can be just as implicated in this mutilation as other forms of organizational materiality. The razing to the ground of the building works of a rival is often regarded as key to strong leadership (Dale and Burrell, 2011). This material violence has to be contrasted to the 'problem' of the lived integrity of the inhabitants of the building, the lived body of the academics, and also the collective corporate body of the 'community of scholars'. Uniformity may be desired by architects and the leaders of their client organizations to keep control over an external image but the complexity of life inside organizations suggests pluralities of forms are everywhere. Instead of the gravitas of the leader pulling all orbiting bodies into her or his grasp by sheer size and will, the organizational universe is much more capable of escaping the weak bond of monolithic gravity. The gravitas of most leaders cannot withstand a first major failure.

CONCLUSIONS

We began by saying our case of a new university building would demonstrate the absence of those monolithic edifices that spoke only of one leader and a monument to his or her leadership. Throughout history, monumental monoliths have been constructed by and for the dictatorial head of state (Spotts, 2002). They were often ruined and plundered by the populace wherever they existed. The reality of organizational arrangements is such that dictatorial dreams must still be brought into being by architects, construction workers and suppliers of building materials. And as soon as one tries to put together the interorganizational network to manage these huge projects one runs into the problems of 'distributed leadership' and 'leaderism'. The leader cannot spend his or her own time putting brick upon brick, mixing mortar and concrete and engaging in quantity surveying. The project must be managed and the leader immediately cedes control to middle-ranking bureaucrats. The leadership today may feel the need to pander to the militant consumer but often this is rhetoric and not the reality as perceived by senior executives. The consumer can be duped, just as staff can, by good public relations and persuasive impression management techniques (Olins, 1989). Yet most university Vice-Chancellors have to carry some vestiges of popular support with them. They have to surround themselves with the flag of staff involvement and participation and pay lip service to the respect they hold for the professional groupings with which they surround themselves. A senior management team charged with the construction of a new university building must manage the coalition that the project management team represents. In other words, there is a pluralistic command structure in evidence on most university building sites.

But the usual coalition in the British context increasingly has less staff involvement in the project. This is because of changes to public sector management techniques and processes more generally, but specifically in relation to university administration. Councils have overtaken Senates to bring this shift about. But because of increasing perceived need to take into account the wishes of the student body for up-to-date facilities, university buildings are becoming more orientated to the supposed needs of the undergraduate user much more than they are to academic staff. The twin thrusts of 'managerialism' and 'leaderism' are very evident in this case presented here, and we must face the reality that permanent academic staff are seen as less important to the corporate mission than transient students within both these overlapping processes. Without question, this reshaping of universities over the next decade will throw up some very interesting evidence regarding the distancing, the dissent and the disembodiment of the typical university academic. It will point to the importance of a perspective based on the notion of 'sociomateriality' in which the material and ideational, action and structure, human and non-human are all allowed to play a role of significance (Dale, 2005). And it will continue to problematize the conventional notions of the 'leader' and of 'leadership' (Alvesson and Spicer, 2012; Collinson, 2012) in institutions that contain highly skilled and qualified subject experts who have a vested interest in professional, quasi-participative control systems.

REFERENCES

Allen, T., A. Bell, R. Graham, B. Hardy and F. Swaffer (2004), *Working Without Walls: An Insight into the Transforming Government Workplace*, Norwich, UK: HMSO.

Alvesson, M. and A. Spicer (2012), 'Critical leadership studies: The case for critical performativity', *Human Relations*, **65** (3), 367–90.

Anderson, G. (2008), 'Mapping academic resistance in the managerial university', *Organization*, **15** (2), 251–70.

Bachelard, G. ([1957] 1994), *The Poetics of Space*, Boston, MA: Beacon Press.

Banham, R. (1986), *A Concrete Atlantis*, Cambridge, MA: MIT Press.

BBC (2014), *W1A*, Episode 4: BBC 2, Producer P. Schlesinger.

Braverman, H. (1974), *Labor and Monopoly Capital*, New York: Monthly Review Press

British Council for Offices (n.d.), 'About the BCO', accessed 28 January 2015 at www.bco.org.uk/AboutUs/About-BCO.aspx.

Calas, M. and L. Smircich (1991), 'Voicing seduction to silence leadership', *Organization Studies*, **12** (4), 567–602.

Clarke, J. and J. Newman (1997), *The Managerial State: Power, Politics and Ideology in the Remaking of the Welfare State*, London: Sage.

Clarke, J., J. Newman, N. Smith, E. Vidler and L. Westmarland (2007), *Creating Citizen Consumers*, London: Sage.

Clegg, S. and M. Kornberger (eds) (2006), *Space, Organizations and Management Theory*, Copenhagen: Liber.

Cohen, L., A. Wilkinson, J. Arnold and R. Finn (2005), 'Remember I'm the bloody architect', *Work, Employment and Society*, **19** (4), 775–96.

Collinson, D. (2012), 'Prozac leadership and the limits of positive thinking', *Leadership*, **8** (2), 87–107.

Dale, K. (2005), 'Building a social materiality', *Organization*, **12** (5), 649–78.

Dale, K. and G. Burrell (2003), 'Aesthetics and anaesthetics', in A. Carr and P. Hancock (eds), *Art and Aesthetics in Organisation Studies*, Basingstoke, UK: Palgrave Macmillan, pp. 155–73.

Dale, K. and G. Burrell (2008), *The Spaces of Organization and the Organization of Space*, Basingstoke, UK: Palgrave Macmillan.

Dale, K. and G. Burrell (2011), 'Disturbing structure, reading the ruins', *Culture and Organization*, **17** (2), 107–21.

Duffy, F. (1980), 'Office buildings and organisational change', in A. King (ed.), *Buildings and Society*, London: RKP, pp. 255–82.

Duffy, F. (1982), 'Introduction', in J. Klein, *The Office Book*, London: Frederick Muller.

Duffy, F. (1992), *The Changing Workplace*, London: Phaidon.

Ford, J. (2010), 'Studying leadership critically: A psychosocial lens on leadership identities', *Leadership*, **6** (1), 47–65.

Foucault, M. (1977), *Discipline and Punish*, Harmondsworth, UK: Penguin.

Gosling, J., R. Bolden and G. Petrov (2009), 'Distributed leadership in higher education: What does it accomplish?' *Leadership*, **5** (3), 299–310.

Hernes, T. (2004), *The Spatial Construction of Organization*, London: John Benjamins.

Hofbauer, J. (2000), 'Bodies in a landscape', in J. Hassard, R. Holliday and H. Willmott (eds), *Body and Organisation*, London: Sage, pp. 166–91.

Knights, D. and T. Vurdubakis (1994), 'Foucault, power, resistance and all that', in J. Jermier, D. Knights and W. Nord (eds), *Resistance and Power in Organizations*, London: Routledge, pp. 167–98.

Lefebvre, H. (1991), *The Production of Space*, Oxford: Basil Blackwell.

Marshall, J. (1995), 'Gender and management: A critical review of research', *British Journal of Management*, **6** (S1), S53–S62.

Marshall, J. (2007), 'The gendering of leadership in corporate social responsibility', *Journal of Organizational Change Management*, **20** (2), 165–81.

Martin, P.Y. (2002), 'Sensations, bodies, and the "spirit of a place": Aesthetics in residential organizations for the elderly', *Human Relations*, **55** (7), 861–85.

Massey, D. (1995), 'Places and their pasts', *History Workshop*, **39** (1), 182–93.

Olins, W. (1989), *Corporate Identity: Making Business Strategy Visible by Design*, Cambridge, MA: Harvard University Press.

O'Reilly, D. and M. Reed (2010), 'Leaderism': An evolution of managerialism in UK public service reform', *Public Administration*, **88** (4), 960–78.

O'Reilly, D. and M. Reed (2011), 'The grit in the oyster: Professionalism, managerialism and leaderism as discourses of UK public services modernization', *Organization Studies*, **32** (8), 1079–101.

Orwell, G. (1949), *Nineteen Eighty-Four*, Harmondsworth, UK: Penguin.

Parker, M. (2013), 'Vertical capitalism and the sublime: Skyscrapers and organization', *Culture and Organization* [online], accessed 28 January 2015 at http://www.tandfonline.com/doi/full/10.1080/14759551.2013.845566#tab Module.

Ritzer, G. (2001), *McDonaldization*, London: Sage.

Ropo, A., E. Sauer and P. Salovaara (2013), 'Embodiment of leadership through material place', *Leadership*, **9** (3), 378–95.

Shattock, M. (2009), *Managing Successful Universities*, Milton Keynes, UK: Open University Press.

Shields, R. (1997), 'Spatial stress and resistance: Social meanings of spatialisation', in G. Benko and U. Strohmayer (eds), *Space and Social Theory*, Oxford: Blackwell.

Shields, R. (1999), *Lefebvre, Love and Struggle: Spatial Dialectics*, London: Routledge.

Spillane, J.P., R. Halverson and J.B. Diamond (2004), 'Towards a theory of leadership practice: A distributed perspective', *Journal of Curriculum Studies*, **36** (1), 3–34.

Spotts, F. (2002), *Hitler and the Power of Aesthetics*, London: Hutchinson.

Stoller, P. (1997), *Sensuous Scholarship*, Philadelphia, PA: University of Pennsylvania Press.

Storey, J. (1983), *Managerial Prerogative and the Question of Control*, London: Routledge and Kegan Paul.

Strati, A. (1999), *Organisation and Aesthetics*, London: Sage.

Taylor, S. and A. Spicer (2007), 'Time for space: A narrative review of research on organizational spaces', *International Journal of Management Reviews*, **9** (4), 325–46.

Urry, J. (2013), *Societies Beyond Oil: Oil Dregs and Social Futures*, London: Zed Books.

Wajcman, J. (1996), 'Desperately seeking differences: Is management style gendered?' *British Journal of Industrial Relations*, **34** (3), 339–49.

Wasserman, V. (2011), 'To be (alike) or not to be (at all): Aesthetic isomorphism in organisational spaces', *International Journal of Work Organisation and Emotion*, **4** (1), 22–41.

Yanow, D. and A. van Marrewijk (eds) (2010), *Organizational Spaces: Rematerializing the Workaday World*, Cheltenham, UK and Northampton, MA, USA: Edward Elgar Publishing.

12. The hospital as a space of power: ownership of space and symbols of power in the hospital setting

Erika Sauer

> To live in an environment that has to be endured or ignored rather than
> enjoyed is to be diminished as a human being.
> (Gauldie, 1969, p. 182)

In this chapter I take a closer look at the hospital space in order to see what kinds of power structures the architecture, design and use of space suggest. I work in the spirit of Foucault, who analyses the relationship of space and power in regard to the power enacted by the individuals in space, the symbolic power enacted by organizations through the use of space and the power that space carries in and of itself so that space structures relationships. We can say that space and power coexist. Space allows some functions to operate while it restricts or prohibits others.

This research is based on the thought of built spaces as storytellers that 'communicate values, beliefs and feelings using vocabularies of construction materials' (Yanow, 1998, abstract). According to Lefebvre, however, the messages of power in space are often confusing: space talks, but it does not tell all (Lefebvre [1974] 1991). My main interest here is to study how the power structures between the staff and the patients play out in the use of spaces in hospitals and in hospital design overall. Does the hospital environment bring feelings of personal power or significance, of security or of fear? How do subordinance and hierarchy present themselves?

SPACE AND POWER

The recognition of space as a 'key dynamic in understanding management and organization' (Taylor and Spicer, 2007) is quite recent (Dale and Burrell, 2003; Hernes, 2004). Today, a number of researchers point out a 'spatial turn' in organizational literature (Kornberger and Clegg, 2003; Taylor and Spicer, 2007; Ropo et al., 2013). However, while space is certainly receiving more attention than before, it still remains on the fringe of the discipline (Clegg and Kornberger, 2006). As Hernes (2004) points out 'Because we have been busy describing organizations with other terms, the meaning of space as applied to organizations has not been subject to systematic exploration' (p. xiii). This chapter seeks then to contribute to a growing body of literature that explores how space is constructed, how we construct it and how we are constructed by it.

In everyday life, institutional space is often regarded as a mere stage or a background for what is being said and what is happening, so most of our attention is spent on dialogue and behaviour, leaving space unnamed. We seldom consider how spaces mould our relationships, power structures and actions. However, what is *not* spoken, named or made explicit is often what defines power or at the very least what defines normal (Dovey, 1999). How often do we question what is considered normal in the designs of institutional spaces such as hospitals?

Power 'is at its most salient when it is embedded, embodied and thus taken as natural and inevitable' (Dale and Burrell, 2008, p. 44). The naturalness or normality of organizational space is the focus of this chapter. Space communicates in a pre-linguistic cultural language about what certain aspects of space mean. For example, we accept that those with a lot of power and higher salaries have larger offices with windows and closed doors and that people with less power will congregate in cubicles in open-floor settings. This simple example of codified spatial language reflects cultural understandings of power, which offer important insights into the world of organizations (Panatoyiou and Kafiris, 2011).

Architecture is never neutral and it is never just a backdrop. The dissemination of power, central to the function of health spaces, is contained in the very fabric of the built form (Gillespie, 2002). In its consideration of institutions such as hospitals, Foucault's analysis of medical power through the 'medical gaze' provides a critique of the social effects of public architecture and the ways power came to be institutionalized in the built form. His account of the clinic, the asylum and the prison as representations of Jeremy Bentham's Panopticon exemplified the exercising of power through surveillance in ways that resulted in subjects being disciplined and controlled. Foucault's account of the regulation of bodies through disciplinary power highlights interdependence between architecture, space and professional power. In particular, his account examines the ways the medical gaze exerts highly specific forms of power and control over the human body (Foucault, 1963). Furthermore, in the post-industrial, information technology age medical surveillance has become yet more sophisticated through ever-increasing complex systems of medical histories or medical records. For example, computer storage, cataloguing and retrieval of personal information from the 'cradle to the grave' constitute a form of electronic Panopticon (Lyon, 1993) contained in 'virtual' health space.

In the *History of Madness*, Foucault ([1961] 2006) was enticed by the void of understanding regarding what power has to do with the histories of buildings and institutions. He insists that 'we have to write the history of the use of power. . .ranging from institutional architecture to the hierarchies in classrooms and hospitals seen through the political and financial ties'. According to Foucault, the spaces and places themselves produce meanings, practices and norms, because buildings are not just symbols of power or reflectors of social order and cultural meanings, but play an active part in producing them through their interaction with the world.

Foucault suggests that space is central when we try to analyse the relationship between knowledge, power and body. Space is a part of a network of power relationships and it is there to control the human body. His analyses of power are linked to human sexuality, self-control and punishment. Foucault thinks that the practices of modern biopower are more linked to the normalization of human behaviour (that is, self-control, norms, values) than law or punishment. In one example of architecture as normalization practice, Foucault analysed the boarding schools of the eighteenth and nineteenth centuries by looking at architecture, placement of furniture, possibilities of movement, sleeping arrangements and sleeping positions. All these suggest in a silent, non-verbal way how sexuality was thought of and thus restricted. The spaces tell us how social norms, habits and practices are internalized in the use of space.

Elizabeth Prescott (1979, p.40) has written about spaces of care, especially the hazards of schools as closed structures:

> [Requirements] stem from the restrictions necessary to maintain the structure: requirements to maintain specific bodily positions, limits on mobility, absence of opportunity for tactical sensory stimulation and performance demands that may undermine self-esteem (or self-worth) (for example 'All right children, sit up straight, don't wiggle, don't touch your neighbour and be ready for my question').

It is not hard to transfer this notion of requirement to the hospital environment: 'All right patients, lie down nicely, keep still, don't go wandering around, don't bother your neighbour or the staff, and be ready to answer the doctor's questions whenever he may turn up'.

SPACE AND POWER IN THE HOSPITAL CONTEXT

The architecture of hospitals is traditionally assumed to contribute to the wellbeing and recovery of patients. This highly idealistic proposition dates back to the late eighteenth century, and has been a recurring theme in the functional development of hospital architecture ever since. The hospital, being a public and representative building with a special societal function, is the ideal vehicle to express this cultural dimension.

As Rosemary Gillespie (2002) notes in her article on power and architecture in family planning clinics, we must study the power relations in healthcare spaces when thinking about the effects of architecture upon healthcare. Social scientists have focused on human relationships in their analysis of healthcare, and medical sociologists have considered power relations in terms of professional interrelationships and medical power and dominance in health care. As Gillespie (2002) details, researchers have traditionally focused on doctor–patient relationships (Parsons, 1951; Freidson, 1970; Byrne and Long, 1976; Stewart and Roter, 1989); healthcare staff and clients (Hugson, 1991); and access to services and gatekeeping (Rummery and Glendinning, 1999; McEnvoy, 2000).

Feminist analyses of power in healthcare delivery have focused specifically on the entrenched power of the male-dominated medical profession and its relationships with both the subordinated and predominantly female professions within medicine and with female clients (Ehrenreich and English, 1979; Bleir, 1988; Stacey, 1988; Kohler-Reissman, 1989; Foster, 1989; Witz, 1992; Hoffman and Massion, 2000).

Gieryn (1999) has suggested that the very existence, appearance and internal spatial arrangements of buildings characterize identities of the people, organizations and practices they house. Brandt and Stone (1999) suggest that spaces designed for healthcare such as hospitals exist between the world of science and the world of culture, as they implicitly represent ideologies and discourses of professional power. Hospitals have traditionally carried a disciplinary message to patients, doctors and healthcare staff as to their social location (Galison, 1999). Studying the changing landscape of hospital architecture, Brandt and Stone (1999) suggest that dominant normative cultural values are represented in the structures and spatial arrangements. Inequalities between doctors, healthcare workers and patients, and medical and scientific authority, come to light in design. These authors argue that nineteenth-century hospitals embodied the nobility and grandeur of benefactors whose ideals of civic duty and philanthropy show in the very fabric of the structures. The importance of benefactors and medical science contrasted with how the patients were arranged and located in the hospital space. The relative powerlessness of the patients actualized in the functional utility, regimentation and discipline of the long common wards. Similarly, during the late nineteenth and early twentieth centuries the growing importance of laboratory and other medical spaces served as a metaphor for the increasing power of the medical profession and of the importance of scientific method in the wider society (Jewson, 1976).

For the reader to be able to put the description below into context, basic healthcare in Finland is almost free of charge, organized by municipalities and the state and is financed by taxpayers. There are private healthcare providers where people can obtain services, and national social security covers a percentage of the costs even in the private sector. The municipal hospitals provide basic care and common procedures to patients, whereas the central hospitals, financed by the state, provide complex procedures and function as teaching hospitals.

Even before World War II, hospital architecture in Finland started to reflect an architectural emphasis on functional design, reflecting notions of efficiency and effectiveness. The clean lines of buildings embodied the accessibility, convenience and universal availability associated with modernism. This was synonymous with a social democratic political ideology, the development of the welfare state and an increased reliance on the scientific method (Gillespie, 2002). According perfectly with social democratic ideology, the Finnish state and municipalities began to display visual art within hospital premises so as to promote wellbeing and to expose all citizens to art. This tradition still prevails.

The second half of the twentieth century saw the emergence of modernist and minimalist architectural designs (Photo 12.1) in health spaces denoting 'scientific management' and the 'new managerialism' in health care delivery (Davidson, 1987). As medical science developed and became more sophisticated, hospital architecture increasingly became contextualized around departments associated with expertise, and synonymous with medical power (Mitchell, 1996). Despite the occasional artwork on the wall of a ward, or sculpture in the lobby, in everyday hospital settings it is obvious that the cultural practices underlying the importance and superior position of the medical staff and undermining the patient's position continue to this day: the aesthetic pleasure or the enjoyment of the patients plays no role in the typical community hospital of a wealthy Northern European welfare state.

Photo 12.1   *Example of Finnish twentieth-century functionalist hospital architecture*

METHOD

I collected my ethnographic data in a city hospital in Finland, where I was working for a project for three weeks in 2013. The project concerned developing the managerial skills of the hospital staff, and it brought me into close interaction with all the professional groups, nurses, doctors, concierges, administrators and cleaning personnel in the hospital. These interactions took place in the administrative areas of the hospital.

By coincidence, at the same time, I had a second role of family member visiting a patient in the same hospital every day. During the period of two weeks (within that three-week project span) I observed the use of space, the talk about space and how the space influenced people, as both a patient's relative and a researcher. I also tried to pay attention to how I myself experienced, behaved in and reacted to different hospital spaces in different roles. I asked the following questions: How is power over a space enacted in a hospital setting? How is power otherwise signalled, symbolized and constructed in a hospital ward?

Dale and Burrell (2008) state that places tell stories: places can intimidate, manipulate and seduce. Places build people's identities and buildings can function as classifying devices. I relate below the story of visiting a hospital paying attention to how people, myself included enacted, functioned and felt in the ward of a municipal hospital. Inspired by Foucault, the relationship of power and space is interrogated in regard to three interrelated dimensions:

1. *Power of individuals in a space.* What are the routines and the acts of inhabiting? How are the rituals of life and work accommodated in different settings? What kinds of rituals? Who controls the space and how? How does one know one's place? Who gets in and where? What role do concierges, security personnel and receptionists play?
2. *Symbols of power through the use of space.* Interior decoration, furniture, lighting, plants, and so on: What signs and symbols are there to suggest the ownership of space or different power positions? What kinds of invitations, permissions, identification cards, money do we need to enter and to be accepted? Signs and keys? Lights and colours, symbols and labels? Uniforms and dress codes?
3. *Architectural structures and power of space.* Layout of the wards, including enclosures and barriers, doors and windows, the spaces allocated for different groups of people. How do doors divide and join different spaces? What kinds of doors? Why do metal doors and glass doors have different functions? What about handles and locks? Windows, views?

The dimensions above are presented in interrelated form in the description below.

OWNERSHIP OF SPACE AND SYMBOLS OF POWER IN THE WARD OF A CITY HOSPITAL IN FINLAND

Sometimes explicit and sometimes hidden, power encoded in built space marks the everyday lives of individuals and shapes relationships. In fact, the way that power is sometimes obscured and mediated in the built form may be what makes it most salient (Dale and Burrell, 2008). Hospitals provide a stimulating and revealing juxtaposition of individual needs and behaviours and professional hierarchies and institutional structures.

My notes from Monday 14 January 2013:

Photo 12.2   Old brick hospital building

The hospital building is located on a piece of land on the bay of a lake a few kilometres outside the city centre. On a grey winter day it looks like a sad, faded construction of Lego blocks, though less colourful. The building complex is mainly functionalist in style, though the oldest parts date back over 100 years and are red brick and more of a classical design, looking hopelessly gloomy and outdated compared to the more modern parts of the complex [Photo 12.2].

The main building is six stories high, a yellow-greyish concrete mass overlooking the more modern and shorter additions. After I found a parking space reasonably close to the entrance, it dawns on me that decades ago, instead of being parking places, the entrance was more of a garden or a festive pathway to a majestic entrance; not anymore.

The automated glass doors hiss as they open for me to enter. The warm breeze of a blowing heater in the roof greets me before I am able to locate a receptionist's booth, unassuming, almost hiding to my left.

Even though visitors are officially welcome at the hospital, and it is clearly stated on bulletin boards and the website that visits from family and friends tend to help a patient recover more quickly, I do feel like an intruder entering the hospital. When discussing this feeling and the tasks of the concierges with the concierges themselves, it seemed that they were not quite sure if they were guards, security personnel or serving the customers, that is, visitors and patients coming to the hospital. This somewhat dual and often contradictory role is visible also in the architecture, decor and uniforms. The uniforms resemble old-fashioned desk officer police uniforms, with pale blue shirts, dark blue trousers and a belt. When entering the hospital, they sit in the cubicle with a glass window just by the main door. The concierges are mostly indifferent to people entering the building, following them with their gaze, and at best, nodding when someone greets them. If the visitor does not know which ward the patient is in, the concierge can help by checking it on the computer. In this case one has to approach the glass window and talk through the opening, which requires bending down a bit, awkwardly. It is clear that the computers have not been a part of the concierge office routine for very long, which is why it takes a while for them to type the name and find out which ward where my relative is in. All interaction is done in a calm, distantly polite manner. However, the uniforms, the cubicle and the code of conduct seem still far from the customer service aspect in the job of the concierge.

On my way to the lifts, I pass a small café. There are a few patients in hospital pyjamas and robes, some having the IV stands beside their tables ensuring the steady flow of liquid and medicine into their bodies. The visitors are dressed in warm winter clothes that make them sweat in the almost too hot environment. Their outdoor clothing is packed between the backs of their chairs and their bodies, making them look even more uncomfortable and out of place.

All the areas are lit by extremely unflattering light from fluorescent tubes. The shiny clean grey linoleum floors and pale yellow walls do not help in making the space feel any cosier. The pale yellow paint, grey-green linoleum with grim neon lights seem to belong to every hospital decoration scheme. I am pressing the button for the elevator, and as it arrives, I suddenly understand why there are lines of different colours painted to the floor: some of the lines continue to the lifts that are spacious enough to fit in a bed or two.

I press the button for the third floor, and lean on the steel wall of the lift. When exiting that elevator, which is big enough to take a hospital bed, one steps out to a small foyer that leads to a ward on the right and one on the left. I cannot enter the one where I know my aunt is, as the security glass door is locked. After some confusion I see there is a button I am supposed to press. The door opens, and I am hit by damp, smelly air. The smell of the disinfectant, the human smells mixed with the smell of the food makes for a strong concoction. After opening a fire door, made of fortified glass, one finds oneself at one end of the ward corridor. The corridor seems to be a democratic zone, used by everyone but claimed by nobody. In the corridor there are nurses, cleaning personnel, patients and visitors all moving at their own pace to complete their own tasks. The cleaning equipment stands in the corridor while the cleaners clean the floor. Food carts and rollaway linen storage bins pack the corridors as well.

The staff come and go in and out of patient rooms, and visitors with overcoats and street clothes, both of which signal their not belonging, wander to and from the rooms of their loved ones. Some patients use the corridor as a training track to get up and start moving again after an operation. Sometimes visitors and nurses stand in the corridor having a discussion on a patient's care, hardly a cosy and discreet environment for that, but there simply is no better place.

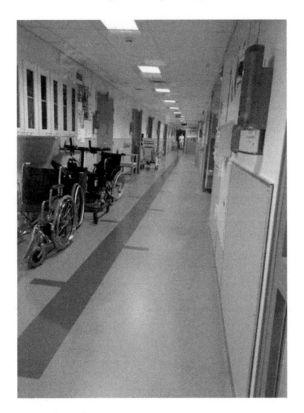

Photo 12.3   Corridor of a ward

There are a couple of chairs in the corridor by the patient rooms for those patients or relatives who wish to sit down [Photo 12.3]. It is a rare sight, however, that someone would actually sit there. It looks more like the chairs are stored in the corridor in case a bunch of relatives arrived to see a patient and there were not enough chairs in the room.

The food wagon makes me think that I have arrived at the wrong time. Even though nobody says anything I still get the feeling that the staff do not like visitors to be there when the patients are eating. There is a doctor speaking with a nurse and a family member, and some patients moving either in or out of their rooms.

On my right there is a day room, with some tables and chairs as well as a bookshelf and television. There is often also a balcony for the patients to get some fresh air (or to smoke). In the corridor there are lower cupboards or storage shelves for flower vases and on the walls there are information boards full of instructions to visitors ('Wash your hands when entering and exiting!'), warnings about MRSA bacteria and information on how to stop smoking. As I walk down the corridor there are the staff areas to my right (locker room, coffee area, food preparation) and after them, the nerve centre of the ward, the

glass-walled administrative hub where the nurses can be reached to get information about the patients and where all the paperwork is done. However, the
big window of the office to the corridor resembles the idea of the Panopticon:
the nurses in the office are able to see who moves up or down the aisle. As access
to the office is restricted to only these personnel, it feels as if the nurses behind
the glass are supervising the space. Especially at night, when there are no visitors or other outsiders in the ward, the nurses are able to keep an eye on any
traffic there.

I introduce myself, explain my relationship to the patient and ask for her
room number. Actually, I know the room number already, but perhaps out of
consideration for the personnel I think it is a necessary gesture.

I knock on the door of the room that is very clearly marked as number six.
Nobody answers. The door is big and wide but surprisingly easy to open. In
the ward visitors most often go straight to the rooms of their loved ones. If the
patient can walk or sit in a wheelchair, the cafeteria or the day room offer more
privacy than the patient room. As there seldom is any possibility of leaving
overcoats outside in the corridor, the visitors carry them. In hospitals the
temperature is set quite high, so very soon the winter boots and wool sweaters
start to feel uncomfortable. The temperature must be set to suit patients in thin
pyjamas, not the wishes of those outsiders, who come and go as they please.
In the patient rooms, there are a couple of chairs meant for the visitors. The
chairs have metal legs and wooden seats and backs. They are very uncomfortable to sit in for a longer time, which may be the purpose, because visitors, no
matter how much the patients expect them to come, are in the way of the hospital staff. The rooms are not designed for hosting the visiting relatives. One
feels that the other people in the room might get disturbed by the discussion,
or that one is in the way of the nurse who comes to help the other patient in the
next bed.

Inside the room there are three beds all in one row. Nearest to the door on
the left there is a large bathroom. I see that my aunt half-sits and half-lies in
the bed right by the window. She tells me she just got that bed today. She likes
it as she has the view at least and there are no people walking by her bed if
they have not come for her. The nurse comes to bring some medicine and picks
up the dinner plate, still half-full. The nurse greets me and we talk for a while
about my aunt's health. My aunt does not hear well so I am not too irritated
by her talking about my aunt in the third person even though she is less than
2 metres away. After the nurse is gone, my aunt tells me that the doctor comes
twice a day and talks with everyone in the room for a long time. However, she
thinks that the doctor might be a bit demented, because he looks very old and
asks the same questions over and over again. Then my aunt remembers that
the ward she is in is especially designed for people with dementia. We both
burst into laughter.

WHOSE SPACE?

Residents of the city can receive medical care services in the municipal hospital. The wards in the hospital described here include surgery, medical,
infectious diseases and general practice wards, all located in the main

hospital. Neurology and geriatrics are in the park hospital. The hospital has 368 beds.

Hospitals are workplaces for several professions. The chief physician is in charge of one or more wards, with the help of the deputy chief physician. Even if doctors in the hospital hierarchy are often said to outrank nurses, the senior nurse or nursing director is a very prominent position in that hierarchy. In fact in this particular hospital the nursing director was most often described as the chief physician's closest colleague. Doctors and nurses have a separate hierarchical structure: the chief physician is the supervisor of the doctors, whereas the nurses are overseen by the administrative director of the hospital. The director of the hospital is the supervisor of both the chief physician and the administrative director.

Traditionally, doctors hold a dominant position in the hierarchy of hospitals, as they are the ultimate decision-makers concerning the procedures, care and medication involving patients. In this particular hospital, an example of this structure had played out a couple of years earlier, when city officials appointed an engineer as a director of the hospital. The city wanted to emphasize the benefits of a market economy and started appointing managers with business backgrounds to lead healthcare institutions. This resulted in the resignations of several doctors and a severe lack of trust among key people in hospital management. After a period of just four years, the hospital returned to the old model, and the seemingly eternal hegemony of the medical profession was restored, as an experienced doctor was appointed to lead the institution.

Residents and attending physicians are in charge of medical treatment, while staff nurses, nurses and orderlies, along with instrument technicians, are responsible for the care and nursing of patients. The cleaning personnel and instrument technicians are working in wards to distribute meals and to clean the premises. Working outside the wards and thus invisible to patients and visitors are the people responsible for the laundry, laboratory, imaging, documenting and administration. However, everyone who enters and exits the hospital meets the concierges.

EFFECTIVE CURE, LOW COST, ERGONOMICS AND IMMACULATE HYGIENE AS DRIVERS OF HOSPITAL SPACE DESIGN

In the first place, hospital facilities are built to stage effective medical care for a large number of people using the lowest possible amount of taxpayer money. Optimizing the use of space for combined medical and economical effectiveness perspective makes it look very different than it would if designed, for example, for patient comfort and privacy. The size of the ward, the position of the patient rooms, the width of the corridor and the size of the doors are designed specifically for the patient/nurse ratio, the size of the hospital bed and easy access of medical staff to patients. Nowadays it is increasingly common to have different machines brought to the patients rather than vice versa, meaning that space continues to play an important role. Through the open scheme of the patient rooms, nurses can check the overall peacefulness of the room at a glance. The corridor is straight and well lit at all times, so both moving around and monitoring it are easy.

Doors to patients' rooms are wide, thick, soundproof and very easy to open. The handle is a sanded, bent metal bar that is comfortable for the hand that pulls it open. The doors have gas springs, so they easily stay wide open. Ergonomic aspects are very important in the work of a nurse. The work is very physical, lifting and turning the patients, helping them stand and walk, moving around beds and machines. In addition to hygienic demands, the equipment and the furniture in the wards need to be ergonomic for the staff.

One of the most important perspectives for hospital spaces is hygiene, which (together with fire safety) determines many surface material choices. Cleanliness is an absolute must in a hospital. In this chapter, I criticize the type of clothing worn by the patients, but much is explained by how well the materials endure high-temperature washing year after year. The same goes for all the textiles in the premises. The pale hard plastic floors and the soft yellow-painted walls reveal every soot mark and stain. The stainless steel metal beds are easy to wipe or power-clean, the white porcelain and chrome in the wet area are hygienic choices. The patients are discouraged from keeping much personal stuff in drawers or cupboards, with one exception: the very traditional expression of love, care and individuality are the flowers that visitors often bring to the patients. The hospital has vases, the staff take care of disposing them afterwards and despite the fact that flowers make cleaning up the laminate tables and drawers more difficult, the practice is not just approved, but very much encouraged.

In the wards the nurses, orderlies and the cleaning personnel walk effectively from one room to another delivering medicine, taking samples and tests, measuring temperatures and changing bandages. They open the doors without knocking, once in a while leaving them open to the corridor. Inside the rooms they address the patients sometimes by first name, sometimes with the title Mr or Mrs, and the family name. When doing tests, the nurses often draw curtains around the bed. Visual privacy seems important but everything that is said behind the closed curtains can still be heard. The nurses often speak in a loud voice, because many of the patients do not hear well due to old age. The voices take over whole rooms, making it impossible for other patients not to overhear whatever might be going on with the patient in the next bed.

The orderlies change bedclothes and the sheets, help the patients into the bathroom and wash them if they cannot do that themselves. The smells and the sounds arising from these activities are shared by all in the room and sometimes by everyone in the corridor too. Even as a visitor, not to mention as a patient, one becomes a witness to things that would be considered extremely private outside hospital setting.

It has been stated that patients with a view of nature improve more quickly and completely than other patients. All patient rooms have large windows, but in this hospital the windowsill is quite high. This means that a patient, when lying in the bed, cannot see the landscape, only a part of the sky. The patient needs to be able to sit up to enjoy any actual view. This applies only to the patient whose bed is by the window and who can sit up; the others do not have this luxury. In the city hospital that I studied, the patient rooms are most often designed for three to four patients. Every patient has a bed and a drawer and a cupboard for clothes. They share the toilet. The beds are arranged in a row, which means that one bed is close to the toilet, and the third has the window view. The middle bed, exactly as the middle seat in airplanes, remains without obvious benefits and is thus the least desirable one. The door to the room is located at the foot of the beds, so that at least theoretically the patients can see anyone who comes in.

The patient room is first of all a space where capacitated subjects (doctors, nurses) wearing signs of their professional status, meet their objects, the patients, for whom they allocate time as they see fit. Staff, and visitors for that matter, enter patients' rooms whenever and however they like. Patients are powerless to forbid entry. They are sick objects receiving care, and if in the room, expected to stay in their beds, as there is no other allocated space in the room for the patient but the bed.

The routine of a hospital day starts when the night shift ends and the morning shift starts. At night, there is minimum staffing at the hospital, whereas most nurses come in at six o'clock for the morning shift. The lights of the patient rooms are turned on and the acute cases brought to bathrooms right away, while other patients wait for breakfast and the morning toiletry in their beds. Breakfast is served at seven, lunch at 11 o'clock, coffee around two in the afternoon and dinner between four and five. The cleaning personnel serve the meals to the patients at the bedside. There is not much flexibility in the timing or choice of foods. You eat what you get.

The doctor comes according to his or her schedule (busy, his or her time is most valuable, others wait). When the doctor speaks and addresses the patient, only the patient's illness matters. During rounds, the doctors stand by the patient's bed, ask questions and possibly speak with the nursing personnel or relatives who are present. Patients are expected to answer the doctor, but not to ask questions about, for example, the doctor's professional background and capabilities. Patients either lie down or sit on their bed while the doctor stands, appearing exponentially taller and more powerful than the patient. The doctor's tone of voice is empathetic yet slightly distant. Details of illnesses and conditions at home are discussed quite openly in front of multiple strangers. The doctor decides what is enough attention for each individual as it is the doctor who initiates and ends the discussion, which resembles more a mild interrogation or an interview.

On one Wednesday in January 2013 my notes suggest it went like this:

Doctor knocks on the door and opens it without waiting for an answer. He says 'Good afternoon' and steps briskly toward the bed by the window. The door to the patient room is left open. Doctor wears a white long coat, and he has tucked his hands into the coat pockets.

The nurse is in tow. She is carrying some patient charts with her. They both smile and look sympathetically and encouragingly at the patients. The discussion goes like this:

'Ok, here we have Mrs Salonen. Hello Mrs Salonen, how do you feel today?' (In a loud voice, as the patient cannot hear well.)

'The usual. . .my leg does not hurt that much anymore, so I was wondering when can I go home?'

Doctor talks to the responsible nurse in a low voice about medication and its effects on Mrs Salonen's health. It is still intended that Mrs Salonen should hear this, but I doubt she actually has, as her hearing is bad.

'I think it is best if you rest here still over the weekend, at least. Now we have Wednesday, yes. Is there someone who can take care of you at home?'

'Yes, my daughter'.

'Yes, very good! However I think it would be difficult for her to lift you, so perhaps we will let her rest over the weekend, but let us talk about this again on Friday, shall we? Take care now, see you tomorrow!'

Everyone in the room has overheard the discussion, as the room is small and the beds are separated only during private procedures by thin curtains. The voices in the room are there for everyone to hear. During rounds the curtains are not drawn to separate the bed areas.

The nurse and the doctor say goodbye to Mrs Salonen and turn to the middle bed in the room. The same discussion is repeated, except that the patient's husband takes part in it. He sits by the patient's bed, as the nurse and the doctor talk with both of them. The doctor asks also him how he is holding up and if he feels comfortable taking his wife home, even if it means a lot of care. When the doctor and the nurse arrive at the last bed, nearest to the door, the nurse continues standing with her papers a bit behind the doctor, who clearly plays the leading role in this daily theatre. The nurse reminds the doctor in a low voice that the patient has dementia, then she steps in front of the doctor and gently rouses the sleeping little old lady in the bed. She wakes up, opens her eyes, but she is still drowsy. The doctor asks the same questions very patiently, which the patient does not actively answer. She says she wants to go home. The doctor explains very sensitively that the patient should stay in the hospital a bit more, that it would do her good. She repeats that she wants to go home and the doctor gives a slightly shorter version of his previous answer. The nurse cuts in and starts talking about the lunch that will be served shortly. The patient asks for water and then for the possibility of going to the bathroom. The nurse says she will call for help for that, as they need to continue the rounds. The doctor smiles and stops at the door to wish a great day to all three ladies and their families in the room. The door closes and he and the nurse are gone. The highlight of the day is over.

The nurses' office is in the middle of the corridor, opposite the patient rooms. It is a clearly distinguishable space because of a large glass window facing the corridor. Only staff are supposed to enter the room, which can be done only through the staff coffee room. Patients or relatives are not expected to go in there or to bother the people sitting inside. On the glass wall, there is no opening through which one could make contact with the people inside. Mostly, however, the room stays empty, as all hands are needed in the work of patient care. Inside the room the light is a bit dimmer, with the desks positioned so that their backs face the people walking down the corridor. The volume of paper and messages meant only for these personnel signal that this area is not for the uninitiated. The coffee room is clearly a private space, with postcards, plants and cheerful tablecloths. It is another kind of an environment completely compared to the other spaces on the ward.

In general, aesthetically pleasing areas or spaces within the wards are difficult, if not impossible, to find. The harsh lightning, the austere pale colours, the cold metal, all the bodily odours and non-existent privacy make hospitals fiercely if awkwardly unpleasing, even though they are designed for human beings to heal. A modest exception to this rule in Ward B3 is a set of old-fashioned chairs and a table placed near the window at the end of the corridor.

UNIFORMS AND DIGNITY

People possessing various skills and thus performing different tasks in the hospital turn into representatives of their professions. They have different uniforms. A trained eye can distinguish the professional groups' uniforms automatically without any problem. Doctors have white coats, while nurses wear pastel colours, mostly green and blue trousers and shirts, sometimes with white jackets. Concierges wear light-blue collared shirts and dark trousers. Cleaning personnel and instrument technicians sport very similar outfits, in their case dark blue trousers with dark blue jackets. It also seemed to be true that one could distinguish a doctor from all the others by looking for the person in the white coat with dozens of pens in the breast pocket. Many of the nurses, by contrast, have the white and blue pin of the Finnish Nurses Association. If all else fails, the ultimate and explicit symbol of one's hierarchy is the name and title plate on the uniform jacket. The caretakers have name tags, key cards and pressed, clean, fitted uniforms. The uniforms divide those that are in a position to make decisions and to invade the privacy of others from those who remain objects and instruments of those decisions and invasions.

It is interesting that in such a culture, patients are stripped of all of their status symbols. By storing personal items such as clothes, shoes, watches, jewels, business cards and name tags behind the locked cabinet door, people turn into 'patients', meaning they wait patiently in their beds to be attended to, and into docile bodies examined by the medical gaze and cared for according to pre-set standards (Foucault [1975] 1995).

Architectural conventions in designing institutions, lack of munici-pal resources and effectiveness of care are all factors that contribute to patients being deprived of privacy, individuality and sexuality (Goffman, 1963, 1971). In their unisex loose-hanging faded jersey night-gowns, and stripped of all hierarchical or gendered signs, patients look like walking examples of their diseases instead of valued citizens, respected taxpayers and stimulating individuals with private lives, pasts and futures.

Some patients are dressed in hospital pyjamas, perhaps the most unflat-tering garments on the planet (Photo 12.4). The patient pyjama turns independent individuals into ugly, sick matter that needs to be fixed. However, the pyjamas are very soft, comfortable and hygienically wash-able in boiling water, with side-effect of fading the colours. The pink and green cotton jersey garments are a must for all patients, as the hospital cannot guarantee the cleanliness of individual outfits brought from home. The robes are made of pastel-coloured or brown-patterned cotton, and cut in a kimono style to fit every body shape. Their elegance is crowned with brown plastic slippers and white socks without heels and elastic, which means that they are crumpled around the ankles at all times. Not exactly a power suit. . .

Photo 12.4   Hospital pyjamas and nightgowns

TOUCHING, SEXUALITY AND BEAUTY

The uniformed staff's central role is to provide medical care to patients. The uniform gives them permission to do so. Caring for and curing patients in hospital settings requires touching. Patients become objects of touch. Doctors and nurses constantly touch patients without asking for permission. The uniform also somehow takes away the individuality of the caretakers, and downplays their personality, thus perhaps making it easier for them to approach the patients in a purely professional capacity. Nursing and care require touching, but the touching in hospitals seems somehow a bit tough, purposeful, efficient and matter of fact. Patients rarely touch doctors. With nurses, it is often a handshake or gentle touch on the arm to get attention, but in general the public and the professionals are well trained to avoid unnecessary touching, due to the spread of germs. When visitors come, they do not necessarily touch the patient. Holding and caressing the hand of their loved one is quite common, perhaps even a short hug. The idea is that the patients do not touch each other, not even when they are in small rooms, beds just an arm's-length away. Doctors or nurses rarely touch each other, nor do the visitors touch them.

Despite nurses and doctors being a popular pictorial and textual genre within erotic literature, the looks, smells, sounds and feels are supposed to turn hospitals into de-sexualized and de-sensualized zones, however inevitably doomed to fail this requirement may be (Baillie et al., 2008). Most nurses are women, but more men have recently entered the profession. All nurses care for both men and women. Due to cultural norms and values in hospitals in Finland, men and women are only put in the same room under special circumstances, which hardly guarantees that sexual deeds or erotic encounters do not take place in them.

In this vein, we must ask if the unflattering pyjama is designed, consciously or not, to serve a purpose. Hospitals are places where the sexuality *of the patients* is excluded, or at least very much downplayed, in an effort to avoid the open enactment of erotic subjectivism that could occur in circumstances where there is no equality or balance of power and status (ibid.). Zero tolerance of eroticism, and ugly clothing to discourage, curb and control the patients' behaviour might all be part of the effort to keep up the high morale expected of a hospital institution.

As an interesting anecdote, after the Balkan Wars of the 1990s, women refugees who fled to Croatia were given small vouchers to go to hair salons and to shops to buy new clothes. They openly stated that this gesture was an effective method to help relieve the trauma they had suffered. 'Beauty on the outside helps healing inside', they said. The pyjamas and night-gowns people wear in the Finnish city hospital, and in most public hospitals, do not respect this concept.

CONCLUDING REMARKS

Dignified surroundings make people able to respect themselves (Baillie et al., 2008). In hospitals, patients lose all signs of their individuality, dignity, privacy and autonomy. Goffman (1971) insists that personal space functions as a protective shield between individuals. Personal space is an integral part of individuals' representations of self and sense of subjectivity (Goffman, 1963, 1971). Losing personal space makes the individual vulnerable. By invading personal space hospitals minimize all signs of individuality and power, thus turning the patients, as prisoners, into 'docile bodies' (Foucault [1975] 1995).

In contemporary public hospitals in Finland, patients lose not only the command over the use of space but also the use of their time: hence the use of the term 'patient' in English. A hospital has regulated schedules (doctor's rounds, meals, medicine, shower, etc.) that leave little room for individual wishes. The control of space and time goes hand in hand.

Architecture is never neutral and it is never just a backdrop. The dissemination of power, central to the function of health spaces, is contained in the fabric of the built form (Gillespie, 2002). As the spaces and places themselves produce meanings, practices and norms, buildings are not just symbols of power or reflectors of social order and cultural meanings. They take part in producing them, interacting with the world. Today, hospitals represent individual leadership thinking, where the people are controlled by the building.

Gazing into the future, late twentieth- and twenty-first-century (private) hospital architecture has been said to increasingly embrace the service space or the open space model of the shopping mall, exhibiting the luxuriousness of a nice hotel, housing commercial spaces such as shops, banks and restaurants. Patients will be presented with choices and services far beyond today's scope.

It is possible, however, that postmodern hospitals have come to embody the power of commercialism (Brandt and Stone, 1999). Nevertheless, despite displays of opulence, spatial arrangements continue to control and exclude as well as welcome and embrace (Gillespie, 2002). In the case that the new way of thinking of hospitals as service spaces is only limited to private hospitals, the new paradigm will contribute to the experience of health inequalities, as style and luxury in the private hospitals reproduces wider social exclusions. Hospital architecture comes to represent and embody social division instead of the equal care that has been the norm in the Finnish health system.

REFERENCES

Baillie, L., A. Gallagher and P. Wainwright (2008), *Defending Dignity: Challenges and Opportunities of Nursing*, London: Royal College of Nursing.

Bleir, R. (1988), *Feminist Approaches to Science*, New York: Pergamon Press.

Brandt, A.M. and D.C. Stone (1999), 'Of beds and benches: Building the modern hospital', in P. Galison and E. Thompson (eds), *The Architecture of Science*, Cambridge, MA: MIT Press.

Byrne, P.S. and B.L. Long (1976), *Doctors Talking to Patients*, London: HMSO.

Clegg, S. and M. Kornberger (2006), *Space, Organizations and Management Theory*, Oslo: Liber.

Dale, K. and G. Burrell (2003), 'An-aesthetics and architecture', in P. Hancock and A. Carr (eds), *Art and Aesthetics at Work*, Basingstoke, UK: Palgrave Macmillan, pp. 155–73.

Dale, K. and G. Burrell (2008), *Spaces of Organization and the Organization of Space*, Basingstoke, UK: Palgrave Macmillan.

Davidson, N. (1987), *A Question of Care: The Changing Face of the NHS*, London: Michael Joseph.

Dovey, K. (1999), *Framing Places: Mediating Power in Built Form*, London: Routledge.

Ehrenreich, B. and D. English (1979), *For Her Own Good: 150 Years of the Expert's Advice to Women*, London: Pluto Press.

Foster, P. (1989), 'Improving the doctor/patient relationship: A feminist perspective', *Journal of Social Policy*, **18** (3), 215–36.

Foucault, M. ([1961] 2006), *History of Madness* (original French title: *Histoire de la Folie*), ed. and trans. J. Khalfa and J. Murphy, London: Routledge.

Foucault, M. (1963), *The Birth of the Clinic: An Archaeology of Medical Perception* (in French), Paris: Presses universitaires.

Foucault, M. ([1975] 1995), *Discipline and Punish: The Birth of the Prison* (original French title: *Surveiller et Punir: Naissance de la Prison*), trans. A. Sheridan, Second Vintage Books edition, New York: Random House.

Freidson, E. (1970), *The Profession of Medicine*, New York: Dodd, Mead & Co.

Galison, P. (1999), 'Buildings and the subject of science', in P. Galison and E. Thompson (eds), *The Architecture of Science*, Cambridge, MA: The MIT Press.

Gauldie, S. (1969), *Architecture: The Application of the Arts*, Oxford: Oxford University Press.

Gieryn, T.F. (1999), 'Two faces on science: Building identities for molecular biology and biotechnology', in P. Galison and E. Thompson (eds), *The Architecture of Science*, Cambridge MA: MIT Press, pp. 423–55.

Gillespie, R. (2002), 'Architecture and power: A family planning clinic as a case study', *Health and Place*, **8** (3), 211–20.

Goffman, E. (1963), *Behavior in Public Places: Notes on the Social Organization of Gatherings*, New York: The Free Press.

Goffman, E. (1971), *Relations in Public: Microstudies of the Public Order*, New York: Basic Books.

Hernes, T. (2004), *Spatial Construction of Organization*, Amsterdam: John Benjamins.

Hoffman, E. and C. Massion (2000), 'Women's health as a medical specialty and a clinical science', in L. Sherr and J. St. Lawrence (eds), *Women, Health and the Mind*, Chichester, UK: Wiley.

Hugson, R. (1991), *Power in the Caring Professions*, London: Macmillan.

Jewson, N. (1976), 'The disappearance of the sick-man from medical cosmology', *Sociology*, **10** (2), 225–44.

Kohler-Reissman, C. (1989), 'Women and medicalisation: A new perspective', in P. Brown (ed.), *Perspectives in Medical Sociology*, Belmont, CA: Wadsworth.

Kornberger, M. and S. Clegg (2003), 'The architecture of complexity', *Culture and Organization*, **9** (2), 75–91.

Lefebvre, H. ([1974] 1991), *The Production of Space*, English translation from French, Oxford: Blackwell.

Lyon, D. (1993), 'An electronic panopticon? A sociological critique of surveillance theory', *Sociological Review*, **41** (4), 653–78.

McEnvoy, P. (2000), 'Gatekeeping access to services at the primary/secondary interface', *Journal of Psychiatric & Mental Health Nursing*, **7** (3), 241–7.

Mitchell, W.J. (1996), *City of Bits: Space, Place, and the Infobahn*, Cambridge, MA: MIT Press.

Panayiotou, A. and K. Kafiris (2011), 'Viewing the language of space: Organizational spaces, power, and resistance in popular films', *Journal of Management Inquiry*, **20** (3), 264–84.

Parsons, T. (1951), *The Social System*, New York: Free Press.

Prescott, E. (1979), 'The physical environment: A powerful regulator of experience', *Child Care Information Exchange*, No. 100, 9–15.

Ropo, A., E. Sauer and P. Salovaara (2013), 'Embodiment of leadership through material place', *Leadership*, **9** (3), 378–95.

Rummery, K. and C. Glendinning (1999), 'Negotiating needs, access and gate-keeping: Developments in health and community care policies in the UK and the rights of disabled and older citizens', *Critical Social Policy*, **19** (3), 335–51.

Stacey, M. (1988), *The Sociology of Health and Healing*, London: Routledge.

Stewart, M. and D. Roter (1989), *Communicating with Medical Patients*, New York: Sage.

Taylor, S. and A. Spicer (2007), 'Time for space: A narrative review of research on organizational spaces', *International Journal of Management Reviews*, **9** (4), 325–46.

Witz, A. (1992), *Professions and Patriarchy*, London: Routledge.

Yanow, D. (1998), 'Space stories: Studying museum buildings as organizational spaces while reflecting on interpretive methods and their narration', *Journal of Management Inquiry*, **7** (3), 215–39.

Index

Academy of Finland 3
action and structure 238
activity-based offices 57–8
Adams, S. 30
advanced information technology
    (AIT) 110
aesthetic epistemology 186
aesthetic leadership 61, 64, 123–4, 125,
    184
aesthetics 3, 6–7, 8, 9, 220, 257
    organizational 179
affordances of virtual worlds 136–8
airports 12, 133
Al-Ani, B. 110
Alahuhta, P. 137
alienation and estrangement 97
Allen, T.J. 31
Alvesson, M. 149, 155, 157
ambient conditions *see* heating and
    ventilation
Anthony, S. 7
Apple 42
Arab countries 203
architectural characteristics 101
architectural motives 5
architectural structures and power of
    space 248
architecture 4
    and aesthetics 6–7
    cities 186–9, 192–3
    hospital 245–6, 260–61
    office 10–11
Arge, K. 6
arrangements of space 159
    see also design; layout
artefacts 8
    see also symbolic dimension of space
        and artefacts in a bookstore
        (Finland)
Asian cultures 202, 203, 207–9
assignments and tasks 131

A.T. Kearney Inc. 184
atrium 219
authority 120, 203, 207
avatars 128, 129–30, 131, 132, 134, 137
    anthropomorphic (clones) 139
    as geometrical shapes 139
    as leaders 139–40
    social influence 139
    social relations between 138–40
Axtell, C. 133

ba 79–80, 134
Bacigalupo, T. 34–6
Bandura, A. 80
Bat Haus 29, 39
Becker, F. 6, 7, 135
behavioural aspects and new
        technology 113
beliefs 242
Bentham, J. 243
Berg, P.O. 149, 155, 157
Bevort, F. 209
Beyes, T. 7
Bezos, J. 42–3
Blair, M. 6
bodily leadership 64
Boje, D.M. 94–5, 102
Bosch-Sijtsema, P.M. 140–41
branding corporate image and identity
        5–7
Brandt, A.M. 245
Brazil 202
Brewster, C. 204
British Council for Offices 226
Burrell, G. 53, 248
business-driven strategies 6

cafés 133, 250
Calas, M. 229
Canon 54
Carlopio, J.R. 206

cars 133
Castells, M. 33
Caulat, G. 112
centralized organizations 201
chairs/sofas 223–4
changes in ways of working 1–4
charisma 120
cities (New York and Jakarta) 183–96
  architecture 186–9, 192–3
  atmosphere 185
  community, sense of 191
  divisions according to ethnicity,
    religion and like-minded people
    188
  divisions between rich and poor 187
  divisions into work, recreation,
    relaxation and consumerism
    187, 194–5
  divisions of specific professions
    188–9
  gentrification 187–8
  grid pattern 189–90
  housing projects/subsidized housing
    188
  kampung (traditional village) within
    the city 192
  planning 189–90
  political monuments and memorials
    192–3
  public transport system 191
  rush hours 191–2
  safety 191
  theoretical underpinnings and
    method 184–6
  traffic, water and waste 189–92
  United Nations Human Settlements
    Programme 188
  urban informal settlements and/or
    illegal constructions 188
  walking and biking 191
Citizen Space (San Francisco) 35
clothing 156, 258–9
  see also uniforms
co-customers 173–4
coincidental meetings (serendipity)
  62–3
collaboration 9, 35, 43, 138, 201, 209
  from multiple locations 132
collaborative meetings, small 140–41,
  142

collaborative working environment
  (CWE) 130
collective leadership 122
collectivistic values 203, 207–8
colour schemes/decor 74, 152–3, 159,
  250, 257
combi-office (open-plan/cellular
  hybrid) 54, 74
communal idealism 36
communication 9, 201
  control over 118
  tools 141
  in virtual space 115–16
community, sense of 97, 191
community-building 34–6, 140
community space 236
competencies in knowledge-intensive
  setting 72
competitive advantage 5
conceived space 5, 9, 101
conferences 141
conformity 235
congruence hypothesis 6, 205
consensus 209
contextual affordances 131–2, 134
control and hierarchy 202, 235
cooperation 44, 64, 209
  cross-cultural 112
  informal 62
corporate branding 5–7
corporate values and management
  principles 200
corridors 9, 12, 219, 224, 250–51,
  254
cost-efficiency 5, 72
costs 253–7
cotivation 39
Country Fire Office 52
Coworking Conference Europe (2013)
  31
coworking movement 1, 13, 27–44
  benefits 31–2
  community-building 34–6
  internal leadership 38
  Jellies (casual working events) 31–2,
    35
  negative features 32
  plural leadership 37–9, 43
  principles in business organizations
    39–43

social aspects 34, 36
  sustainability 34–5
  values 35–6
Coworking Wiki 34
creativity 116
critical post-structuralist approach 8
cross-functionality 72
crowd funding 43
crowdsourcing 43
cultural meaning and symbolic
  meaning 159
cultural norms and values 260
cultural studies 160
cultural values 205, 245
culture/cross-cultural factors 1, 97, 188
  in virtual space 114, 115, 117
  see also Telenor
customers *see* self-service hotels;
  symbolic dimension of space and
  artefacts in a bookstore

Dale, K. 53, 248
Davis, M.C. 5, 7
De Certeau, M. 97
de Dear, R. 42
De Paoli, D. 6, 59, 61
Deal, T.E. 7
decor *see* colour schemes/decor
Denis, J.-L. 38
Denmark 207
dependence and hierarchical
  relationships 202
design 246
  features 5
  hospital 246
  office 54–5
  physical 204
  strategy 205
  workplace 7
  workspace 6–7
Deskmag 31
desks/work stations 5, 223, 236
Dickinson, P. 6
Digital 51, 54
digital representations 136
disembodiment 236–7, 238
dissent and resistance to project 234–6,
  238
distancing 230–34, 238
  see also power distance

distributed leadership 61, 229–30,
  238
distributed teamwork 132, 133
domesticating the space 222–4
doors 12, 254
Dourish, P. 128
dual competency leadership 65
Duffy, F. 5, 57

e-leadership 111, 113, 120
Edelberg, G.S. 33–4
effectiveness in design 246
efficiency in design 5, 246
efficiency of space 54
Elsbach, K.D. 9, 74, 101
embodied leadership 119, 123–4, 125
embodiment 3, 8–9
emotion 149
emotional connection 116
employee wellbeing and workspace
  experiences 1, 87–103
  data collection and materials
    89–90
  giving way and adapting 95–100
  narrative approach 89–90, 91,
    95–100
  noise (hustle and bustle) in open-
    plan office space 90–95
  privacy, loss of and surveillance
    92–4
  'stage' 88–9
  tensions 94–5
empowered leadership 119, 124
enablers of leadership 135–6
enclosure and barriers 101
entrance (of a building) 133, 149–50,
  219
environmental psychology 11
epistemology 3
  aesthetic 186
equality 208–9
equipment and ergonomics 254
ergonomics 253–7
Ericsson 51, 54
experience of space 91

facilities management (FM) 5, 58
factual and impersonal approach
  116
feelings 242

felt experience 2
femininity/feminine culture 208
Finland 39, 40, 51
   see also ownership of space and
       power in hospital (institutional)
       setting; symbolic dimension of
       space and artefacts in a
       bookstore
fire safety 254
flexible office plans 54, 74
floors 254
food 195, 250–51
Ford, J. 217, 229
Foucault, M. 156, 242–4, 248
Frankfurt School: critical theory
   185
Frantic 40–41, 43
Freeman, T. 38
furniture 220–23, 254
  chairs/sofas 223–4
  desks/work stations 5, 223, 236

Gagliardi, P. 8
Gardener, D. 206
Gauldie, S. 242
Germany 53
Gerstberger, P.G. 31
getting lost in the space 97–8
Ghiselli, E.E. 205
Gieryn, T.F. 245
Gillespie, R. 245
GLOBE project 202, 205
Goffman, E. 260
Goh, S. 140
Gosling, J. 230
Grenness, T. 54, 55
groupware 122
Guillén, M. 8

habits and internalization 244
Hair, M. 205
Hakonen, M. 142
Halford, A. 133
HALO rooms 131
Hamel, G. 2
Handy, C. 113–14
Hansen, H. 61
Harrison, S. 128
Hassard, J. 8
Haussmann, Baron G.-E. 192

Hawthorne studies 7
headquarters 8, 200
heating and ventilation 7, 225–6, 227,
   236, 252
Heerwagen, J. 5
Hegel, G.W.F. 35
Henry, S. 189
hermeneutics 160
Hernes, T. 243
hierarchical structure 202, 203, 207,
   235, 253
high-involvement workplace 2
Hislop, D. 133
Hofbauer, J. 9, 201–2
Hofstede, G. 201–3, 208
Holbrook, M.B. 180
'home' space 223
hospital *see* ownership of space and
       power in hospital (institutional)
       setting (Finland)
hot desking 73
hotels *see* self-service hotels
House, R.J. 202–3
hubs 32, 44
human geography 10
human relations studies 7
human/non-human relationship 11–12,
   238
Hurry, C.J.P. 32
hybrid workspace 133

IBM 31, 43
ideals 11, 36, 54, 134, 245
ideation 128–31, 133–4, 238
identity lens 74
image-text 90
imagined space 10
India 207
individual meaning and symbolic
   meaning 159
individualism versus team orientation
   203, 208
individuality, loss of 258, 260
information, access to 43
innovation 235
interaction 9, 64, 77, 201
interdependence 36, 44
interests and knowledge-intensive
   setting 72
internal leadership 38

international business management *see* Telenor and international business management
international human resource management (IHRM) 204, 212
Internet 27, 109–110, 117–18, 130–31, 135–6, 166, 168, 174
Interpolis (Tilburg) 55
interpretation and social constructionism 2
invitation-only spaces 32

Jellies (casual working events) 31–2, 35
job satisfaction 101
Jobs, S. 36
Jones, D. 30–31, 43
Joroff, M. 58

Kampschroer, K. 5
Karanian, B. 9
Kayworth, T.R. 114
Kennedy, A.A. 7
Kim, D. 42
King, N. 4
knowledge 209
   embodied 154
   explicit 79, 81
   tacit 79, 81, 149
knowledge-based organizations 6
knowledge-intensive projects 71–83
   ba 79–80
   open office plans 75–81
   open-plan offices/open zones 73–5
   tacit and explicit knowledge 79, 81

Ladkin, D. 2, 118, 160
language 114, 117
large events 140, 141
Larkin Administration Building 52
layout 5, 101, 159, 235
Le Corbusier 11
leader-centric approach 2, 119–20, 121–2, 124, 160
leader–follower 117, 135
leader member exchange (LMX) theory 140
leader/leadership distinction 2
leaderism 229, 233, 238
Leadership in Place and Space project 3
learning and training 140, 141–2

Lefebvre, H. 5, 9, 42, 100–101, 242
Leidner, D. 114
Levin, A.C. 6
Lewin, K. 134
liberation management 54
life space 134
lighting 101, 152, 236, 250, 257
Lilischkis, S. 133
Lindkvist, L. 209
listening in virtual space 116
lived space 9
lobbies (hotel) 133

Mabey, C. 38
maker movement 44
management of space 58
managerial motives 5
managerial/architectural space 101
managerialism 238
Marshall, J. 229
Martin, P.Y. 218
massively multiplayer online game (MMOG) 140
material aspects of organizational life 7, 9
material spaces 3
materiality 8, 136, 185, 238
   digital 136
   physical 135, 136, 185
   social 185
Mayne, T. 205
meaning and artefacts 157
meaningful places and spaces, importance of 64, 65, 124–5, 147–8
meaningmaking and social constructionism 2
meeting rooms 32, 40, 60–61, 77–8, 226
Meindl, J.R. 2
mental space 134–5
Microsoft 39–40, 43
Milgram, S. 185
Mitchell, W.J.T. 90
mobile telework 133
Morgan, A. 7
motivation 116
multilocational work 133
multinational corporations (MNCs) 199–200, 204, 206
mutual constitution 12

Nadler, D.A. 6
Napoleon III 192
nature of a task 131–2
nature-like surroundings 5, 101
Net Geners 118, 120
Net Work 56–7, 62, 63, 64
Netherlands 39, 55
network model 56–8, 60, 120–21, 141–2
New Work City (Broadway New York)
  28, 39
Nishida, K. 79
nodes: formal and informal places for
  interaction 61–2
noise disturbance and soundproofing
  90–95, 101, 226, 227, 236
non-places 133
non-territorial features 73–4, 75
non-verbal cues 15, 78, 137, 159
Nonaka, I. 79–80
Nordbäck, E. 139
norms and internalization 244
Norway 6, 42, 75
  Work Environment Act 209
  Work-Life Forum 208
  see also Telenor

objective approach to space 8
objective physically oriented space 3
Occupy movement 43
offices 4–17, 51–6
  activity-based 57–8
  architecture 10–11
  design, alternative 54–5
ontology of leadership 185
open source movement 43
open-plan offices/open zones 5, 32, 42,
  73–81, 90–95, 200
  layout 101
openness and transparency 35, 43,
  60–61, 64
O'Reilly, D. 233
organizational change and
  development 5–6
organizational form, culture and
  practice 205
organizational gravitation 58
organizational justice, equality and
  respect 94, 99
organizational pyramids 200–201, 210
organizing space 4

Orlikowski, W.J. 135–6
Orwell, G. 217
ownership of space and power in
  hospital (institutional) setting
  (Finland) 242–61
  aesthetics 257
  architecture 245–6, 260–61
  autonomy 260
  café 250
  coffee room 257
  colour schemes 250, 257
  concierges 249–50
  corridors 250–51, 254
  data collection method 247–8
  design 246
  disciplinary power 243
  doctor's rounds 255–7
  doors 254
  effective cure, low cost and
    ergonomics as drivers of space
    design 253–7
  effectiveness 246
  efficiency 246
  equipment 254
  exterior of building 249
  fire safety 254
  floors 254
  flowers 254
  furniture 254
  heating and ventilation 252
  hierarchical structure of nurses and
    doctors 253
  hospital beds 254
  hygienic demands 253–7
  individuality, loss of 258, 260
  lighting 250, 257
  medical gaze 243
  modernist and minimalist
    architectural designs 246
  night-gowns/pyjamas 258–9
  nurses' office 257
  patient rooms 252, 254, 255
  personal space 260
  power 242–4
  power, dissemination of 260
  privacy 258, 260
  routine of hospital day 255–6
  sexuality, loss of 258, 259–60
  symbols of power 248–52
  touching 259–60

uniforms 250, 257–9, 260
visual art displays 246
visual privacy 254–5
walls 254
ward size 254
wellbeing 246
windows 255

participative leadership 62
particularism versus universalism
    203
paternalistic leadership style 203, 207
patriarchy 229
peer surveillance 75
perceived space 9
performance versus maintenance
    orientation 203
personal abilities, subordinates or rules,
    reliance on 203
personal space 236, 260
personalization of workspace 74,
    101
Pevsner, N. 52
phallogocentrism 229
phenomenological approach to space
    8, 160
physical environment 8–9, 200, 203,
    204, 210
physical position and status 210
physical space 8, 59, 134–5
physical strategy 64
physicality in virtual leadership 115,
    119
places for work 50–51
planes 133
planned space 5, 10, 100, 101
plants 5
plural leadership 37–9, 43, 122–3
Porter, L. 205
power 8, 202, 210, 242–4
    disciplinary 243
    dissemination 260
    distance 200–203, 206, 207, 208,
        210
    of individuals in a space 248
    issues 184
    relations 185–6
    and space 192
    symbols of through use of space
        248–52

theory 156
    see also ownership of space and
        power in hospital (institutional)
        setting (Finland)
practised space 10
Pratt, M.G. 9, 101
prerequisites of leadership 131–2
Prescott, E. 244
presence, sense of 61, 141
presence work 39
pride 94–5
privacy 92–4, 101, 224, 258, 260
    visual 254–5
    see also pseudo-privacy
process approach 119, 121–2
process (challenge in virtual space)
    115
process simulations 140, 142
process-oriented strategies 6
product development 140, 142
product quality 72
productivity tools 141
project work in knowledge-based
    organizations 5
    see also knowledge-intensive
        projects
projectification 33
pseudo-privacy 135
psychological factors 7

Quickborner Team 53
Qvale, T.U. 208

Ramirez, R. 8
rational planning motive 5
rebellion 235
    see also dissent
reciprocity 35
redundancy (and role modelling) 80
Reed, M. 233
regional studies 10
relational process, leadership as 119,
    121–3, 160
religion 114, 117
respect 210, 211
Riessman, C. 100
ritualism 235
role-model learning 80, 82
Ropo, A. 147, 159
Rukmana, D. 184

sabotage (as form of dissent) 235
safety 191, 254
　see also fire-safety; security; video
　　cameras
SAS Frösundavic office building 54
Scandinavia 54–5, 202
Scandinavian leadership model 208
Scharmer, C.O. 10
schools 244
Schramm-Nielsen, J. 209
Schwartz, S.H. 202
Scott, S.V. 135–6
security 169–70, 171, 177, 226
　emotional and psychological 169
self-control 244
self-leadership 118, 119, 123, 143
self-service hotels 163–79
　back-stage employees as virtual
　　human resources 170–71
　co-customers, meaning of 173–4
　consumptionscape 178
　customer perceptions 167–75
　customer segmentation 174–5,
　　178
　customers' experiences 179
　customers' needs for front-stage
　　employees in accommodation
　　encounters 169–70
　customers' perceptions of hospitality
　　171–2
　customers' sensuous experiences in a
　　hotel room (sight/hearing/smell)
　　172–3
　emotional and psychological security
　　169
　experience room 178
　front-stage employees in hospitality
　　services 178
　future research 177–9
　hospitality/hospitableness 169
　interactive, relativistic preference
　　experience 178
　script to guide service encounters
　　165
　security concerns 171, 177
　security service 169–70
　service design when the space is the
　　service 175–7
　service failures 170–71
　service quality 171–2
　service system as a theatrical
　　performance 164–5
　servicescape 178
　target group 174–5, 178
　video cameras 169, 171
self-service restaurants 12
Sennett, R. 27, 33–4
sense of living in someone else's space
　98
senses 172–3, 236
servant leadership 123
shared leadership 61, 62, 64, 119, 122,
　123, 124, 143
shareholder value 53
sharing economy 35, 43
Shortt, H. 42
simplification 232
Sims, W. 135
Sivunen, A. 139, 140–41, 142
Sjöman, S. 54
smells 236
Smircich, L. 229
social aspects 7, 34, 36
social constructionist research
　approach 2, 178
social distancing 230–34, 238
social infrastructure for work 59–63, 64
　coincidental meetings (serendipity)
　　62–3
　nodes: formal and informal places
　　for interaction 61–2
　openness and transparency 60–61
social learning theory 80, 82–3
social needs 43
social networking tools 141–2
social norms and internalization 244
social space 59, 134–5
social strategy 64
societal cultural values 205
societal pyramids 200
sociomateriality of leadership 11–12,
　159, 238
Soeharto, H.M. 192–3
Soekarno 190, 192–4
software 122, 142
SOL 51, 54
spatial leadership 3, 12, 82, 160
spatial production theory 100
spatial turn 3–4, 7–9
Spicer, A. 5, 9–10, 42, 87, 100–101, 156

Spinuzzi, C. 28–9, 32, 33
stairs/staircases 12, 93, 150, 220
stakeholder value 53–4
standardization 232
Standing Conference on
    Organizational Symbolism
    (SCOS) 8
status 202, 206, 210
Steyaert, C. 7
Stoller, P. 218
Stone, D.C. 245
Storey, J. 235
strategic alignment 59
Strati, A. 8, 218
Strauss, K. 29
subgrouping 115
subjective meanings 149
subjectively perceived space 3, 8
sustainability 34–5
Svensen, N. 6
Sweden 51, 52, 54
symbolic dimension of space and
    artefacts in a bookstore (Finland)
    147–60
  being a salesperson: rules and
      routines and mental state 153–6
  break room 154–5, 159
  clothing 156
  colour scheme 152–3, 159
  concept redevelopment 152–3
  dressing room 154–5
  entering bookstore and data
      collection 148–9
  entrance 149–50
  layout 159
  lift 154
  lighting 152
  manager's office 157–8
  meaningfulness 147–8
  meanings attached to different
      spaces 149–53
  retail space 151–3
  sales desk 154, 156–7
  sales personnel's spaces 153–7
  shop area 159
  staircase 150
  toilet 154
  uniform 155–6, 159
  upstairs and downstairs areas 151
  warehouse 154, 159

symbolic meanings 184
symbolic representation of culture of
    organization 203
symbols of power through use of space
    248–52

Tapie, J. 139–40
Tapscott, D. 118
task, control over 118
Taylor, F.W. 4
Taylor, S. 5, 9–10, 42, 87, 100–101, 156
Taylorism 52–3
technology (challenge in virtual space)
    115
Technopolis 40–41, 43
Telenor and international business
    management: culture/cross-
    cultural perspective 42, 55, 60,
    199–212
  age and education (of employers/
      employees) 210, 211
  Arab countries 203
  Asian cultures 202, 203, 207–9
  centralized organizations 201
  challenges 205–6
  collaboration 201, 209
  collectivistic values 203, 207–8
  communication 201
  control 202
  corporate values and management
      principles 200
  dependence 202, 207
  design strategy 205
  equality 208–9
  experience 210
  femininity/feminine culture 208
  hierarchical structure 202, 203, 207
  horizontal relationships 201
  individualism versus team
      orientation 203, 208
  interaction 201
  international human resource
      management 212
  knowledge 209
  lateral relationships 201
  leadership roles 210–212
  obedience 210
  open-space office design 200
  organizational pyramids 200–201,
      210

particularism versus universalism
203
paternalistic leadership style 203,
207
performance versus maintenance
orientation 203
personal abilities, subordinates or
rules, reliance on 203
physical environment 200, 203, 204,
210
power distance 200–203, 206, 207,
208, 210
respect 210, 211
Scandinavian cultures 207–9
Scandinavian leadership model 208
societal pyramids 200
status 202, 206, 210
symbolic representation of culture
of organization 203
traditional leadership 202
uncertainty avoidance 208
vertical relationships 201, 207
visual privileges 203, 207–8
telework 132–3
territorial features 73, 75
3D CAD software 142
tidiness, uniformity and sameness
236–7
time, control over 118
time frames 72
time, task, team and transition (for
projects) 72
Torp, N. 54
trade shows 141
traditional leadership 202
traditional offices 51–6
traffic 189–92
transformational leadership 119
transparency 60–61, 64
Triandis, H.C. 205
Trompenaars, F. 202
trust (challenge in virtual space) 115
Tuan, Y.-F. 10, 149
Turner, F. 36
Tushman, M.L. 6

uncertainty avoidance 208
uniforms 155–6, 159, 250, 257–9, 260
United States 33
university building (UK) 217–39

aesthetics 220
atrium 219
budget 230–31
community space 236
corridors 219, 224
desks/work stations 223, 236
disembodiment 231, 236–7, 238
dissent and resistance to project
234–6, 238
domesticating the space 222–4
ethics 226
exterior of building 218, 219
floor plan 221
furniture 220–22, 223
heating and ventilation 225–6, 227,
236
'home' space 223
layout 235
lighting 236
moving in 218–22
noise disturbance and soundproofing
226, 227, 236
open plan and 'fish tank' analogy
224–8
patriarchy 229
personal space 236
phallogocentrism 229
privacy 224
professionalization of management
231
security 226
senses – sight, sound, taste, touch
and smell 236
simplification 232
social distancing 230–34, 238
sofas/chairs 223–4
staff room 223–4
stairways 220
standardization 232
tidiness, uniformity and sameness
236–7
'user', rhetorical notion of 232
visual distractions 226, 227
us and them distinction 98
usability of work-places 59

Vaagaasar, A.L. 55
values 35–6, 117, 157, 205, 242, 244
collectivistic 203, 207–8
corporate 200

creation 5–6, 59
cultural 205, 260
knowledge-intensive 72
Van Marrewijk, A. 7
Van Meel, J. 55
Värlander, S. 75
ventilation 7, 225–6, 227, 236, 252
video cameras (as security) 169, 171
video-conferencing 65, 112, 131
virtual organizations 37, 65, 109–125
benefits 116
challenges 113–16
embodied and aesthetic approach to
leadership 123–4
meaningful places and spaces,
importance of 124–5
overcoming challenges 119
plural collective phenomenon,
leadership as 122–3
redefining concept of leadership
119–20
relational process, leadership as
121–2
virtual spaces as workplaces 1, 59,
128–43
affordances of virtual worlds 136–8
co-presence 137
enablers of leadership 135–6
frame of references, changing users'
137
high-fidelity video-conferencing
(e.g., HALO rooms) 131
ideation 128–31, 133–4
immersion, experience of 137
multimodality 137

new ways of working 132–3
parallel communication tools 131
prerequisites of leadership 131–2
simulation capabilities 137–8
supporting tools utilized in
collaboration 138
types of places as virtual spaces
130–31
uses of virtual workplaces 140–42
visual information, rich 137
see also avatars
virtual strategy 64
visibility of leader 61
visual privileges (of status) 203,
207–8

Wajcman, J. 229
Walker, J.W. 204
Wallman, S. 6
walls 254
Wasko, M. 140
Weick, K.E. 78
wellbeing 246
see also employee wellbeing
Wenger, E. 78
windows 101, 255
work arrangements, adjustability of
101
work-life model 208
workplace managers and leaders 58–9,
63–5
workplace strategy 7
Wright, F.L. 52

Yanow, D. 7, 8–9